WHAT IT FEELS LIKE

RHETORIC AND DEMOCRATIC DELIBERATION
VOLUME 27

EDITED BY CHERYL GLENN AND STEPHEN BROWNE
THE PENNSYLVANIA STATE UNIVERSITY

Co-founding Editor: J. Michael Hogan

Editorial Board:

Robert Asen (University of Wisconsin–Madison)
Debra Hawhee (The Pennsylvania State University)
J. Michael Hogan (The Pennsylvania State University)
Peter Levine (Tufts University)
Steven J. Mailloux (University of California, Irvine)
Krista Ratcliffe (Marquette University)
Karen Tracy (University of Colorado, Boulder)
Kirt Wilson (The Pennsylvania State University)
David Zarefsky (Northwestern University)

Rhetoric and Democratic Deliberation focuses on the interplay of public discourse, politics, and democratic action. Engaging with diverse theoretical, cultural, and critical perspectives, books published in this series offer fresh perspectives on rhetoric as it relates to education, social movements, and governments throughout the world.
A complete list of books in this series is located at the back of this volume.

WHAT IT FEELS LIKE

VISCERAL RHETORIC AND THE POLITICS OF RAPE CULTURE

STEPHANIE R. LARSON

The Pennsylvania State University Press | University Park, Pennsylvania

This volume is published with the generous support of the Center for Democratic Deliberation at The Pennsylvania State University.

Library of Congress Cataloging-in-Publication Data

Names: Larson, Stephanie R. (Stephanie Rae), 1989– author.
Title: What it feels like : visceral rhetoric and the politics of rape culture / Stephanie R. Larson.
Other titles: Rhetoric and democratic deliberation ; v. 27.
Description: University Park, Pennsylvania : The Pennsylvania State University Press, [2021] | Series: Rhetoric and democratic deliberation ; volume 27 | Includes bibliographical references and index.
Summary: "Investigates contemporary and historical rhetorics of rape culture within institutional, legal, cultural, and medical discourses. Examines how discourses about rape rely on strategies of containment and deny the felt experiences of victims, ultimately stalling broader claims for justice in the United States"—Provided by publisher.
Identifiers: LCCN 2021024884 | ISBN 9780271091433 (hardback)
Subjects: LCSH: Rape culture—Political aspects—United States. | Rhetoric—Political aspects—United States.
Classification: LCC HV6561 .L37 2021 | DDC 362.883920973—dc23
LC record available at https://lccn.loc.gov/2021024884

Copyright © 2021 Stephanie R. Larson
All rights reserved
Printed in the United States of America
Published by The Pennsylvania State University Press,
University Park, PA 16802–1003

The Pennsylvania State University Press is a member of the Association of University Presses.

It is the policy of The Pennsylvania State University Press to use acid-free paper. Publications on uncoated stock satisfy the minimum requirements of American National Standard for Information Sciences—Permanence of Paper for Printed Library Material, ANSI Z39.48–1992.

For Nana

Warning: This book includes graphic depictions of rape and its aftermath and may be triggering, especially for those who have experienced sexual violence. Please do what you need to do to take care of yourself while reading. That might mean reading in a particular location or position, alongside others or in privacy; engaging in physical activities like knitting or swaying while reading; or even pausing at various moments or closing the book entirely.

While I do not intend to know or assume what parts of this book might be triggering for readers, I want to offer a brief description of what chapters include some of the more difficult material as a way to help readers prepare to engage with the book: The introduction includes material about what it feels like to physically and emotionally live in a rape culture. Chapter 1 concludes with a discussion of Brett Kavanaugh's Supreme Court Justice hearing and his assault of Dr. Christine Blasey Ford. Chapter 2 concludes with a discussion of Recy Taylor, who was group raped by six men, and a brief history of sexual abuse against black women by white men in positions of power. Chapter 3 includes descriptions of a sexual assault forensic examination—what is commonly referred to as a "rape kit" or "rape kit exam." Chapter 4 includes graphic accounts of rape from the public performances of Chanel Miller and Emma Sulkowicz. Chapter 5 includes testimonies from the Me Too and #MeToo movements. And finally, the conclusion includes material from Roxane Gay's memoir that documents her experience with rape and living in its aftermath.

CONTENTS

Preface: The Problem with Origin Stories | xi

Acknowledgments | xvii

Introduction: Bodies, Feelings, and the Rhetoric of Rape Culture | 1

1 Sensing the Nation at Risk: Sexual Citizenship and the Meese Commission | 25

2 The Specter of Patriarchy: Imagining Victims in Bystander Discourse | 57

3 The Proof Is in the Body: Transcending Rhetoric with Rape Kits | 85

4 Disrupting Silence: The Law and Visceral Counterpublicity | 112

5 Taking It All In: #MeToo, Feminist *Megethos*, and List Making | 136

Conclusion: "I Was Trapped in My Body": Writing and Living After Rape | 155

Notes | 163

Bibliography | 183

Index | 201

PREFACE: THE PROBLEM WITH ORIGIN STORIES

Many people ask me why I study rape. If they don't come right out and ask directly, they hint around the question. I can practically hear their brains churning, wondering why. It is somewhat common in academia to probe the origin stories from which our work emerges. Whether it is a valid question about positionality or simply curiosity, we are constantly wondering how people come to their research, how they arrive at their topics, questions, methods, and objects. For women, minorities, or those of us who study topics we are personally connected to—topics at the margins or topics of identity—these inquiries are tricky. And sometimes, they are downright hostile.

While I was in graduate school, I attended the 2015 Rhetoric Society of America (RSA) Summer Institute just after finishing my preliminary exams. It was the first time I can remember introducing myself as someone with research interests regarding rape culture and sexual violence. I was young, in my twenties, and deeply unprepared to publicly address the question: What is it that connects you to the topic of rape culture? So, of course, someone asked me exactly that.

The workshop I attended was led by some of my favorite scholars in the field, and we were gathered together to address the topic of field methods and their use and value in rhetorical studies. To be clear, it was one of the most engaging and meaningful experiences I had outside the boundaries of my own graduate program up to this point. I learned a lot that week—about rhetoric, my research, myself, and the thick skin I would need to do the work I wanted to do, the work of this book.

The workshop leaders put us into small groups periodically throughout the week. On a day when we were tasked with discussing our writing, I was paired with two men, one a fellow graduate student and the other an assistant professor, all of us from different institutions. What I shared was admittedly messy. I was coming out of the haze of my preliminary exams and writing the first draft of my dissertation proposal, a project that generated some of my earliest thoughts about rhetoric and rape culture. After trying to talk through the relationship between the embodied risk of violence in public space and rape culture, the assistant professor cut me off and stretched his hand out in front of me on the table. He looked at me, sighed, and said, "Why do you study rape culture?"

I was stunned and speechless. I could feel the lump in my throat forming as I held back tears of anger. He had called me out. He had *outed* me. I should have been ready to justify my research interests, but I was too young, too inexperienced to have prepared a response, especially a pointed one I needed in that moment. I replied cautiously, "What do you mean?" He continued, "I think you should think about what relationship you have to this context and how it's shaping your ability to look critically at it. Perhaps you're too close to it."

I was enraged. My chest began to get hot and my hands started sweating and shaking. I was choking back tears and stumbling over my words. Not only had he labeled me someone unfit for this work, he had marked me weak, emotional—a victim incapable of speaking in a way that he wanted me to, in a way that he thought rhetoricians and scholars should. When it came to theory, I knew all about the gendered implications of testimony, the power dynamics central to feminist deliberation, and the masculine performance of expertise. I knew the theories, but I didn't know what to say.

While the assistant professor remained oblivious to both what he had just asked me and how it made me feel, the other graduate student could sense my anger and frustration. He also did research around a sensitive topic, studying how the shifting US/Mexico border violently displaces people and disrupts cultural life in communities close to his own. We were just strangers at the time and, furthermore, in much less powerful positions than this faculty member. But in that moment, he looked at me with care in his eyes and said, "I love this project, and I'm glad you're doing it." My heart lifted. He had restored the smallest inkling of faith I needed to escape what had just happened and find a way forward. He didn't perform or posture; he didn't offer some tidy, pseudo-profound academic response. He responded as a human, someone who could sense how vulnerable I felt. I've never thanked this person before, but one day I will.

From that moment on, I told myself that I would never publicly disclose my own relationship to rape culture—my own experiences with sexual violence—even when people implicitly or explicitly try to force disclosure of it. For those of us who are intimately tied to our research, admitting our own experiences and the origins of our stories runs (at least) two risks: On the one hand, we risk our audiences thinking us weak, broken, angry, or bitter. On the other, we risk receiving responses to our work that position us as "too close," biased because of what happened to us. When I entered academia, I did not anticipate writing about rape culture. It was not a professional part of me. But I came to write it. I came to write this project as a way to make sense of all the questions my nineteen-year-old self couldn't answer. It was a way for me to think through why really terrible, traumatic, and violent things happen to people all the time and go unnoticed, neglected, or even doubted. Writing about rape became a necessity.

I wrote this book because my orientation to the world changed when I was just barely becoming an adult. My body and my relationship to it took on new meaning in public, with new fears about what had happened, who would find out about it, and what could happen again. In many ways, writing this book was a search to figure out why I felt the way I felt about the world, why my body reacted the way it did on days like the one at the RSA Summer Institute when someone asked me about why I study rape. The book began as a quest to understand how the contours of our environments seep with such visceral, bodily feelings. Along the way, I met some key people working on the body and affect, people who gave me a way to make sense of all the feelings I had, scholars that helped me understand seriously in conversation or through their writing that we are constituted through our attachments to others, attachments that can, at times, turn violent.[1] Researching how people protest the limits imposed upon them to fight for equity and challenge an epidemic of violence, I learned to take seriously the old adage that you should "trust your gut." Our guts are suspicious and filled with insights. Meaning is not only made in words, of course, but rather made in and transpiring from deep within us, at the level of our organs and our bone-deep, felt sense of harm and risk. Anger and sadness are embodied experiences. But felt emotions like these rooted deep within our bodies also compel us to act. As a rhetorician, theories of the body and affect drew me to consider how symbols not only have meanings but also have feelings—symbols incite feelings, circulate them, and confront publics with them. *What It Feels Like* uses a paradigm of feeling and sensation to uncover the mood of this world, the mood of rape culture. It is a study about a society in which a commonplace reality of violence persists, a study of how bodies are wrapped up in our very ability to make meaning and be heard among others.

Knowing all of this, though—knowing that what has happened to me has most certainly shaped how I wrote this book—I am sure that my experiences are not unique. That's the thing about rape culture: it affects all of us, whether we choose to acknowledge it or not. But writing about rape as a white, straight, and cis woman in the academy no doubt comes with its privileges. I'm not as much at risk of retribution when I speak of my experience, unlike many others in this world, people much more vulnerable than me. People with disabilities are almost three times as likely to experience violent assault when compared to people without disabilities.[2] Nearly 50 percent of people from trans communities report an experience with sexual assault at some point in their lifetime.[3] Black women have long been far more at risk of rape, less likely to report it, and even less so heard or believed when they disclose it.[4] Our society is steeped in sexual violence, a form of violence that coincides with the very founding and development of this country, violence that frequently denies the bodies subject to it while failing to reprimand those who perpetuate it. In 2016, a known sexual predator was elected president of the United States and in 2018, another was sworn into the US Supreme Court. While I know that I will never be able to fully capture the experiences of those most at risk—that my own subjectivity and privilege in this world are and will always be a limitation of my work—this book seeks to understand why and how some voices are so often excluded from public discourse, how they go unseen, unheard, or disbelieved.

At conferences, workshops, and institutes, in classrooms, hallways, and meetings, I know that people wonder, both to my face and behind my back, why I study rape culture. They're often not as direct or condescending as the man who interrogated me at the RSA Summer Institute in 2015. But they're curious, and I don't blame them. I'm curious, too, why people come to research what they research. In writing this preface, my intention is not to suggest that asking about these origin stories is always inherently problematic. But for those of us who are implicated in our contexts—close to the experiences of those we study—these kinds of questions can expose us and put us at risk. At the core of these inquiries is the question: Do you study [insert context] because you've been a victim of [insert context] before? For me, layered underneath the question of my origin story is always a question of whether or not I have been raped and the potential desire to ogle my own pain. So, for people in the future who confront this problem of addressing their own origin stories in front of others, I'll tell you a few things I wish I would have said to that man at the Institute:

> *I study rape culture because it's a pressing public problem.*
> *Your question tells me more about your desire to gaze at and peer into my life than it does about your concern for my actual research.*
> *Suggesting that I am not capable of researching this topic is exactly the reason I study rape culture.*

The truth is, I study rape culture because I do not want to live in a society where people experience violence and then have no way to talk about it or are met with skepticism when they try. I study rape culture because I know it to be a true and pervasive reality. Maybe that will shape how you read the pages that follow in this book, but I would be remiss if I didn't say it. Aside from these reasons, hope also motivates why I study rape culture—hope that as a society we may try and understand how particular bodies are consistently confronted with tactics that seek to contain them, deny them, and silence them—a version of hope that is simultaneously seething with anger, frustration, resentment, and pain, one grounded in what this book terms "visceral rhetorics." I'm not naïve about the world around us, but I believe we can do better, that we can engage in the needed struggle to be better, that we can work to uncover and respect the histories of trauma and shame that many have endured and actively endeavor to change discourse and behavior and norms and even laws. The resilience demonstrated by many studied in this book make me believe that struggle is not only essential but that change is possible. Perhaps that hope is too optimistic, cruel, as Lauren Berlant reminds.[5] But perhaps it's all we have.

ACKNOWLEDGMENTS

This book was written because of many feminists who came before me, paved a path for a book like this, and supported and nourished its development throughout the process. I am indebted in equal parts to your brilliance and kindness, and I promise to pay it forward whenever and wherever possible. To begin, my warmest thanks to some of my earliest teachers I met while at the University of Wisconsin–Madison: Christa Olson, Kate Vieira, Morris Young, Jenell Johnson, Sara McKinnon, Michael Bernard-Donals, Karma Chávez, Brad Hughes, Mary Fiorenza, Jim Brown, Caroline Gottschalk Druschke, and Rob Asen. Your teachings can be traced through literally every page of this book. Kate, you introduced me to this field, taught me how to write about something that matters so deeply to me, and helped me navigate the process when it felt scary. Morris, I will forever be grateful for your honesty and your generosity with time. I am still on the hunt for an academic hangout spot equivalent to Wisconsin's resource room, though I know it will never be filled with as much laughter or warmth without you in it. I owe my deepest gratitude to my advisor, Christa. This book would not exist if it were not for your willingness to guide and push me. You continue to model for me what it means to be an ethical scholar, teacher, mentor, writer, and human in this world, and I feel incredibly fortunate to have crossed paths with you.

Many thanks to a broad circle of academic friends, readers, and mentors near and far who have been generous with their time and energy, graciously commenting on various drafts of this project or lending their wisdom and support when I needed it: Anna Floch Arcello, Marian Aguiar, Karma Chávez, Doug Coulson, Chris Earle, Brandee Easter, Jess Enoch, Elisa Findlay, Natalie Fixmer-Oraiz, Cheryl Glenn, Debbie Hawhee, Stephanie Kerschbaum, Annika Konrad, Meg Marquardt, Elisabeth Miller, John Oddo, Tori Peters, Rich Purcell, Candice Rai, Liam Randall, Andreea Ritivoi, Brandi Rogers, Neil Simpkins, Kristina Straub, Emily Winderman, and Sharon Yam. Candice, your comments on an early draft of my introduction clarified for me the work of this book, and I'm so grateful that such an important piece of this project passed through the hands of someone who takes such care in their comments. Natalie, your feedback on a draft of chapter 1 helped me pull my central argument forward, pushing me to be bolder and sharper in my claims. Elisa and Elisabeth, our writing groups don't just motivate me but keep me grounded. You are two of the smartest readers I know, but I feel most fortunate to have your friendship. I am grateful to have participated in the 2019 RSA Institute seminar "At the Intersections of Rhetorics & Feminisms," with Karma Chávez and Cheryl Glenn, and the workshop "Writing Sensory Rhetorics," with Debbie Hawhee, at a time when I was preparing to submit the first draft of this manuscript. My conversations with both these leaders and those in my various working groups were pivotal in helping me drive the project forward, especially Earl Brooks, Nancy Henaku, Heather Palmer, Holland Prior, and Candice Rai. Thank you for engaging with my work and giving me some encouragement at a time when I really needed it.

To my colleagues at Carnegie Mellon University (CMU), thank you for welcoming me into the English department and embracing my scholarship, especially Marian Aguiar, David Brown, Doug Coulson, Sharon Dilworth, Jason England, Linda Flower, Kevin González, Suguru Ishizaki, David Kaufer, Jon Klancher, Jane McCafferty, Chris Neuwirth, Kathy Newman, John Oddo, Rich Purcell, Andreea Ritivoi, Lauren Shapiro, Kristina Straub, Chris Warren, Necia Werner, Danielle Wetzel, Stephen Wittek, Joanna Wolfe, and James Wynn. I feel lucky to work alongside such brilliant people. Andreea and Dave K., thank you for your steadfast support and mentorship. Kristina and Marian, thank you for being badass feminists and scholars—there's no other way I can put it. Kristina, thank you for reading one of the earliest drafts of my book proposal; it undoubtedly helped me shape the project. John and Marian, thank you for the many, many conversations about publishing and the profession; your advice has been crucial. Doug, thank you for reading an earlier version of chapter 3; your comments were sharp and insightful, guiding me toward the product it is here. Rich, every new faculty member should be blessed with an office neighbor who is a "Rich Purcell"; no one could have helped me navigate being a new faculty member better than you. Danielle, Dave B., and Rich, when I think of you, I think of my Pittsburgh family; thank you for the many venting sessions, drinks, laughs, and conversations. Candace Skibba and Lisa Tetrault, thank you for providing much needed support and guidance, and modeling how to maintain your ethics when navigating the complexities of academia. Many thanks to the undergraduate and graduate students in my "Feminist Rhetorics" and "Rhetoric and the Body" courses for pushing me to see scholarship I care so deeply about in new ways. To the students who have moved in and out of my mentor group, especially Sam Garfinkel, Russell Holbert, Cody Januszko, Madison

Maher, Nisha Shanmugaraj, and Sam Turner, our conversations about your scholarship and the profession continue to inspire and sustain me. Eyona Bivins, Mike Brokos, Laura Donaldson, Jen Loughran, Vickie McKay, and Nick Ryan, you are the backbone of the English Department. Thank you for keeping the ship afloat.

Many programs, individuals, and institutions made the research and writing for *What It Feels Like* possible. The UW–Madison Graduate School provided funding for an early research trip to the archives at the University of Virginia's Law Library. The Department of English at UW–Madison granted me an A.W. Mellon–Wisconsin Fellowship, giving me necessary and sustained time to write. CMU funded me with two research grants, including college-wide and university-wide awards used to support two research assistants, Richard Branscomb and Amy Thompson, who were invaluable in tracking down last-minute citations or transcribing archived letters for me, often with the speediest of turnarounds. The Department of English at CMU provided a semester of leave that was essential to completing and submitting the first draft of this manuscript. The staff at the archives at the University of Virginia Law Library, especially special collections archivist Cecilia Brown, provided warm and welcoming support during my research trip. An earlier version of chapter 4 appeared as "'Everything Inside Me Was Silenced': (Re)defining Rape Through Visceral Counterpublicity," *Quarterly Journal of Speech* 104, no. 2 (2018): 1–22. A version of chapter 5 appeared as "'Just Let This Sink In': Feminist *Megethos* and the Role of Lists in #MeToo," *Rhetoric Review* 38, no. 4 (2019): 432–44. Thank you to Taylor & Francis for allowing me to reprint them here.

My sincerest thanks to the folks at Penn State University Press, particularly Ryan Peterson, who kindly supported this project with grace from the beginning and encouraged me throughout every step of the process. To Stephen Howard Browne and Cheryl Glenn, my deepest gratitude for including this book in the Rhetoric and Democratic Deliberation series. It is an honor to be in the company of you and the other authors in this series. Beth Britt and an anonymous reader provided so much energy and care in their feedback, and this book is a better product because of it. While I couldn't have written *What It Feels Like* alone, the faults and flaws are entirely mine.

And finally, to my family, including those I've known all my life and those I've adopted along the way, I feel overwhelmingly fortunate to have a safety net filled with all of your laughter, dysfunction, and love. To my grandpa, Edwin Wijas, who would tell anyone he loved to "be smart" when he said goodbye, I hope writing this book does your advice justice—I miss you very much. To my Nana, Katherine Wijas, to whom I dedicate this book, you have guided so much of my life, I know my path would not be the same without you. Jon and Kristen Larson, thank you for always being the big brother and big sister that I have needed, and adding even more love and laughter to our family with your partners, Jessie Larson and Pat Burns. Thank you to my friends, especially Joey Chemello, Evan Dunn, Elisa Findlay, Jordan Gorrell, Taylor How, Emer Lucey, and Evan Munch, and all of my extended family, especially Karen Pennington and Marianne Denkewalter—between warm hugs and uncontrollable laughs, you keep me sane. Evan M., thank you for always being my sounding board and biggest cheerleader; this project grew and developed because of countless conversations with you. To Kevin, Kristi, Lisa, and Tom McGuire, thank you for welcoming me into your family. To my parents, Rick and Marcia Larson, I am forever grateful that you let me chart my own path and supported me as I worked to find it in more ways than I can list here. Finally, Ryan, who let me vent about this project in its many stages and pulled me away from it when I needed it most, you are my partner in everything—I love you. And to all of you who shared your own experiences with me, whether you are students, colleagues, family members, friends, and even strangers, I will forever hold your stories close to my heart. This book is for you.

INTRODUCTION: BODIES, FEELINGS, AND THE RHETORIC OF RAPE CULTURE

We talk about rape, but we don't carefully talk about rape.
—Roxane Gay, *Bad Feminist* (2014)

On January 16, 2018, former gymnast Megan Halicek testified to the abuse she endured by Dr. Larry Nassar while being treated for back pain at the young age of fifteen. Speaking in a Michigan courtroom in front of Judge Rosemarie Aquilina and Nassar himself, she recounted her feelings about the assault committed in and on her body:

> I am disgusted—disgusted that Larry Nassar, the trusted adult, authority figure, and famous doctor had the audacity to use his incredible power, prestige, and influence to sexually abuse me, a little girl, right there in his office in the safest and warmest of places with such an overlying sense of healing and recovery. [. . .] He broke in loudly without consent or restraint. He was an unwarranted intruder to my most private, intimate, never before touched places without warning, without gloves, and without explanation. [. . .] Treatment after treatment with Nassar I closed my eyes tight, I held my breath, and I wanted to puke. My stomach pierced me with pain. To this day that pain and these feelings are still there.[1]

Over 160 other young women who had been previously silenced testified in Aquilina's courtroom to their experiences of being violated by Nassar, marking the case as a remarkable shift in legal proceedings regarding rape and sexual assault. Unlike other cases, dozens of young women entered the courtroom, one after the other after the other, testifying to being assaulted by Nassar—touched, stroked, pinched, penetrated, and invaded. But what made the Nassar case exceptional was not just that the judge welcomed a magnitude of victims into her courtroom.[2] Rather, the sheer power and volume of their testimonies, which were widely circulated and publicly revered, gave audiences a way to experience the felt sense of violation—how his fingers crossed the boundaries of young girls' and women's bodies, how their bodies clenched in response, how the painful memories and trauma of being trespassed lingered for years.[3] That is, the vast circulation of these testimonies emphasized a visceral account of violation, provoking a bodily response in audiences. Hearing testimonies like Halicek's over and again prompted audiences to feel their stomachs sink, their throats tighten, or their chests burn—examples of what this book terms "visceral rhetorics," or instances when the body responds, reacting to certain words or actions.

This book takes interest in moments like the Nassar case when discourses about the embodied experience of rape and sexual assault circulate within public discourse. It ruminates on the extent to which a focus on what violation feels like is able to disrupt and shift public understandings of sexual violence. It considers why the visceral and embodied required this scale of testimony to "count" as evidence, how personal narratives laced with pain are often contained, dismissed, or denied by more authoritative voices—a symptom and outcome of rape culture. But this book also remains keenly aware of the fact that Nassar's actual conviction of 40 to 175 years in prison unfortunately remains a notable exception. Even though the Nassar case is distinctive in that the judge invited victims into her courtroom, that immediate and wider audiences largely validated their testimonies, that the perpetrator was actually convicted and essentially sentenced to life in prison, it falls short of bringing justice to bear on rape culture. That is, relying on the Nassar case as a symbol of change demonstrates an embrace of the law and criminalization, what Elizabeth Bernstein has called "carceral feminism," as systems used to respond to sexual violence, systems that continually leave people from trans and queer communities, women of color, and immigrant women—those most structurally vulnerable to violence—often more at risk of violence.[4] Celebrating Nassar's outcome fails to disrupt the pervasive logics of rape culture because it aligns justice and progress with punitive action, eliding the insidious everyday acts of violence that occur in rape culture but are hard to pin down. It suggests that response and change can happen under certain conditions: when a serial offender commits a vast slew of sexual abuse crimes against women who were largely in privileged positions and predominantly white, heteronormative, and cisgender—women who fit our recognized notions of victimhood.

While scholars and activists have long sought redress for crimes of sexual violence, *What It Feels Like* addresses an underexamined reason why efforts to abolish rape culture struggle to achieve wider public success: a denial of the embodied experiences of those who have been raped or sexually assaulted within public discourse. This book builds from scholars who have helped define rape culture, illuminating how it "encourages male sexual aggression," how it "condones physical and emotional terrorism against women and presents it as a norm."[5] Scholars have exposed how within a rape culture "sexual violence is a fact of life," seen as typical and even "sexy."[6] In other words, we know that we live in a society that frequently "excuse[s] perpetrators and demean[s] victims," a society that cultivates "a cultural climate whereby sexual violence can flourish."[7] But rape culture operates through social norms, practices, and scripts that affectively and symbolically support logics of aggression, violence, and sexism—logics that, for instance, allow a doctor to violate his patient during a checkup and then silence that patient when she speaks up—logics that disseminate widely beyond the capacities of a courtroom and continue to go unquestioned in social and cultural life. As a result, *What It Feels Like* examines mainstream public discourse, finding that what stalls progress and change is not so much the need to convict perpetrators like Nassar (though we most certainly should) but rather how patriarchal structures and their influence over public conversations limit the options available for disclosure, curbing the available frameworks for understanding the scope of rape culture today and how it manifests in more ordinary, insidious ways. As noted by Roxane Gay in the epigraph to this introduction, we, as a society today, certainly talk about rape, but we don't do so carefully, in ways that could respect the felt experiences of victims and furthermore effectively scrutinize the problem and its rhetorical dimensions.

To apprehend rape culture's commonplaces—its norms, practices, and scripts—*What It Feels Like* asks the following set of questions: What happens when publics deny the embodied experiences of victims? How do these denials happen in legal, medical, or institutional contexts and organize public meaning about rape and the bodies subject to it? And finally, how do bodies and their capacity to provoke feeling serve as powerful resources for challenging public discourse in their efforts to transform rape culture into a more just society? To answer these questions, this book considers how patriarchal definitions of and responses to sexual violence permeate public discourse, shaping and influencing how we talk about rape and those who experience it.

For instance, publics adopt discursive frameworks that center an ideal, white, male, rational speaker and constitute an archetype of the victim that is white, able-bodied, cisgender, and female, bypassing the experiences of women of color and trans women, in particular. When assessing an alleged act, publics often favor a perpetrator's perception of what happened, configuring women's bodies through male desire. Mainstream discourses mimic a legal quest to assign guilt and responsibility and, in the process, target certain bodies as blameworthy or make excuses for why the harms committed against others do not amount to that of assault or rape. Yet the law, as many feminist legal and rhetorical scholars have pointed out, is a system built to ignore or, worse, deny women and minorities and their accounts of injustice.[8] Over and over again, the law fails to hold perpetrators accountable and properly assess risk and harm. It "does not favor fairness and due process," as Leigh Gilmore has maintained, but instead "produces general, default notions of women's unreliability."[9] In short, dominant deliberative frameworks prioritize a normative subjectivity that works to obscure victims' own experiences with their bodies, overlooking the roots of power *over the body* central to the violence of rape.[10] Casting aside such evidence reveals how patriarchal structures exercise power over victims by silencing them, how it takes over 160 testimonies to sway the legal system and the public of the malicious gravity of perpetrators like Nassar when only one should have sufficed.

What It Feels Like submits that this failure to understand embodied experiences stems from a range of discourses constituted in public that govern how justice claims are made. I attend to this problem by interrogating how patriarchal perspectives rooted in a desire for rationality, heteronormativity, ableism, white supremacy, and male dominance establish the grounds for public discourse about rape, comprised in mainstream conversations in seemingly benign ways. As a result, widespread public opinion of rape largely negates testimonies rooted in feeling, marking such embodied sources of knowledge as gendered and untrustworthy while eschewing the bodies and forms of communication that defy the norms of discourse. To make that case, *What It Feels Like* examines how the laws about, tools that document and adjudicate, and responses to sexual violence are rooted in the need to manage and restrain women's bodies. In the process, I analyze disruptions that illuminate how discussions of the fleshy, bloody, and corporeal body—disruptions like the testimony of Megan Halicek—reveal a new vantage point from which to examine rape culture, one with potential to shift public opinion and provoke change. Probing how the threat of violence can be communicated through affect and feeling sheds light on the repeated, ignored, mundane instances of rape or sexual assault that chronicle an embodied understanding of violence as an act of power. Put differently, centering the body and embodiment exposes how and in what ways publics fail to take rape seriously, how simply being in public puts some bodies at greater risk, how the violence of rape culture gets disregarded in everyday life. Taken together, this book argues that discourses about rape culture rely on strategies of containment to assert control over a presumed affective excess of femininity but also that those discourses can be challenged by mobilizing forms of embodiment that stress what it feels like to be raped.

In tracing the material and embodied force of rape culture, this book theorizes what I call visceral rhetorics through historic and contemporary case studies to better account for the affective dimensions that accumulate, circulate, and regulate public debates. Across contexts including anti-pornography debates from the 1980s, Violence Against Women Act (VAWA) advocacy materials, sexual assault forensic kits, public performances by survivors, and online social movements, I account for how bodies and their residue of feeling—residue layered with historical, material, and cultural notions of violence—can serve to generate a bodily intensity in audiences with powerful potential for feminist protest.[11] Visceral rhetorics foreground how judgment is a process that forms deep within our gut, a process in need of attention when traditional deliberative frameworks do not work as well for inspiring change. For instance, when our hearts race, our teeth grind, or our palms sweat, these are visceral rhetorics at work, rhetorics guiding us toward a force of feeling, one that can serve as an alternative mode of understanding the world around us. Yet, in investigating how patriarchal concepts, definitions, and procedures influence and limit public deliberation in a variety of forums, I show how institutions, groups, and individuals work to quell or control the visceral nature of bodies, concealing their agential and rhetorical capacities, and consequently stall claims for justice.

In other words, I define visceral rhetorics as the bone-deep, felt sense of communication that transpires from a position of flesh and wound in addition to the processes that seek to erase the bodies communicating from this very perspective. Attention to visceral rhetorics, I argue, provides (1) a conceptual framework for exploring how certain modes of recognition central to discussions of injustice deny or ignore bodies and embodied forms of communication; and (2) a hermeneutic for examining alternative modes of embodied protest, intervention, and change. Together, this book's examination into visceral rhetorics reminds us, as rhetorical scholars, how bodies don't simply aid in persuasion or provide an opportunity to theorize the sites of argumentation or invention in abstract terms. Rather, visceral rhetorics demonstrate how bodies—their very fleshy, corporeal, material, and sensory nature—become caught up in arguments, fueling a rhetoricity that works with and through our embodied attachments to others. Expanding a feminist rhetorical commitment to understand how those who do not fall under the category of Man (read white, male, able-bodied, and cisgender) are excluded from mainstream publics, *What It Feels Like* initiates a new move in feminist rhetorics' long interest in the silencing of women's voices by demonstrating how silencing not only suppresses voices but also suppresses bodies—both the discourse about bodies and their affective capacities.[12]

To elucidate the tensions surrounding fleshy, visceral, and feminized bodies, *What It Feels Like* takes up historical and contemporary artifacts and events that deal with the problem of rape culture. As a feminist rhetorical critic, I have gathered, read, and analyzed a range of artifacts including archived letters; newspaper articles; public campaigns, advertisements, and speeches; medical, political, and legal documents; advocacy efforts; performance art pieces; and Twitter feeds. Throughout, the book places legal, institutional, and medical claims about the raped body alongside testimonial and embodied accounts and analyzes how these juxtapositions reveal arguments that sustain an unequal treatment of violence committed against marginalized bodies. Thus, *What It Feels Like* engages a dual approach: first, it identifies how historical and official discourses narrowly define the act of rape through procedural, linguistic frameworks, and second, it locates embodied acts that call those definitions into question. Examining discourse about women's bodies through these two interpretive lenses illustrates how sensation works alongside more traditional, discursive tools in both propagating and resisting rape culture. Together, its case studies find that while policy makers, judicial authorities, and medical professionals deploy methods that serve to control women's bodies, public performances and creative genres that use bodies in disruptive capacities emerge as fierce ethical interruptions that challenge the operations of power present in political life. Through this broad examination of affect, feminism, and publicity, *What It Feels Like* maintains that investigating how women's bodies serve both to manage and oppose rape culture sheds light on how bodies become necessary for responding to the exigencies of violence, even when their present contexts seek to ensure their erasure.

In what follows, I outline the scholarly contours of this project, situating it in rhetorical, feminist, and affect studies while foregrounding the theoretical and scholarly framework of the book. I then offer a brief discussion of visceral rhetorics in relation to the structure of the book. The arguments I make here are especially pertinent today given the gridlock of public discourse about rape, a discourse in which gender, embodiment, and language are complexly enmeshed in ways that serve to constrain people's abilities to speak about their own experiences with violence committed against their bodies. My hope is that this book addresses this problem by guiding us toward potential solutions that (1) acknowledge how embodied forms of meaning making have been ignored and silenced and (2) take seriously the role and value visceral rhetorics can play in attempting to reshape public opinion and disrupt the power patriarchy holds over public life. To do so, I examine past legacies of rape culture, how those legacies currently operate in different contexts, and what rhetorical strategies have been and might be effective for uprooting it. Together, we must understand how women's symbolic and material bodies are problematically foreclosed in these arguments in ways that deserve our attention if we desire any sort of change to the status of violence in everyday life. Following the work of Annie Hill, turning toward, not away from, the violated body "proceed[s] from the assumption that feminism is far from finished" and "insist[s] on the urgent need for feminist intervention now."[13]

Rape Culture and Its US Legacies

Feminist scholars from a range of disciplines have intervened in the problem of rape, analyzing how within its discourses, gender and power are deeply and troublingly intertwined.[14] "Rape is part of a system of male dominance," writes Patricia Hill Collins, and has consequently naturalized relationships of fear among certain bodies.[15] Gender roles have been shaped by the everyday nature of rape culture, leaving many in public to assume certain behaviors are normal or acceptable. But because sexual violence is so pervasive, so commonplace, so profoundly chronic, ironically, the actual *violence* of rape or sexual assault is rendered invisible in mainstream conversations. To make legible these invisibilities, this study centers public deliberation to interrogate the logics of rape culture, revealing how contemporary modes of defining and responding to rape and sexual assault reinforce patriarchal approaches that diminish space for embodied, feminist perspectives. In this section, I foreground a brief history of rape culture in the United States in relation to the current project, elucidating how a rhetorical perspective grounded in the body and attuned to difference is critical for exposing how and why the violence of sexual abuse persists uncontested for many in everyday life.

As a term, "rape culture" originally came into public vocabulary during the second-wave feminist movement specifically in the 1970s and remains in usage today.[16] When anti-rape feminists first began using it in public dialogue, they did so to highlight the commonplace dismissal of rape crimes, crimes in which victims of rape were discredited for assaults committed against them. "In 'rape culture,'" writes Maria Bevacqua, "sexual assault is tolerated, [. . .] women are blamed for being raped, sexist attitudes prevail, and male sexual privilege goes unquestioned."[17] Rape myths are one of the dominant vehicles responsible for circulating and emboldening such ideas and serve to mark women's bodies as inherently untrustworthy: "women lie about being raped"; "rape only happens by strangers"; "it only counts as rape if she was physically abused"; "she was drunk, therefore responsible." Even though these myths are widely false, negative beliefs about victims sponsored by these ideas are "persistently held" and ultimately "serve to deny and justify male sexual aggression against women."[18] As a result, women's bodies are too often subject to scrutiny: what she was wearing, how she acted, where the rape occurred, and how she retaliated "all become evidence for whether a woman was even raped at all."[19]

Understanding how contemporary rape prevention efforts operate through both discursive and sensory means, directing women to comport themselves through disparaging gender norms in order to ward off violence, drives this book's analytical approach. Because rape myths are so pervasive, normalized in how we talk and move in society, women's bodies have been coded as "risky spaces" within mainstream rape prevention efforts that focus on things like statistics or the role of the bystander.[20] Contemporary prevention efforts turn scrutiny over women's bodies into foreboding prophecies that direct women not to drink, dress like a whore, or, essentially, *ask for it*. As Catharine MacKinnon has provocatively written, "To be rapable, a position that is social not biological, defines what a woman is."[21] Consequently, "the goal" for women, argues Rachel Hall, "is to become physically impenetrable."[22] The very possibility of invasion marks a woman's body as an unsafe space: "quite literally, she has too many orifices."[23] In other words, to prevent rape, mainstream discourses ask rapists not to change their own behavior or recognize how rape is a crime of power; rather, they encourage women to deploy self-surveillance tactics that require her to be vigilant of her own body, sustaining the gender imbalance central to the violence of rape. To put it bluntly, women in US society have been taught that the best kind of surveillance is that which performs a virginal subjectivity. A woman who behaves chastely, modestly, and most importantly, quietly—characteristics akin to how Cheree Carlson has defined "True Womanhood"—may have a better chance of escaping rape by remaining appropriately fearful of what is otherwise doomed to happen.[24]

But the risk of rape is not shared equally by all, a fact largely unacknowledged in mainstream publics as a result of the discourses of rape that do circulate. That is, rape prevention discourses are grounded in a whitewashed history that has failed to account for how women of color, people from trans and queer communities, and working-class women are significantly more at risk of rape. Part of this problem can be attributed to cases that *do* take shape in the mainstream media, cases that are typically oversensationalized and focus on a particular type of victim. That is, when rape is given a public platform, it is frequently the result of some of the most gruesome, violent, gut-wrenching cases that simultaneously involve victims deemed appropriate for public sympathy. In addition to the Nassar case, for example, take the 1983 New Bedford rape, in which Cheryl Araujo was brutally group-raped in a bar in New Bedford, Massachusetts, or the 1989 Central Park Jogger rape, in which Trisha Meili was attacked and raped while running in Manhattan. Both cases stole the national spotlight and still inhabit a public memory about rape today. They involved beatings in which each woman was brutally attacked, raped by multiple men, and left as a spectacle outside in public. What happened to these women was horrific, tragic, and deserving of national coverage. But the public broadcasting of these and other events like it work to categorize an archetypal victim and obscure the everyday violence of rape culture that still lives on today.[25] Put differently, the legacy of women like Araujo or Meili serves to represent all cases of rape, "reinforc[ing] iconic representations of victims (as innocent, white, and/or angelic)" that deflect the affective valences of rape culture that are pervasive yet hard to see when committed against bodies and in contexts other than these.[26] Thus, the rhetorical perspective I take here seeks not to weigh one case of rape as more or less gruesome than the next but rather to illustrate how media portrayals such as these provide a framework of assessment that works to persuade publics of the forms of violence and violated bodies worthy of public outcry. The debate comes down to flesh and wound.

This book examines how this archetypal victim can be traced in contemporary prevention and response efforts, shaping how publics fail to understand a variety of cases that count as rape. For instance, legislative efforts today that center their attention on the college campus still carry this image of the rape victim: she is college-aged, cisgender, white, upper-middle-class, educated, heterosexual, and able-bodied. In other words, the typified victim of rape is always imagined as white and female in public discourse, foreclosing a broader awareness of the range of bodies subject to sexual violence. Thus, I use "woman" or "women" in this book not to ignore femmes, queer women, people from trans or nonbinary communities, or men, who most certainly experience rape and sexual assault, but rather to acknowledge a public obsession with focusing solely on cis, white women in predominant rape prevention discourse. Furthermore, while these discourses may encourage us to characterize rape as a problem of *male* dominance and control over *female* sexuality, this book understands the problems inherent to rape and its influence over public discourse as those of *"white* male regulation of *white* female sexuality," as Kimberlé Crenshaw reminds us, a problem rooted in a history of rape statutes that obscures the legacy of rape and sexual assault for women of color, specifically.[27]

Apprehending why this archetype surfaced and took grip in the 1980s and still exists today requires examination of the history of rape in this country and how anti-rape measures first began politically. When anti-rape feminists such as Andrea Dworkin and Susan Brownmiller started to protest rape, they did so by organizing as a grassroots, anti-state movement committed to helping the needs of battered women. While critiquing the state's failure to protect women, second-wave feminists applied for and received government grants to help target the issue of rape culture and raise public awareness of it. Yet, as Kristin Bumiller has pointed out, accepting money from the government left these second wavers—who were already part of a movement problematically tied up in white feminism—permanently tied to the state, specifically at a time when the fear of violence (due to things like the war on drugs and the AIDS crisis) circulated widely. The anti-rape movement thus coincided with a "crime control mentality" that typified not only the rape victim but also the perpetrator and the act of rape.[28] Placing sex in the context of what were then perceived as social ills "resulted in a panic over sex crimes that contributed to wrongly directed fears about the omnipresence of predators and to opportunistic prosecutions."[29] State-sponsored efforts—particularly those that formed the foundation of VAWA—constructed the rapist as a stranger, racialized as nonwhite and typically black, and generalized the fear of the sex criminal who lurks in a dark alley, preying on young, innocent, white women. With the help of advocacy centers today such as the Rape, Abuse & Incest National Network (RAINN), we know and can confirm that the majority of rape cases, however, simply don't occur like this.[30] And yet, the legacy of these archetypes largely circulates in the public imaginary about rape, how it happens, and who experiences it, emerging throughout several cases examined in this book.

Along with interrogating sensationalized rape cases, the second-wave feminist movement, or VAWA, scholars have also pointed out how perceptions of rape and its stereotypes stem far deeper in this country's founding history. For instance, Collins has turned to the early twentieth century and the legacy of enslavement in the United States to unveil a much more complex and intersectional understanding of rape and its naturalized presence in society. In *Black Sexual Politics: African Americans, Gender, and the New Racism*, she underscores how black women and their experiences with rape have largely been erased historically, given "no public name [. . .] or significant public censure."[31] This failure to acknowledge the plight of rape for black women, she argues, is a complicated result of advancing the rights of black people more broadly in the decades following the American Civil War, particularly at the height of the Jim Crow era. Though black women were commonly at risk of rape, it was far easier, Collins argues, to outline the injustices of lynching—a spectacle that intentionally took place in public—than it was to argue the injustice of rape—an act committed against black women who were often the target of violence by powerful white men. "Whereas lynching (racism) was a public spectacle," she writes, "rape (sexism) signaled *private* humiliation."[32] Black women were overwhelmingly subject to sexual abuse by slave holders in the Antebellum South but also white men in law enforcement during the mid-twentieth century. Yet, the pervasiveness of these actions went largely unnoticed in public, engendering the central linking of toxic masculinity and white supremacy that began centuries ago yet still grossly persists today.[33] In other words, the maintenance of white male dominance in the United States does not only include sexual violence; rather, it is predicated on a history of normalized sexual abuse largely committed against women of color by white men in power.

To be clear, this book recognizes that rape is a central component of this country's foundation, its very presence as a nation-state and economic world power, supported by a powerful legacy of misogyny and white supremacy. This history establishes what I take "rape culture" to mean in this book, embedded into this country's very civic and political makeup from the beginning, a history that buttresses current exercises of power and abuse that occur in ordinary interactions and continue to go unaccounted for or ignored, seen as normal, if not logical. Most certainly, colonization and slavery in the United States were perpetuated by rape, and, consequently, their mechanisms simultaneously served to control and populate enslaved people through the proliferation of sexual abuse.[34] "The reproductive capacity of enslaved and native women," writes historian Rickie Solinger, "was the resource whites relied on to produce an enslaved labor force, to produce and transmit property and wealth across generations, to consolidate white control over land in North America, and to produce a class of human beings who, in their ineligibility for citizenship, underwrote the exclusivity and value of white citizenship."[35] Sexual violence served "as weapons of racial domination," weapons of "white supremacy, patriarchy, and genocide" that have long been overshadowed by the colonized stories we continue to tell of the nation's founding.[36] What's worse is that the laws protected slave holders from punishment. According to Virginia state legislation passed in 1662, "the children resulting from rape of enslaved women by white men were not considered legally free, nor were they recognized as part of the white family, which enabled free white men to conceal their sexual behavior with enslaved women and avoid responsibility for their actions."[37] In other words, the law "financially incentivized rape of enslaved women," writes Rachel Feinstein, because slave holders profited off the children born into their households.[38]

What It Feels Like builds from scholars who have investigated how the law has skirted rape in the United States to understand how central the history of paternalism and masculinity is to rape culture, demonstrating how the legacy of this history lives on today in how rape laws are classified and understood publicly. In addition to this dark, underacknowledged but powerful legacy of sexual violence, one other reason for this historical and public erasure of rape deals with where the act of rape often happens. Because rape is understood legally to take place in private, historically, rape has been framed not as a criminal matter, but rather one that requires civil intervention on behalf of the (male) head of the household. For much of US history, the home operated outside of the "law's sovereign domain," as Jennifer Andrus has argued, and "because it [was] the duty of the husband to control the world within it, [. . .] he had the power to exercise sovereign control by punishing the bodies of his subjects."[39] Thus, in cases of rape that occurred between a husband and wife or master and enslaved person, the private sphere of the home constituted rape as an issue outside of the rule of law. Rape was "presented unapologetically as common sense," an unfortunate consequence, or even a regrettable outcome of marital relations, if recognized at all.[40] It was not until the late twentieth century—well after the Nineteenth Amendment was passed—that paternalistic laws of property were finally broken.[41]

If and when a person does choose to report a case of rape or sexual assault, the offense is categorized by degrees of severity that vary state by state, both in number of degrees and how they are termed. While rape law within the latter half of the twentieth century and current twenty-first century has undergone several changes in definition, rape is typically thought of today as *sexual intercourse without consent*, intercourse imagined with a man and woman. Sexual assault, however, is often defined as *unwanted or nonconsensual touching* (for instance, with one's mouth, fingers, or fists), which may include attempt to rape. Thus, as legal scholars have pointed out, "the crime of rape centers on penetration"; adjudication procedures operate "from the male standpoint"; a man's bodily parts determine how to catalog, measure, and account for violation.[42] While the majority of sexual assault cases, including rape, are classified as felony offenses, some states categorize sexual assault cases as misdemeanors, which receive a lesser sentence and are those typically involving nonconsensual touching such as grabbing someone else's genitalia without permission. With all of this said, however, it must be noted that rarely are those who commit rape or sexual assault convicted of such crimes. For instance, according to RAINN, out of every thousand cases of sexual assault reported, only forty-six will lead to an arrest and of those, only five will receive a felony conviction.[43] We still see that, as Judith Butler has described, "the status given to the law is precisely the status given to the phallus, the symbolic place of the father, the indisputable and incontestable."[44]

Sexual violence has been ingrained in the very institutions that define this country, making rape a central component of our cultural DNA, invisible yet fundamental to US identity. Rape culture has flourished in this country since before it was even recognized as one. Yet testimonies that women or those feminized by discourses of rape offer of their own experiences with their bodies are often viewed as inherently unfit for the public sphere, marked as less valuable, irrational, or excessive.[45] Debates about rape cases quickly devolve into cases of he-said, she-said—a binary that, as Gilmore has argued, will always seek "to taint" her words in the service of supporting his.[46] Victims' testimonies are denigrated as private and personal, biased on the grounds that they are not perceived as universal or of public concern, compounded by discriminations that pile up for women, women of color, poor women, people from trans or queer communities, and so on. In response to these gendered injustices, *What It Feels Like* investigates how prioritizing the male perspective at the expense of hearing from a variety of people targeted by rape carries over into the way we talk about, investigate, and adjudicate rape, a perspective nearly indistinguishable yet integral to these discussions. Examining rape culture in this book, thus, goes far beyond analyzing individual acts; rather, this book uses a rhetorical approach to apprehend how everyday life is saturated with a network of violence seen as commonplace, an approach equipped to interrogate how such insidious acts are linked to a uniquely sexist and racialized history of power that has long operated for financial, colonial, legal, and political gains at the expense of justice and equity for all.

Fleshy Bodies and the (Im)Possibility of Being Heard

In *Living a Feminist Life*, Sara Ahmed argues that "feminist history is affective."[47] "Words surround us," she writes, "thick with meaning and intensity."[48] When I invoke the discourse of sensation, feeling, or embodiment, I am thinking of scholars like Ahmed. Words and actions make us feel a certain way, feelings that have potential to sink in deep within our bones. When people use their bodies to articulate violence, however, they draw upon alternative communicative frameworks to express the experience of harm from a perspective grounded in these exact feelings. In the case of rape culture, I view these actions as rhetorical forms seeking to combat the stigmas projected onto victims. Honing how meaning can be made at the fleshy sites of violation illustrates how affect operates at the "edges of language," to borrow from Debra Hawhee.[49] Language leaves felt residue; belief is sensed in the gut; persuasion is never an entirely rational operation that acts outside of the physical body. This book aims to shift rhetorical scholars' sense (pun intended) of the material body to grasp how feelings transpire in ways that not only circulate arguments but also constitute their very being. Bodies are corralled by institutions, tinkered with by tools; judgment percolates under the surface; fear is felt; women seethe with anger. The goal of this book is to understand how visceral rhetorics—these thick, material, bone-deep, gut-felt sensations—illuminate the body's capacity to expose a reality of inequity and the need for change, a powerful capacity that operates with and beyond language and reveals the fictional promises of rationality patriarchal discourses seek to promote. In this section, I begin to unpack how rhetorics like these interact with publics, theorizing visceral rhetorics as a tool equipped for attending to women's experiences and justice claims broadly.

While rhetorical study has long considered the body, this book moves beyond theories that have treated the body as an abstract concept or in two-dimensional fashion by viewing it solely in terms of representation and image.[50] When first approaching the body, scholars viewed it as a site of persuasion akin to a visual object, a representation or protest, a place where arguments could form.[51] Best said by Hawhee, "Contemporary theory [. . .] has a tendency to freeze bodies, to analyze them for their symbolic properties, thereby evacuating and ignoring their capacity to sense and to move through time."[52] When unquestioned, the abstract body, Karma Chávez argues, may serve to amplify "taken-for-granted values like civility, respectability, and normative identity," further producing theories and practices of rhetoric that continue to identify certain bodies as important, and, thus, as the grounds for theories and practices that remain deeply entrenched in unmarked power.[53] I echo Chávez and seek to understand material bodies at the intersections of race, class, gender, dis/ability, location, and sexuality. I treat the body as Hawhee does, as a "vital, connective, mobile, transformative force, a force that exceeds—even as it bends and bends with—discourse."[54] This study follows Jay Dolmage, who defines rhetoric as the circulation of power in communication by specifically tracing the body's fleshy, moving capacities, "its phenomenological and persuasive importance," to understand how bodies mingle with perceptions of rape culture in public.[55] Working from this groundwork, I consider how bodies *make meaning*—how bodies break with convention; how bodily differences emerge and call into question our theories of rhetoric; how fleshy, corporeal forms of embodiment shift the modes available for making meaning.

But this rhetorical attention to fleshiness and corporeality is inspired by a feminist goal. That is, *What It Feels Like* critically expands this body of scholarship by interrogating how assumptions about material bodies serve as a primary motivator for silencing women, theorizing the body in relation to the feminist rhetorical trajectory of silence. Rape, as Hill has argued, continually shapes women's words and actions: "Fear of rape, and of being accused of inviting assault, influences where women go, to whom they speak, and how they experience public and private spaces. It affects what they wear based on the pervasive belief that a woman's appearance can communicate consent to sex."[56] Rape culture, in other words, is an enterprise of power over one's body and one's voice. While women's mental capacities and bodily processes have long been subject to stigmas that serve to define women as incapable of speaking rationally or meaningfully, a woman's body becomes a key source of public anxiety when assessing an act of rape: her body appears weak, meager, or angry after an alleged attack; she cries uncontrollably or yells loudly when she speaks of what happened; her drunken altered mental state marks her as untrustworthy; blood could mean anything. These bodies seep unwanted excess—both material and symbolic—that mark them as awkward, tainted, or even out of control. Amy Koerber writes that "the idea [is] that women are motivated by something inside themselves that they cannot control, whereas men control themselves through rationality and the male brain."[57] Consequently, speakers responding to victim disclosures employ rhetorical tactics that seek to circumvent women's bodies, the wounded sites of trespass, and the feelings that result from rape.

Thus, while the concept of visceral rhetorics, as this section suggests, carries implications for a variety of rhetorical studies, I theorize it in this book as a feminist rhetorical project. Attention to physical bodies and embodiment illuminates the constraints of disclosure, placing this book in conversation with a long history of feminist scholarship that has investigated the genre of personal testimony.[58] Examining how silencing permeates our entire notion of gender and embodiment allows me to locate how patriarchy trickles into the rhetorical situation beyond what gets spoken and who speaks, how mechanisms that restrict, limit, or render impossible the act of women speaking operate both generally in public but specifically in the case of sexual violence. As a result, this book remains aware of how discourses about rape serve to keep women in their "proper place" by denying the discourses they offer of their own bodies.[59] Taken together, it reveals how the surveillance of behavior and embodiment become tools to manage and assess the experience of rape, invoking old strategies in new forms that serve to deny a woman's place in the public sphere.

In addressing the body's capacity to transpire visceral meaning, *What It Feels Like* stems from recent scholars who have advanced the rhetorical study of affect and sensation by uncovering its critical role in public engagement and belonging.[60] Feeling acts as a kind of circuitry to any rhetorical situation, and traces of such affective phenomena, as Jenell Johnson has argued, "tell us *a public was here.*"[61] This book builds critically from the work of Johnson, who defines the capacity of the visceral as an "*intensity* of feeling," an intensity different than Brian Massumi's initial theorizing of affect and one more akin to "a matter of scale, of saturation, what physicists would describe as power per square unit and what rhetoricians might describe as magnitude."[62] As Jenny Rice argues, "The problem is not that public subjects feel. Rather, the problem is that feeling too often serves as the primary connective tissue to our public spaces."[63] Bodies engage, are subject to, and even challenge ideas about rape culture, constituting affect as a tool of public formation in addition to the tools of discourse and the visual. What sets this study apart, though, is that it demonstrates how visceral phenomena not only congeal publics but also serve as strategic sources of counterpublicity. That is, while fleeting, feeling moments of connection emerge from and converge publics, they can also tell us *this public is hostile*, unwelcoming of certain bodies and their forces.

Because this study deals with the violence of rape, it cautions against treating pain solely in terms of representation and instead calls us to understand its visceral impressions with the outside world, how the physical experience of pain moves us to judgment in ways that words alone might not. For rhetorical scholars, experiencing pain demonstrates how meaning circulates and calls audiences to connect with a speaker at the level of feeling. That is, *feeling pain*, as opposed to simply hearing about pain, as Elaine Scarry has famously theorized, encourages a level of certainty unavailable under strictly discursive frameworks.[64] We come to know and understand our embodied existence when we feel, when we grasp—even if only for a moment—a sense of harm or wound. The experience of pain is "bound up with how we inhabit the world, how we live in relationship to the surfaces, bodies, and objects that make up our dwelling places."[65] Pain transcends discursive frameworks, it moves audiences to certainty, and it illuminates an experience of violence beyond language—all of which reveal how central feeling is to meaning making. But "pain leaks," as Margrit Shildrick points out, and attention to visceral feelings, specifically, locates the intricate connection between the body's insides and outsides that highlight the production of boundaries.[66] Understanding how people use their bodies to make audiences feel the violation of a boundary in an effort to protest institutions that failed to recognize what happened to them as rape illustrates how the body becomes necessary for foregrounding identification and subjectivity in contexts that have so desperately sought to ignore them. In the process, this book explores how our lived, embodied experiences are not simply shaped by our relation to others; rather they are *constituted* by such communal, potentially dangerous, and even painful public encounters.

Witnessing the sensation of pain encourages us, or rather, demands that we confront the inequity among bodies who move through public space. In other words, reckoning with justice and its limits requires moving beyond language. To understand how humanity is granted to some bodies and not others, I draw from Hortense Spillers, who has carefully argued that some bodies are merely granted "flesh" (instead of marked as Man or even a whole body) and dehumanized as a result.[67] The flesh, as Spillers theorized it, is a distinctively gendered concept, drawn from the experiences of black women in slavery. Being "flesh," for those made captive under enslavement, is different than having "a body," for those granted the recognition of humanity, in that the flesh occupies "that zero degree of social conceptualization that does not escape concealment under the brush of discourse, or the reflexes of iconography."[68] The flesh persists within capitalist society even if it functions outside of subjectivity or ideology, rendered legible often in commodity form. Black female flesh has always been "unprotected," a "materialized scene" that "offers a praxis and a theory, a text for living and for dying, and a method for reading both through their diverse mediations."[69] This idea of the flesh leaves the "marks of a cultural text whose inside has been turned outside," marks of violence that can be traced in what Spillers views as the internalization of violence, or what this book cites as visceral phenomena.[70] By pressing on naming practices, she guides our thinking to investigate how identities are formed through corporeal power and meaning, articulations that are never fixed, past the limits of ideology or what ideology seems to refuse.

Interrogating how the state manufactures norms that restrict protection over certain bodies, Alexander Weheliye, building on Spillers, invites scholars to focus on the "zones between the flesh and the law" to render these bodies visible, an approach I take in this book.[71] He urges scholars to note "the importance of miniscule movements, glimmers of hope, scraps of food, the interrupted dreams of freedom found in those spaces deemed devoid of full human life."[72] In other words, expanding attention toward these moments where humanity is *barely graspable* sheds light on how the state disregards certain bodies as abject forms of life. Following Spiller's and Weheliye's guidance, I trace the grit of pavement that brushes with a victim's body or the tools deployed to scrape a body's orifices to capture visceral moments of flesh present in my objects of study. These messy, dirty, and earthy encounters call me to see how the state participates in a body's capacity to be seen as human, foregrounding the processes of racialization, debilitation, and gendering that so often shape a rhetor's ability to speak and be heard. A focus on the flesh—skin, bones, and everything in between—illuminates the biopolitical processes that deny certain bodies the subjectivity of hu/man and exposes how affective safety is granted to few.

In uncovering how certain bodies are perceived as at risk while others are constituted as risky, this project asks that rhetorical scholars and others who are committed to interrogating questions of injustice attend to moments of flesh and feeling—prickles of pain that jolt us, instinctive or knee-jerk reactions that attempt to tell us something's not right.[73] Institutions endeavor to monitor and assess risk through their own frameworks, and yet "a gut has its own intelligence," one that is consumed with the capacity to persuade only if we let it.[74] While discourses about rape strive to contain the body and all of its visceral, fleshy, and generative modes of articulation, these are exactly the forms of communication that hold potential to break the status of rape culture. In these moments of deeply constrained engagement, one may require a sort of "affective whiplash" that strives to smack us back into reality and restore a sense of equity in public life, a form of persuasion yet to be given its due attention.[75]

Even as this book adds to a legacy of scholars dedicated to unveiling the injustices committed against women and their bodies, the tactics of visceral protest and disruption found in performances by Emma Sulkowicz or the virality of #MeToo demonstrate possibilities for change. Acts such as these—while not without flaws—explicitly move beyond rational discourse and instead employ tactics of feeling, visceral rhetorics, or what we might even consider rhetorical tactics of the last resort deemed necessary when communicative mechanisms continue to limit the testimony of rape. This book argues that protests and responses that call upon the body as a central rhetorical tool are deployed to make audiences *feel the pain of rape*. They invoke what Teresa Brennan terms the "transmission of affect," that which is a "physiological shift accompanying a judgment."[76] When victims turn toward their own embodied sources of meaning making, they offer a glimpse into how feelings transpire viscerally in ways that make and move powerful arguments otherwise ignored in public. They provoke audiences to feel how they feel by coming into contact with other people and other environments, demonstrating how affect holds the potential to "enter into another" and inspire audiences to act.[77] Words have not always worked well for people attempting to disclose rape, but perhaps feelings can.

Visceral Rhetorics: On Methodology and Chapter Outline

My analysis is guided by my own training as a feminist rhetorical critic and an ethics of recognition informed by rhetorical and cultural theorists of affect and the body I outline here. When I trace *feelings*, I follow rhetorical scholars like Hawhee and Johnson, who have turned to the work of Ann Cvetkovich when tracking such extra-discursive material.[78] For Cvetkovich, "retaining the ambiguity between feelings as embodied sensations and feelings as psychic or cognitive experiences" is important.[79] Feelings are "intentionally imprecise," she maintains, and allow for a fluidity in understanding the relationship between affect and emotion.[80] To avoid going down a rabbit hole of distinguishing the differences between affect and emotion, as Massumi famously underscored, I, too, use the word "feeling" for such reasons.[81] On the one hand, I search for how bodies are described, portrayed, and discursively constructed in ways that associate women's bodies with particular feelings. On the other, I locate how affective responses to rape "become not just the basis but the very stuff of ideation and of critique."[82] Meaning has the capacity to "take hold," as Butler has described; responses to rape are layered with affect and constitute certain feelings about rape that move us closer to a physical, material understanding of violence.[83] In short, feelings construct our primary interpretations, compelling us to make certain judgments about the world and those around us.

In theorizing visceral rhetorics, I extend these ruminations of feeling and affect to account, in material terms, for how bodies communicate the raw, vulnerable threat of violence. The visceral regards "the surfaces and orifices—the skin, the mouth, the lungs, the alimentary tract," according to Johnson, the boundaries between the body's insides and outsides.[84] Attention to the visceral offers us a glimpse into the felt experience of violation, what Spillers calls "an interiorized violation of body and mind," or what we might consider the material, felt, fleshy experience of violence.[85] Building from Johnson's work on bodily intensity, I trace how feelings illuminate a deeply vulnerable and internal understanding of violation and, in the process, can serve to connect publics but also to violate them, to rupture them and call for change. Viscerality has the capacity to "reveal primal truth" about our relationships to others; it communicates meaning felt deep within the body; it draws acute attention to the body's edges as sites of potential danger and as sites of action, praxis, and change.[86] Pushing rhetorical scholarship to reconsider rhetoricity at the level of feeling, I trace what Ahmed refers to as an "affectivity of pain" across changing contexts, locating its force in encouraging audiences to *feel* certainty and believability—a rejoinder to Scarry's theory of pain.[87] In considering this affective, felt capacity, I argue for an understanding of rhetoric as "a feeling of bodily change."[88] When my stomach knots, my skin crawls, or my heart feels heavy—these are all forms of visceral rhetorics that guide us toward recognition and judgment. Visceral rhetorics that communicate by way of the body's organs, I suggest, are powerful for moving audiences to persuasion. When victims call us to consider the earthy, gritty, and even bloody accounts of rape, we are invited to engage with these forms of visceral rhetorics, forms that work with and beyond language, calling us to reconsider our relational lives in public.

Bringing together an interdisciplinary perspective informed by gender, publicity, and affect studies, *What It Feels Like* makes two important contributions.

First, the various perspectives mobilized in this book expand what constitutes the ground of rhetorical work specifically in a context of violence. Focusing on meaning made about violation and wound from a visceral perspective moves rhetorical theories of affect and sensation further into the realm of politics and ethics and expands feminist materialist theories within rhetoric to better account for how bodies become tangled up in arguments.[89] In the process, *What It Feels Like* demonstrates a methodology for how rhetorical scholars can capture these fleeting, affective, and visceral engagements by attending to how communication interacts with and engages the flesh and the internal nature of bodies, illustrating opportunities for examining affect's force and effect on discursive interactions more broadly. As a whole, this study offers utility for examining how bodies collide with language and are subjected to communicative frameworks that, together, serve various instances of violence and injustice in US society today, emphasizing a range of stakes for scholars across disciplines.

Second, demonstrating how individuals are subjected to a variety of tactics that function to contain their bodies and deny their felt experience of violence marks visceral rhetorics not only as a tool for apprehending women's experiences but one capable of interrogating rape culture more broadly. Within institutional, medical, and official discourses of rape, rhetorical tactics are deployed to circumvent victims' testimonies of what happened, serving to manage victims' bodies by dismissing what is often portrayed as an excess of feelings. Seeing, hearing, and sensing victims' bodies on their own terms, however, exposes these limits and offers a chance to understand contemporary prejudices due to sexual violence present in everyday life in new and necessary ways. Moving beyond efforts to recover women's voices in history, this renewed feminist rhetorical approach better accounts for how commonplace presumptions about women's bodies undergird a widely acknowledged silencing of women's voices in US publics.

To begin, I turn to the 1980s to understand how and when certain legacies of rape culture have taken hold in US society, leaving a mark we still feel today. In 1985, President Ronald Reagan appointed Attorney General Edwin Meese to spearhead the second national commission aimed at assessing the effects of pornography on public life. Like the Antipornography Civil Rights Ordinance hearings led by Dworkin and MacKinnon just a few years earlier, the US Attorney General's Commission on Pornography (popularly termed the Meese Commission) invited victims of sexual assault to testify during six public hearings across the country to their experiences with sexual violence. In 1986, the Commission issued a final report that drew a causal link between "substantial exposure to sexually violent materials" and "antisocial acts of sexual violence."[90]

In chapter 1, I investigate what frames are available for deliberating sexual violence by exploring citizen letters sent to the Meese Commission. Through the lens of Butler's theory of grievable bodies and Jasbir Puar's concept of debilitation, I examine how letter writers circumvented women's actual experiences with violence and instead focused on what seeing naked women's bodies does to the health of the nation.[91] In making claims to legally censor pornography, letter writers generated hysteria over male bodies and linked the experience of sexual violence with contemporary fears of social deviance, aligning raped, violated bodies with nonnormative, nonwhite, poor, single or nonmonogamous, and queer bodies—those perceived outside the boundaries of the nation-state. I argue that this case reveals a tacit linking among sexual citizenship, risk, and sensation that lives on today and ultimately serves to generate panic over those accused of rape or sexual assault while disregarding those made victim to violence.

Chapter 2 extends the concern for how publics deliberate the problem of rape by examining two contemporary VAWA rape prevention campaigns: It's on Us and 1 is 2 Many. In 2014, each of these government-sponsored campaigns entered into mainstream media by including in their promotional materials high-profile celebrities who identified as bystanders also responsible for rape culture. By suggesting that the problem of rape is "on all of us" or that "one case of rape is too many," these campaigns revived attention to the problem of rape. Drawing from each campaign's public advocacy and marketing materials, this chapter examines how the specter of patriarchy looms in the background of the voices of bystanders, who are given center stage, haunting public knowledge produced about rape and who experiences it. Investigating how speakers frame a heteronormative "victim"—a heterosexual, cis, white, able-bodied, US American, middle-class woman—in need of protection from a male body and male gaze, I theorize a new methodology, what I call "patriarchal spectrality," a methodology capable of hailing those who remain present in the discourse but ignored in state-sponsored conversations about rape. By looking to a contemporary focus on the bystander, this chapter explores how publics understand solutions to rape culture as those supported by white and male subjectivities, subjectivities that serve to codify contemporary anxieties over normative sexual and political identities. Taken together, these first two chapters identify how institutional discourses construct the problem of and solutions to rape culture through male-centric lenses, lenses that seek to contain and expel bodies deemed unfit for the body politic and normative social order.

The next two chapters examine how women's bodies are leveraged politically to respond to sexual violence. Chapter 3 considers how sexual assault forensic evidence kits—commonly referred to as "rape kits"—serve as powerful tools for rape adjudication even though a backlog of tens of thousands of untested and unprocessed rape kits has accumulated on law enforcement shelves. Tracing the rhetoricity of women's bodies through an analysis of public conversations about the backlog, this chapter reveals how assumptions about these medico-legal tools play out in public discourse to suppress embodied, visceral accounts of rape and privilege technological sources of evidence for adjudicating rape. In the process of prioritizing the need for "hard" evidence, I argue that legislative support for the use of such technological tools constitutes an attempt to remove rape justice from the realm of the rhetorical.

Chapter 4 turns to recent high-profile public performances by survivors who used embodied forms to protest institutional and legal failures to understand what counts as rape. During 2014 to 2015, Emma Sulkowicz engaged in a series of public art performances that sought to comment on the faulty institutional standards and procedures universities and colleges use when assessing rape. In 2016, Chanel Miller (anonymized during and after the case as Emily Doe) read her victim impact statement aloud in court during the trial of the *People of the State of California v. Brock Allen Turner*, a man who raped Miller behind a dumpster at a party on the Stanford University campus. In this chapter, I theorize how each individual calls upon their body as a source of evidence and protest, constituting what I call "visceral counterpublicity," acts that seek to shift the grounds by which we understand what counts as rape. By calling into question how mainstream publics define and discuss rape by way of the law, this chapter exposes the need for public opinion over cases of embodied violence to include visceral frameworks when deliberating the problem of rape.

The final chapter and conclusion consider the role of embodiment in writing for people living in the aftermath of rape. In 2017, the hashtag movement #MeToo went viral, leading millions across the globe to participate in a conversation about rape culture unlike any before it to date. Chapter 5 argues that what happened during #MeToo reveals a feminist deployment of an old strategy, *megethos*, or magnitude, matters of scale like those deployed in the Nassar case. People engaged with the #MeToo movement in multiple social media platforms by linking together intentionally brief disclosures or commentaries about rape culture, which formed a massive list that documented a multitude of experiences about sexual harassment, sexual assault, and rape. I maintain that listing tweet after tweet generated a visceral magnitude of testimonies that served to establish a collective believability about the contemporary realities of rape culture and overwhelm viewers into feeling the pervasive ubiquity of sexual violence in US society. Theorizing what I term "feminist *megethos*" through the idea of a list extends theories of magnitude beyond the ideas of coherence or amounting excessive detail and toward a theory that captures how magnitude can work to replace problematic assumptions about rape culture with a collective understanding of sexual violence central to victims' actual experiences.

In the conclusion, I reflect on how we move forward in US society knowing the limits of political, cultural, and public life by turning to the writing of popular writer and scholar Roxane Gay. Here, I examine how Gay has consistently employed strategies of viscerality and embodiment in her critiques of rape culture. I suggest that the rhetorical tactic of seething demonstrated throughout her work as a black woman living and writing in the aftermath of rape today offers a methodology for change, one that calls attention to how anger manifests across time and history in and through the body. In attending to how anger seethes, boils, and percolates silently yet viscerally, I conceptualize justice as a matter of visceral safety, a form of justice that might lead to an ethical possibility of interconnection if (and only if) the risk of harm is acknowledged in everyday life, material risk most certainly not equally shared by all.

I
SENSING THE NATION AT RISK: SEXUAL CITIZENSHIP AND THE MEESE COMMISSION

During the mid-1980s, President Ronald Reagan appointed Attorney General Edwin Meese to direct the second national commission aimed at assessing the effects of pornography on public life.[1] The goal of the Attorney General's Commission on Pornography (often referred to as the Meese Commission) was "to determine the nature, extent, and impact on society of pornography in the United States, and to make specific recommendations to the Attorney General concerning more effective ways in which the spread of pornography could be constrained, consistent with constitutional guarantees."[2] While a prior Presidential Commission (the 1970 Presidential Commission on Obscenity and Pornography) found that no public harm results from viewing pornography, the attorney general's commission issued a final report in July 1986 concluding "substantial exposure to sexually violent materials [. . .] bears a causal relationship to antisocial acts of sexual violence, and for some subgroups, possibly to unlawful acts of sexual violence."[3]

Shortly after its release, the report received harsh criticisms from legal, public, and scholarly audiences. After observing and testifying to the commission during its hearings, ACLU lawyer Barry Lynn published a summary of the commission titled "Polluting the Censorship Debate," calling the report "unsatisfying" and a "document [that] often reads more like a moral or religious tract than a serious legal or scientific work."[4] Public figures such as Betty Friedan, Colleen Dewhurst, and Kurt Vonnegut gathered at a National Coalition Against Censorship briefing just months before the release of the report and eventually published their critiques of the commission in *The Meese Commission Exposed*.[5] Scholars, too, echoed these and other critiques of the commission, citing faulty standards of proof, the absence of a warrant supporting the causal relationship between pornography and harmful behavior, vague definitions of pornography, and personal biases that presented a conflict of interest for the commission.[6] Overall, critics largely argued that the commission's work was an assault on First Amendment rights and a misuse of censorship for rape prevention advocacy.[7]

Not all reactions were negative, however. During the investigation, citizens wrote to the commission expressing concern over the state of pornography in the United States, declaring an anxiety over changing US sexual and gender roles as effects of viewing pornography.[8] In these letters, variously written by religiously affiliated members, former and then current sex industry workers, local politicians, popular fiction writers, and self-identified parents, among others, writers enlisted available cultural scripts that framed the effects of pornography within constructions of bodies—the bodies of children and family, the bodies of men who view pornography, and the bodies of women most valued in society. Their letters illuminate how investigation into the relationship between pornography and the causes of sexual violence quickly devolved into public debates about sexuality and the nation-state, eclipsing an initial inquiry into a public concern for sexual assault and rape. Instead of concerning themselves with bodies who had been subject to sexual violence, letter writers articulated what seeing naked women's bodies does to the health of the nation—a vision of the nation grounded in a white, heteronuclear fantasy—as justification for censoring pornography. Put differently, the concern for sexual violence faded from view, while heteronormative, masculine, ableist, white, and nationalist ideals were perceived as at risk and marshalled into the debate, rerouting and reframing public conversations about sexual violence that ensued during and after the actual hearings.

In this chapter, I argue that the Meese Commission manufactured norms around sexuality and violence that served to envision raped bodies out of the national imaginary, an imaginary grounded in normative embodied faculties. To make this argument, I use this case study to ask the following questions: What are the available frames for recognizing sexual violence? Whose bodies are subject to risk within these frames? And finally, how are bodily metaphors and images used when articulating a vision of a public good? In answering these questions, I examine dozens of letters that were submitted to the Meese Commission. In these letters, writers attempted to convince the commission (and, thus, the state) that risky bodily behavior was permeating every corner of society, but this concern was not one of power or the kind of violent, yet mundane, behavior central to acts of sexual violence. Rather, the proliferation of sexual materials—the very presence of women's sexuality—many argued, was the cause of a deterioration of society, which included a perceived uptick in rape crimes. Instead of uncovering the underlying causes of repeated instances of sexual violence, letter writers collectively sought to intervene in the debate by rehabilitating an alternative subjectivity: heteronormative, white, male bodies who presumably had "fallen off track" and been wrongly seduced by the evils of female sexuality. While the next chapter examines how the subjectivity of the victim is constructed and imagined in contemporary public discourse, this chapter traces its historical legacy in relation to a cultural idea of violence, advancing feminist, sociological, and cultural theories that have examined the relationship among criminality, race, and nonnormativity, one that maps onto perceptions of perpetrators, troubles discussions of justice, and, ultimately, operates in ways that overlook or forgive white, male perpetrators of the crimes they committed while casting aside actual victims.

Drawing upon crip and queer frameworks, I extend this body of scholarship and this book's interest in rhetorics of containment by examining how the commission and its surrounding discourses aligned raped or sexually assaulted bodies with nonnormative, nonwhite, poor, single or nonmonogamous, and queer bodies, those perceived outside the boundaries of normative social order and, consequently, not worth grieving.[9] Letter writers, I maintain, grieved what they believed to be the most worthwhile members of society—children, men, and mothers—and, in the process, sought to regulate certain forms of embodiment. As a result, the Meese Commission's investigation into erotic materials and its influence over the perception of a public good constituted victims as synonymous with those who were perceived as socially deviant figures. That is, the Meese Commission generated a specter of violence in which arguments against pornography operated through heteronormative-, ableist-, white-, and male-centric frames that dictated which bodies and bodily processes were deemed properly American, an imaginary in which raped, violated bodies had no place. Taken together, my analysis reveals how debates about sexual violence are haunted by a desire to contain the nation-state and its neoliberal imaginary, an imaginary leveraged in this case to preserve, first and foremost, the subjectivity of white, heteronormative, male members of society—members who might otherwise be identified as perpetrators responsible for violent crimes—while ridding victims and their actual experiences from this national vision.

The stakes of this argument, I suggest, are high and carry deep implications that foreshadow how we understand and frame perpetrators and victims of sexual assault today. In manufacturing male hysteria, the Meese Commission deflected interrogation into the conditions that foster sexually violent behavior and, consequently, created a culture of surveillance over sexual activities that ultimately served to redirect responsibility of rape onto the individual victim, a form of responsibility pervasively still present. Instead of grieving what, at the time, had been cited as a rape culture, letter writers circumvented the problem of sexual violence and alternately submitted sanitized sensations around sex and sexuality as grounds for establishing a healthy citizen and citizenry body.[10] Put another way, analysis of the letters sent to the commission illuminate how the available frameworks for responding to the debate were layered with a visceral anxiety about the proliferation of sexuality and difference that was grounded in a fear of the Other, someone who could infiltrate and contaminate both individual bodies and the body of the nation. To respond to that fear, letter writers invoked visceral reactions that served to bound belonging in the United States by blaming those who had ostensibly participated in sexual acts deemed most unfit.

In illustrating these larger stakes, this chapter lays an important groundwork for what follows in this book, establishing how public deliberation over rape functions through a rhetoric of containment that stems from patriarchy and heteronormativity, one akin to what scholars such as Jasbir Puar and others have theorized as an affective politics deeply entrenched in the promises of neoliberalism.[11] Tracing how claims against pornography became yoked to raced, gendered, and classed ideas of the experience of rape reveals the "nonconscious and unnamed, but nevertheless registered, experiences of bodily energy and intensity that arise in response to stimuli impinging on the body."[12] Analyzing how letter writers deployed visceral rhetorics central to this cultural moment that operated to protect white male subjectivity and generate sensations that served to mark women's violated bodies as abject unearths how national security is always subtly, yet powerfully, invoked in discussions of sexual violence, ultimately constraining larger discussions of rape culture in the service of containing the nation-state.

In what follows, I begin outlining the theoretical framework used in this chapter to foreground containment as a neoliberal concern of the nation-state that operated through visceral rhetorics of belonging during the Meese Commission. Using this groundwork, I then analyze how letter writers framed their concerns through the following three constructions: visions of the heteronormative, nuclear family; assessments of the contaminated male mind that viewed pornography; and abject perceptions of female sexuality. Taken as a whole, my analysis uncovers how certain bodies were labelled *risky* (and imagined out of a state investigation into sexual violence and its causes) while others were deemed *at risk* (and, thus, in need of rehabilitation), demonstrating the relationship sexual violence has to American identity and bodily regulation.[13] In closing, this chapter turns to the case of Brett Kavanaugh and his 2018 US Supreme Court Justice hearing, revealing how the connection among containment, national security, and sexual violence played out in a more recent, highly publicized debate about sexual assault. This tenacious linking among sexual citizenship, risk, and sensation, I argue, pervades our contemporary moment and ultimately serves to generate panic over *what could happen* to accused bodies in cases of sexual assault while ignoring *what has already happened* to actual victims' bodies. If rhetorical historians are tasked with understanding "how messages are created and used by people to influence and relate to one another," my conclusion explores how this case study bears serious implications for how publics relate to and understand those who experience sexual violence today.[14]

Containing the Nation's Grievable Lives

As a concept, neoliberalism surfaced after World War II among economic and legal scholars tied to both the Freiburg School in Germany and later Latin American scholars dubbed the "Chicago Boys" at the University of Chicago. Eventually imposed by Ronald Reagan in the United States, Augusto Pinochet in Chile, and Margaret Thatcher in the United Kingdom, neoliberalism became associated with several policies that supported pro-business programs, privatization, and free market expansion. It led to the creation of what Lisa Duggan calls "master categories" of "the *state*, the *economy*, and the *family*" that sought to manufacture nationality around a strict set of values.[15] Thus, while the neoliberal state is often "imagined," as Robert McRuer puts it, "positioned rhetorically, as a small, supposedly noninterventionist and nonregulatory state," its effects are grippingly felt in everyday life.[16] That is, neoliberalism not only serves to dictate economic policies but also "trickles into [. . .] everyday lived experiences," writes Rebecca Dingo, shaping "how individuals ought to act."[17]

The Meese Commission was born out of this political and cultural moment, one of heightened sexual panic that circulated broad rhetorics of emergency and wrongly directed fears about bodies that fell outside of a heteronormative, white, male ideal.[18] Alongside the neoliberal pillars of personal responsibility, austerity, and a harsh disciplining of law and order, newly marshalled in policies produced anxieties about sexual desire and sexual terror that circulated during this time and influenced the work of the commission. These anxieties played out in letter writers' constructions of risk, a version of risk consumed with feelings of harm that ultimately failed to account for sexual assault or rape. This chapter argues that one major reason why victims' actual experiences with rape and sexual assault were not taken as the primary frame for deliberating sexual violence can be traced in what motivations facilitated the politics of recognition that were used during the Meese Commission. In this case, labeling some bodies *risky* and others *at risk* invoked a boundary, a porous discourse of exclusion and inclusion that was tied to the nation and unfolded through sense-oriented faculties grounded in affect that served to hierarchically organize certain lives over others. In this section, I theorize containment in relation to the nation-state and the bodies imagined within it, sketching a framework for capturing how visceral boundaries worked in the service of an oppression that shaped defining and assessing risk.

Prior to the Meese Commission, several "porn wars" erupted, first in San Francisco and then migrating to places like Minneapolis, Indianapolis, Los Angeles, Madison, and Suffolk County. One of the most notable campaigns was introduced by anti-rape feminists Andrea Dworkin and Catharine MacKinnon, who composed the Antipornography Civil Rights Ordinance for the city of Minneapolis, arguing that pornography was a violation of women's rights. Following their methods, the Meese Commission called upon women who had experienced gender-based violence and aggression to testify to their experiences and their ostensible connection to pornography during the hearings. Unlike the Minneapolis hearings, however, which were concerned with civil rights and gender equality, the Meese Commission narrowed in on pornography as a dangerous form of moral turpitude. As such, the commission neglected responding to the ideological and cultural problems of gender inequity prompting sexual violence and instead chose to focus on the commission's objective of censoring pornography and identifying social deviance.

This fear of deviance, however, was not generated solely in response to the perception of sexual promiscuity at this time. A range of domestic policies responded to perceived social threats and helped disseminate a wider culture of fear in the United States during the 1980s. The use of statistics for issues like sexually transmitted diseases, the war on drugs, the AIDS crisis, domestic crime, rising divorce rates, and changing gender roles all led to what criminologist David Garland has called a "culture of control," and this new attitude encouraged people to identify "social deviants" who participated in what were portrayed as "social ills" at this time.[19] The numbers generated panic, covering over the fact that sexual abuse had long been occurring, troublingly yet intricately linked to the very formation of the state as the introduction to this book discussed. Amid these ideas of violence, panic, and disorder, the body served as a site of surveillance and regulation in which danger became tied to sexualized, racialized, classed, and gendered bodies. Certain bodies—often nonwhite and male—inhabited the gaze of many and were racialized as a social Other that was responsible for violence and disarray in US society.

As fear of the Other began to occupy a cultural backdrop more broadly, perceptions of sexual violence, too, took on new meaning. Sexual violence as a "social problem" emerged during the commission alongside this growing push for crime control, insecurity over minorities, and increasing penal reform. In the process, neoliberalism, argues Kristen Bumiller, circulated false fears about "the omnipresence of predators" lurking on the fringes of society.[20] While second-wave feminists of the 1960s and 70s called for state responsibility and aimed to show how women were subject to sexual violence by men they frequently already knew, neoliberalism helped reconstruct the rapist as a stranger, a distant, deviant, and racialized social Other. In other words, surveillance tactics led to the belief that those who participate in criminal activity—such as sexual assault or rape—must be an Other, someone far outside normative social order. Imagining a perpetrator as cisgender, straight, white, and male—a subjectivity otherwise deemed normative in society—became virtually impossible. Criminality was constituted through this raced, masculine figure. During the 1980s, "the feminist movement" thus "became a partner in the unforeseen growth of criminalized society," making strange bedfellows out of radical feminists and moral conservatives.[21]

While the Meese Commission initially emerged specifically concerned with what were perceived as rising rates of sexual violence, I maintain that it developed by constituting certain lives as worthy of protection, lives Judith Butler might label as grievable or losable.[22] Like all modes of recognition, those informing this moment were certainly historically, socially, and politically contingent and rooted in contextual frames that served to elicit political judgment. Writes Butler, "The frames through which we apprehend or, indeed, fail to apprehend the lives of others as lost or injured (lose-able or injurable) are politically saturated. They themselves are operations of power."[23] Lives not recognized and, as a result, not deemed worthy of public grief risk becoming unknown. Grief, in other words, functions as a political resource that forms a foundation for recognition, "a point of identification with suffering itself."[24] Lives that were given attention during the commission, seen as suffering—what Butler might view as mourned for their risk of loss—illuminate who was privileged and recognized in the public sphere at this time, constituted as *a life that matters*. Such public-facing grief subtly operated as a tool of the nation-state, serving to recognize and materialize certain lives as worthy of state protection. In ignoring the actual violence of rape already inflicted against some bodies, the Meese Commission constructed a boundary of the nation that served to contain those perceived as at risk, thus grievable, represented as important to the future of the nation and the body politic.

These modes of recognition, which functioned to include and exclude, however, were not simply dictated to letter writers through language or communication given by the commission. Rather, they disseminated through a wider biopolitical agenda that forced certain bodies into a state of abjection, one overwhelmed with feelings. Once used by the commission to raise attention and then later framed as risky, women who had experienced rape or sexual assault were folded into this concern for sexuality, encompassed by a space akin to what Puar has termed "debilitation," those chronically disempowered in public life, forced to endure bodily injury and political exclusion as a result of state efforts influenced by neoliberalism.[25] In other words, debility, as a framework, locates how bodies are disabled by the state, not necessarily identified under the category of disability but rather oppressed by the state in its effort to protect others. Those who did experience rape or sexual assault during this time, I suggest, dwell in this space, leveraged politically for a conservative agenda and then expelled afterward. In particular, those who testified during the commission hearings "[were] made to pay for 'progress,'" subjected to "increasingly demanding neoliberal formulations of health, agency, and choice," or what Puar defines as "a liberal eugenics of lifestyle programming."[26] That is, while victims' testimonies expressed violence committed against them in an attempt to redress inequality and call for state protection, their lives were ultimately foreclosed access and legibility—debilitated—in a context that explicitly began with a concern for the violence committed against them.

As the following analysis demonstrates, containing the nation-state through modes of grieving and debilitation functioned through the production of "ecologies of sensation, technics, and affect" that arranged some bodies as in danger.[27] Facilitating arguments about what it means to feel American, the Meese Commission thus coopted a visceral rhetoric of containment and deployed it as an object of control. If you feel fearful about the bodies of others, the sheer presence of difference—its broader discourses suggested—then those feelings mark you at risk, in danger, potentially the target of a lurking criminal. Such affective identification emerged, linking certain "histories, rhetorics, and images," those not directly conjured, as Jennifer Wingard puts it, "but that circulate to connect our memories and our bodies" with particular feelings tied to discourses of power.[28] Engaging visceral rhetorics, then, letter writers justified their primary sources of critique through images of bodily corruption, a visceral account of exclusion, paving a path for recognizing (or failing to recognize) future cases of sexual abuse. Grieving some bodies while debilitating others functioned through an "allegiance to the state, [in which] surveillance itself [was] rendered mundane and inevitable," facilitated through the feelings associated with the presumption of civic duty.[29] Letter writers most certainly adhered to a sense of belonging; however, it was one deeply rooted in oppression and exploitation, central effects of neoliberal policies. But these neoliberal logics, as transnational feminist scholars have shown, have always been linked to vectors of power that support the subjugation of certain racial, gendered, and differently located groups, ideologies that manifest in severely destructive ways.[30]

The Meese Commission was thus haunted by a reality of the nation that clashed with its imaginary, a reality that included nonwhite bodies, queer bodies, and disabled bodies. Just as feminist and queer theories have been helpful in exposing how contexts not seemingly about gender and sexuality are full of concerns about gender and sexuality, using a disability informed framework here reveals how the desire to ignore raped bodies is really a quest to debilitate them, ignore them, or secure and eliminate them from the nation-state. In other words, I seek to crip the discourses of the Meese Commission, demonstrating how "bodies and bodily imagery [. . .] were being used to send messages of outrage," how "spaces, issues, or discussions [got] 'straightened'" in the service of resisting difference.[31] Cripping is especially powerful for thinking about contexts such as the Meese Commission given its central rhetorics of emergency and risk, rhetorics that always seek a return to an imagined normative state devoid of difference.[32] That state, as this chapter argues, is one filled with an anxiety about sex and sexuality articulated in the service of defining and bordering the nation. Next, I examine how risk is always influenced by a public's shared assumptions, perceptions, and values, illustrating how the frames used by letter writers reveal certain beliefs about which bodies were positioned as most belonging in the nation-state while designating others outside of state protection and recognition.

Framing the Effects of Pornography

Alongside several pornography debates that circulated during this time period, the Meese Commission emerged with a specific concern for sexual violence after a prior commission found no link between violence and the viewing of pornography. In fact, the 1970 Presidential Commission recommended loosening restrictions on the sale of pornographic materials after concluding no connection between harm and viewing. Nonetheless, the Meese Commission gathered together twelve members, held public hearings in six cities across the country over the course of a year, and published an unwieldy 1,960-page final report in July 1986, documenting the commission's findings and recommendations. After observing the hearings, anthropologist Carole Vance suggested that a moral agenda remained at the heart of their work. Writes Vance, "Pornographic images were symbols of what moral conservatives wanted to control: sex for pleasure, sex outside the regulated boundaries of marriage and procreation. Sexually explicit images are dangerous, conservatives believe, because they have the power to spark fantasy, incite lust, and provoke action," subtly defining sexuality writ large as a state of visceral uncontrollability, in other words.[33] Almost immediately following the report's release, several people responded, many of whom were critical of the report, in the form of books, pamphlets, protests, and articles, claiming that the commission was an attack on First Amendment rights. Supporters of the commission and its outcomes, however, framed their opinions around a much different threat to public life, one grounded in a neoliberal fear of the Other and a desire to preserve certain subjectivities within US cultural and political life.

While the majority of letters I found in the archival papers of commission member Park Elliott Dietz argued for censorship, some—very few—did represent arguments against censorship of pornography, one of which I take up in the conclusion to this chapter. Though it is reasonable to assume that the commission solicited letters from the public, that local communities organized letter-writing campaigns, or that commission members preserved letters supportive of the goal of censorship, I found no evidence confirming these actions to explain why the letters archived overwhelmingly served the commission's main interests.[34] At the very least, we might assume that everyday individuals who felt anxious about the perception of deviance more broadly might have been motivated by the commission's goals or even that those who supported the commission may have felt more comfortable producing a private letter, given that critics of the commission vigorously attacked its work in public. Nevertheless, what this focus on letters does reveal is how the nation-state was leveraged into the debate. The final report published after the commission focused mainly on testimonies given by "experts" who spoke of the effects of viewing pornography, yet the letters themselves speak to a wider culture of conservatism that circulated in public and prioritized white male subjectivity at the expense of protecting victims of rape or sexual assault. As my analysis reveals, these letters tap into a public pulse present throughout the commission's work that catalyzed its larger messages, serving to center normativity and national security in a debate about sexual violence and ultimately further shift the discourse of rape culture away from victims' actual experiences.

Pornography as a National Threat

In a letter written to commission member Alan Sears, Bishop E. Harold Jensen wrote, "One need not be a prude or some kind of overly fastidious person to realize that the issues that become commercial merchandise are issues that in human experience ought to be held in private and discreet contexts. The question of taking the human body, sexuality, and sexual impulses as the base material for entertainment or sensation or just simple profit taking is not only abhorrent, it is erratically dangerous to the development of a free people."[35] In his letter, Jensen wrote of a society "speechless" on the subject of pornography, the effects of which "create a dullness and an insensitivity to the observance of basic human dignity."[36] He suggested, "There are indeed some parts of the body that ought to be private property," fearful of what happens when public and economic contexts are exposed to the sensations linked to sexual impulses. But the most nefarious consequences of pornography, he submitted, occur to "the development of a free people."[37]

Several letter writers positioned pornography as a threat to the nation—"a clear and present danger to the very fabric of our society," as Reverend William C. Wantland put it in his letter.[38] This section explores how making claims about what constitutes the sensations of "proper" citizenship formed a foundation to define what counts as dangerous and risky behavior. Sexual desire demonstrates the visceral capacities of a body—its internal ability to feel and respond to external images, sensations, and actions. Yet distinguishing which parts of the body "ought to be private property" imagines a particular type of visceral behavior suited for civic contexts—one controlled and sanitized, monitored and managed through existing fears of sexual panic during this time. In constituting particular behaviors as "erratically dangerous," letter writers like Jensen worked to, in Butler's words, "produce and shift the terms through which subjects are recognized," limiting the scope for examining victims' actual experiences.[39] Sensations associated with pornography—feelings of lust, desire, and pleasure—created a framework for understanding rape and those who experience it. But because public subjects, as the letters examined in this section maintained, should only be recognized through the ability to control their sexual impulses—the visceral boundaries of the body—the affective responses to rape mirrored those of disgust similarly linked to sexual practices that threaten public life, including pornography. Thus, feeling properly American meant excising sexual practices that did not serve a heteronormative, reproductive family, including the act of rape along with the bodies involved, both perpetrator and victim. Constructing a risky body metonymically functioned to define what it meant to be a victim of rape or sexual assault.

In suggesting that pornography leads to societal danger, letter writers contextualized its consequences alongside other common threats to conservative social and sexual norms. For instance, Jane Barnett addressed her letter to the commission with a specific concern for rising cases of "crime and abuse in [her] community."[40] After outlining "the rate that pornography [was] flooding into [her] area," she explored in general detail several sexual abuse crimes that had allegedly occurred in her county involving a murder-rape, incest, and rape cases by adolescent perpetrators.[41] "Pornography," she maintained, "encourages incest, homosexuality, violence against women and child molestation."[42] In defining rape through extreme examples alongside acts deemed improper, Barnett assembled a national threat that registered rape crimes with feelings of impurity, feelings tied to incest, homosexual relationships, and child molestation—all in the same breath, all equally "problematic" from her perspective. She addressed the commission asking, "Should we be surprised at the violence and abuse that is surfacing in our society after allowing the pollution of pornography to flood our country for the past thirty years?"[43] Linking pornography with pollution and national decline positioned rape as a consequence of pornography, as opposed to a condition of sexually violent culture, one that long preceded pornography and its technological affordances. In this vein, rape was understood as a new problem, resulting from new cultural modes and actions. Ultimately, Barnett closed her letter writing, "These kinds of crimes will continue to esculate [sic] if we choose to remain silent and inactive regarding pornography."[44] Her call to act and resist "silence" framed sexual purity politics as civic duty.

Weaved into civic calls such as these, however, is a broad categorization of what constitutes "violence," framing the problem of rape alongside other perceived "social ills." Another writer, Curtis Maynard, echoed similar claims made by Barnett, writing, "The evidence overwhelmingly supports the linkage between pornography and so many of our Nation's social ills: divorce, drugs, rape, child abuse, homosexuality, battered wives, abortion, AIDS, V.D.

and the list goes on and on."⁴⁵ Again, violence such as rape and domestic or child abuse were buried alongside things like homosexuality, divorce, and AIDS and conjured in hypothetical terms. Conflating certain social activities with disease constituted an image of nonnormativity, one that provoked ideas of deficiency as a response to these activities, marking them as deplorable and a threat to civic life. While the presence of violence against women was presented in these letters, it is important to note that it was done so alongside other bodies deemed not grievable—bodies, in fact, designated as pollutants to the nation. That is, like bodies subject to rape, the bodies suffering from AIDS, sexually transmitted diseases, and presumably divorce or queer identity were all perceived as repulsive and aligned with conservative fears tied to moral corruption. As a result, bodies that had been raped carried the affective baggage of disgust that positioned victims and others as unfit for the nation-state.

In framing the nation at risk, writers' claims against pornography invoke Puar's concept of debility. By "evaluating the violences of biopolitical risk" through "metrics of health, fertility, longevity, education, and geography," letter writers built a definition of risk through the valence of personal responsibility and morality.⁴⁶ Put differently, the measurements for proper citizenship were facilitated through the affective work of normativity, identifying a clear distinction between healthy and unhealthy citizenry behaviors grounded in certain feelings about sex. After arguing that the "display of nude females" was bombarding US public space, Nancy Adinolfe closed her letter with the following question: "Do you feel secure about the sexuality in this country?"⁴⁷ Adinolfe's letter alludes to what many viewed as an overwhelming perversion of sexuality—the very spread of nudity spilling over into society—invoking an anxiety about the sexual presence of women's bodies in public. In posing her rhetorical question, though, she echoed a then contemporary form of fear mongering that functioned by "imagining sexuality in the shadow of deaths to be avoided."⁴⁸ In other words, some may hear traces within Adinolfe's letter of the fear of public sexuality more broadly, a sexuality linked to the distress of AIDS looming at this time. In posing an insecurity around sexuality, a fear of queer, nonnormative sexual behaviors—fears shaped by affective frameworks that sought to monitor sexuality—encapsulated a fear of rape. Risky sexual behaviors, including those central to the act of rape, posed unwanted threats to be avoided and generated a citizen behavior rooted in self-surveillance and prevention of such behaviors.

To reclaim an idea of the proper American citizen, writers constructed an image of the family in which sex was used solely for reproduction. Pornography, as Dr. R. Donald Shafer submitted, "is devastating to the home in both marital relationships and the relationships between children and parents."[49] Apocalyptic in tone, threats to the family became threats to society and the state. Letter writers such as Jensen quoted above hailed "the freedom of privacy" as one of America's "profound freedoms" that "includes the private functions of human beings within which context the most sacred of all things happens, conception."[50] In other words, feeling American was grounded in a domestic, family unit upheld by an image of a heterosexual couple whose private sexual lives were based in reproductive purposes. Sexuality was depicted as purposeful, intentional, and solely for conjugal purposes—most certainly private and contained.

In this frame, an imagined future circulated through nostalgic depictions of childhood, fostering state responsibility over the child and the bodies responsible for rearing that child. Writers called for censorship by coupling appeals to democracy with appeals to morality, as was done in a letter jointly written by a husband and wife: "The majority of people in America <u>do not</u> want this destructive, depraved, malignant material in their neighborhoods where they are trying to raise their children. They further believe it is the responsibility of their federal, state and local government to complement the family unit by maintaining a morally sound and safe environment where families and children can become responsible, healthy, confident members of a civilized society."[51] The Pasquini letter puts forth an easy linking between family and the government, marking the private sexual and social activities used for child rearing as the proper sensations central to the national imaginary, bodies and feelings deemed most worthy of government protection. In other words, "responsible, healthy, confident members of a civilized society" are those who engage with sexual activities specifically aimed at parenting the health and future of the nation. Sexual perversion, on the other hand, became associated with national risk, that which needs to be avoided. Calling pornographic materials "destructive, depraved, and malignant" simultaneously marked all forms of sexual pleasure in hostile ways. Visceral impulses associated with sex for pleasure that escape the private confines of the heteronormative home suggested an excess of sexuality, a body at risk for feeling in unruly ways.

Juxtaposing ideas of the ethical subject—"responsible, healthy, confident members of a civilized society"—against "malignant material" served to justify the family as the normative, ideal construction in which parents mold their children into proper citizens through ideas of civil obedience. The letter written by the Pasquinis echoed similar claims made by the Moral Majority, an organization started by the late Rev. Jerry Falwell in the late 1970s that continued into the 1980s in which the conservative agenda took on several platforms of the religious, specifically Christian, right. In closing their letter, "concerned for America," writers Ronald and Leslie Pasquini submitted, "To believe that society can exist without the family unit, as the basic foundation, is suicide."[52] Perhaps the most hyperbolic in tone, these writers generated feelings of shame and even death as descriptions for a nation in which the family was not at the center. Outraged by shifting standards of sexuality in public, these writers called on the government to "take a responsible position and [. . .] set a standard in America that the world can again look to and follow."[53] In reflecting on her 1984 "Thinking Sex" article in 2011, Gayle Rubin notes how panic, specifically the concern for the "sexual welfare of the young," served at this time and has since served as "[a vehicle] for political mobilizations and policies with consequences well beyond their explicit aims."[54] Such visions of the nation, she argues, have ultimately led to "intensifying women's subordinate status, reinforcing hierarchical family structures, curtailing gay citizenship, opposing comprehensive sex education, limiting the availability of contraception, [. . .] restricting abortion," and, in this case, obscuring a reality of sexual violence.[55] Fashioning national security as sexual and familial normativity constituted a set of sexual activities that should be protected by the state, in which the rhetorical use of children served as a symbol for hope, a vehicle for imagining the future. Any mention of sexuality not linked to the family and reproduction incited public fear, making it difficult to understand sex-positive ways of being in the world.

Readers familiar with neoliberalism and its effects will not be surprised to hear that the image of the family served as an important construction for writers in favor of pornography censorship when establishing their idea of community and the nation-state. Queer, feminist, and crip scholars have well documented how neoliberalism has centered heteronormative feelings directly around an idealized image of citizenship, feelings that then serve to generate panic over bodies not deemed heteronormative, middle class, white, able-bodied, or cisgender.[56] As neoliberal policies took stronger grip during the 1980s, the valence of personal responsibility constituted a public mediation of private matters, where "acts that are not civil acts, like sex, [. . .] [bore] the burden of defining proper citizenship."[57] These private acts of intimacy served to authorize the inclusion and exclusion of certain subjects and constituted a national imaginary that worked to regulate intimate activities, sanitize sexuality, and categorize gender identity roles. While the production of normative sexual, marital, and familial roles created a national identity maintained and materialized through the performance of gender, these identities were conjured through a fictional imaginary of the nation, one in which heteronormative "ideologies and institutions of intimacy [were] increasingly offered as a vision of the good life [. . .], the only (fantasy) zone in which a future might be thought and willed, the only (imaginary) place where good citizens might be produced."[58] Letter writers prioritized this fantasy image of the heteronormative family and went so far as to align certain bodily sensations with whom and what they perceived as fit for social, cultural, and political life. Familial normativity, in other words, was used not just to condition sexuality and civic life but also to deny the very presence and ubiquity of rape culture.

Through this frame, writers described the consequences of pornography in terms of national security, and in the process, affirmed heteronormative standards as the boundary of the idealized national body. Those who had experienced rape, however, were positioned as an effect of unwanted and undesirable sexual activities associated with viewing pornography. In this rise of neoliberal society, democracy and its cultures "were often secured through violence, repression, and the literal, state-sanctioned disappearance of dissidents," consequences that most certainly blunted victims' experiences with violence from being heard or valued on their own terms.[59] Even though they were positioned as victims of someone else's wrongdoing—someone else's "disease," as the next section shows—the subjectivity of victims still posed a challenge to the perception of healthy, national well-being, making it difficult to recognize their subjectivity, deliberate the causes of what happened, and further eradicate the conditions of rape culture. In short, victims failed to fit inside a citizenship ideal. In what follows, I extend this investigation into who is imagined as at risk to account for the bodies of those who view pornography.

Contaminated Male Minds

On behalf of the American Coalition for Traditional Values, Maynard addressed the commission and the need to censor pornography by making an argument about pollution. He wrote: "The Bible written thousands of years ago has clearly taught us 'As a man thinketh so is he.' [sic] In other words, its [sic] virtually impossible to pollute the mind without polluting the whole body. We are all products of our thoughts. Our behavior is based on our thought process."[60] In his letter, Maynard drew a strong connection between the mind's ability to influence the body, suggesting that bodily processes are deeply affected by thought processes. He invoked metaphors of consumption to suggest that visual images taken in through the mind hold the capacity to influence and alter the body—to infect it. Alongside his claims of pollution, panic lurks in that which goes unstated in his letter: the fear of uncontained, contaminated, nonnormative male arousal.

This section analyzes how letter writers grounded their claims for censorship in the idea that viewers of pornography risk experiencing an uncontrollability of the senses and, as a result, called for measures that sought to recover and rehabilitate the visceral capacities of the body back to a state of containment. Unlike the previous section, here I focus not on the question of debilitation in the case of rape victims but rather those *at risk of debilitation*, on the edges of society but not yet worth casting out. In other words, not all debilitated bodies are simply ejected and removed from the state. Rather, "debility is profitable for capitalism," Puar maintains; some "debilitated bodies can be reinvigorated for neoliberalism, available and valuable enough for rehabilitation" while some cannot.[61] Here, I attend to how writers make arguments about which bodies are "valuable enough" by drawing upon metaphors of contagion and invasion, producing arguments that ultimately served to mark sexuality as the problem from which male viewers of pornography must be saved. Put differently, employing metaphors of contagion, pollution, or degradation to understand pornography's influence functioned through arguments that suggested viewing pornography held the capacity to control the senses, a visceral state layered with fears regarding the destruction of the white male body who ostensibly views such images.

Maynard invoked a body manipulated by the mind, inundated by the onslaught of "bad" thoughts, susceptible and vulnerable to outside influences. He wrote, "It seems incredible to me that in our society, we recognize the need to control what we eat, breathe and drink to protect our physical bodies from polluted food, air and water but allow the minds of our people to be grossly polluted."[62] On the surface, he raised environmental regulation as a response to the proliferation of pornography. In the process, he aligned pornographic viewing with things like alcohol or smoking, actions that have the capacity to "poison" the body through inhalation or consumption, calling for regulation in order to return the body to a healthy state. I speculate, however, that laden within his claims of pollution rests a homophobic panic in which "gayness form[ed] the motif of a story that [was] not ostensibly about gayness," one in which "homophobia and internalized homophobia ensure[d] that gayness [was] properly abjected."[63] Because sexuality at the time was publicly invoked in the discourse of AIDS, it's not a stretch, in other words, to imagine how stigmas tied to sexuality bolstered Maynard's claim for environmental regulation, that the male body was in need of purification and that it may become out of control because of what has been captured in the mind.[64]

In other words, readers may hear a number of anxieties shaping statements made by Maynard, written at a moment when the norms and subjectivities imagined in the United States were shifting. In subtly defining the means for proper citizenship, neoliberalism simultaneously created a "political rationality," which resulted not only in defining normativity but also in the management and governance of it.[65] Heteronormativity emerged at this time as a measuring stick for citizenship, serving to place boundaries around certain individuals and sexual practices. The dearth of public and presidential remarks made about AIDS led to feelings of ambiguity, uncertainty, and anxiety regarding the disease and cultivated an attitude of surveillance targeting those who had AIDS in addition to those who engaged in sexual activities positioned outside the imagined heteronormative image, activities that were, as a result, deemed risky, capable of spreading. Many letter writers drew on similar motifs when describing sexuality more broadly, inciting fear by suggesting things like bodily corruption and infection as potential outcomes of viewing pornography. The concern for an excess in sexuality thus merged with wider fears of difference, and, more specifically, censorship claims hailed the same ideas of contamination used in AIDS discourses circulating at the time. Whether grounded in homophobia or misogyny, censorship became a plea to cleanse the body from its sexual impulses, ridding it from unwanted thoughts and actions, serving to valorize a heteronormative male identity.

Seeing became the primary sense susceptible to vulnerability in claims concerning bodily invasion. Letter writers imagined consequences to viewing these materials in ways that rhetorically relegated the body to a status below the mind and proceeded by imagining what the mind "takes in," material acting as a parasite living off and in the body. According to one letter writer, "What we put into our minds will ultimately come out as actions," echoing the proverbial "you are what you eat" warning.[66] Like eating or drinking, Eileen Roth argued, viewing and seeing have the potential to alter behavior. Continuing this line of thought, she wrote, "The more filth and perversion people 'feed' on, the more violent and unsafe and degrading our society will become."[67] The metaphor of "feeding" deployed here suggests that viewing bodies have become dependent on pornography in ways that could cause addiction and corrupt their health. The problem, according to Roth, was that explicit images held the potential to cause visceral reactions, in which, when viewing, people would be unable to control their bodies (or their sexuality).

Calling for public action, she wrote, "Each one of us is responsible by what we do to put a stop to it or allow it."[68] Collective responsibility was garnered around a goal of saving the potential viewer from consuming images of naked bodies, which were framed as poisonous material.

Such ideas of contamination were echoed by Sylvia Harbison Phillips, who wrote, "It [pornography] is the most insidious contempt-producing material which plants the seeds of 'disgust of the female' into impressionable minds of all the youth acrossed [sic] this nation."[69] In identifying a female object, Phillips simultaneously invoked a male gaze, situating the fear of contamination within heteronormative gender dynamics in which men—men who otherwise appeared "normal"—view sexualized women for pleasure. Positioning pornographic images as "seeds" implies a growth process, a process ironically sexual and in line with reproduction. However, this seed is a misplaced reproductive seed; planted into the mind, it has the potential to do the most harm to the body, to give birth to libidinous desires feasted on and erected by uncontrollable viewing. Phillips also claimed that this contamination extended to society, suggesting that pornography "erodes moral values of fidelity within a two-parent family unit."[70] The metaphor of erosion—a slow but devastating process—served to imagine for readers altered neurological and biological functioning as a result of viewing pornography.

During the actual hearings, commission members widely suggested the idea that pornography causes a psychological and physical reaction in the body. Arguing that bodily reactions demonstrated in male viewers led to destruction was heavily critiqued by outside observers, yet these ideas concerning an image's power to alter behavioral action circulated in several letters. In Wantland's letter, he wrote, "Numerous studies by medical, legal and ethical scholars show clearly that there is a direct link between prolonged exposure to gratuitous sex and violence and criminal behavior."[71] Wantland extended the idea of altering behavior here to suggest that criminal actions will result from viewing pornography, fearful of "unwanted sights and sounds of deviant sex invading the private homes of citizens."[72] While critics of the Meese Commission balked at this idea, challenging the sources and studies employed as dubious at best, letter writers invoked ideas of physiology, persuaded by a fear of the body's visceral capacities, its "numbing effect," as Wantland cited it.[73] By generating hysteria around male bodies that view pornography—a fear that assumed viewers could turn into criminals—writers called for public protection of these bodies, and, in the process, marked them worthy of grief and in need of revival. Cases of rape were positioned as acts caused by bodies out of control, yet the ideal solutions, writers suggested, were aimed at rehabilitating male bodies instead of responding to those subjected to violence.

This fear of sexuality was certainly influenced by racialized angst stemming from shifting national demographics at the time. For instance, metaphors of infection were used to propagate not only homophobia or misogyny but also racism. "The metaphor of African influence as cultural contagion," Barbara Browning writes, "was constructed in the West as an effort (largely unconscious) to contain or control the diasporic flows, whether migrational or cultural."[74] Thus, the fear of deadly diseases disseminated in metaphors used to discuss both gay men and black bodies more broadly, metaphors similarly used in anti-immigration discourses surrounding the US-Mexico border. Metaphors of spread have functioned through depictions of "immigrants [...] as infections" to suggest "a Third World invasion of the First World."[75] In other words, the "invasion" of queer or nonwhite bodies is often understood through metaphors that contaminate the body politic, positioning it as at risk of disease, as the first section well documented. Thus, the sexual depiction of women served to represent wider social anxieties at the time. Letter writers submitted metaphors of contagion and invasion that stem from such sexualized and racialized fears to describe the spread of pornography, ultimately reaffirming a white male normative center in need of relief. Instead of arguing pornography's effects only on the national body, however, writers drew upon these metaphors to position the effects of viewing pornography on the senses and the body's visceral responses to certain images.

In addition to heteronormative male viewers, writers also feared what could happen to children who encountered pornographic images. Writers worried about how children would view pornography on a supposed "involuntary basis," suggesting that children's bodies could also be controlled by images.[76] Laden within these anxieties was a fear that viewing pornography would lead to improper development, a form of sexuality out of control, unfit for the nation. Self-identified as a "citizen, parent, child advocate, and social woman," Sara Brown wrote, "Please understand how important it is to some of us and to the nation's children that we limit and regulate the production and distribution of pornographic materials in this country. With the technological advances that have made pornography so available to children (home VCRs, video rental stores, cable T.V., etc.) we must take action! This action protects the rights of children to grow-up in a healthy, unpolluted environment."[77] Similar to calls for censorship, arguments fearful of the rise of technology invoke a concern for inactive viewing, wrongful and dangerous visual and visceral persuasion of gross sexuality. Appealing to "a healthy, unpolluted environment" served as a call to purify a space for the development of (white) children, marking them worthy of governmental protection.

To stall corruption of the mind, letter writers invoked arguments of environmental regulation that sought to contain the availability of pornography alongside other risky consumable materials assumed to cause unwanted harm to the body. The risk of overindulgence was echoed and circulated during the hearings as demonstrated by the testimony of Representative Frank Wolf: "To those who would suggest that the viewing of pornography is a right, a freedom that must be protected, a means of self-expression, I would like to leave you with this thought: When an individual takes a drink of alcohol, he or she is exercising a right as a free American citizen. But when that individual overindulges or drinks to the point that that drug threatens the lives of other humans should that person drive a car—then his right to that drink is called into question."[78] In Wolf's testimony, he opened with a narrative about police officers finding pornography in the homes of serial killers, wondering what influence such materials held over their acts to murder. During his closing remarks, Wolf invoked pornography as a public health crisis that could lead to deadly effects akin to drunk driving. Placing his argument in the context of rights served to rouse government oversight and the need to protect male bodies that view pornography to an excessive degree, a protection oriented toward future men that denied past acts of violence. Writers appealed to the destruction of the body and the brain as responses to viewing pornography by conjuring metaphors of contamination and war, and these constructions served to portray the body as deeply susceptible to outside stimuli. But appeals to contamination also framed sexuality in terms of state regulation. Citing pornography as an environmental concern created the idea that perpetrators had been infected by crude or wrongful images of sexuality, that they had simply fallen off the proper path of normalcy, seduced by the "evils" of sexuality, whether female or otherwise.

In all of these cases, writers shed light on pornography's effects through metaphors of destruction. They honed an image of the male viewer and positioned pornography as an infestation of his mind and body. In the process, they circulated rhetorics of contagion and cure that served to diagnose the sexuality present in pornography as the problem while "straightening" male behavior as the solution. In other words, calls for government protection were made by leveraging the demise of male bodies instead of bodies subject to violence. The crime of rape was thus defined through logics of contamination as opposed to normalized sexually violent behavior. Such rhetorics of cure and correction are incredibly powerful when defining a "problem," because as queer and crip theorists have shown, a cure suggests that which should be preserved, made normal, returned to its proper functioning state all for the purposes of advancing the nation. Through these metaphors of contamination, letter writers asserted the men who view pornography as most at risk—the subjectivity that must be rehabilitated—while actual experiences of rape involving perpetrators remained absent from conversation. In what follows, I examine how female sexuality gets further pitted as the problem, a perceived cause of all that is problematic in US society, which formed the foundation for victim blaming as a response vehicle to rape that would go on to thrive in US culture.

Female Sexuality as Un-American

In his letter to the commission, Matthew F. Carney cited the proliferation of danger in the United States, the increase in "alienation, anomie, drug abuse, sexual deviance, and the rising incidence of teenage suicide" as factors that cannot be ignored due to the "simple acceptance of sexual liberation among rebellious youth."[79] Echoing a similar threat to the nation outlined in the first section, Carney feared a society ruined due to "promiscuity and sexual licentiousness" as a result of the proliferation of pornography.[80] But he also recognized another "significant effect"—that of the "dehumanization of women" as one consequence of the rise of pornography. He wrote: "How can a lasting relationship be built between people where there exists no image of *women as friend, companion, teacher, and confidant to man?* How can a strong sense of family unity be built where there is no balance between freedom and responsibility?"[81]

In this last section, I analyze how pornographic representations of women caused anxiety for writers concerning how these images would affect the subjectivity of women in society. Invoking a concern for responsibility, Carney suggested specific conventions through which women should be realized. Freedom, he maintained, had been overextended to the point where visions of sexualized women needed to be contained, that women needed to be relegated back to their former position as an extension of man. In calling for censorship, letter writers analyzed in this section leveraged the idea of an archetypal mother as most threatened by sexualized depictions of women, invoking what Natalie Fixmer-Oraiz has termed a "homeland maternity" or "a project of security that enlists domesticity as requisite to the future of the nation," one that has troublingly led to "the differential surveillance and control of women's bodies and behaviors."[82] Prioritizing this vision of womanhood, I argue, framed feminine sexuality as the problem and laid a foundation for blaming victims for acts like rape or sexual assault. Letter writers grieved a contained, closed form of sexuality projected onto heterosexual, white women and aligned sensations associated with cloistral, conservative depictions of motherhood as the only ideal through which women could be realized in the public sphere. Such limiting constructions of gender, race, and sexuality made it difficult to acknowledge a reality of rape in US society, paving the way for a history of victim blaming and victim shaming that exists today.

As suggested by writers in the first section, the ideal woman framed in the national imaginary was a mother capable of reproduction. Pornography, according to letter writers, harmed this image: "Pornography not only breaks down moral values, thus destroys the family unit, it further destroys the human-status value of womankind thus dismisses the opinion value of a mother trying to raise children."[83] While testimonies like this one emerged from a place of valuing women, they submitted that a woman's subjectivity could only be understood as that of a mother and, as a result, argued for women's rights through the veil of motherhood. They feared that shifting norms around sexuality would consequently shift gendered expectations: "There are a lot of kids out there who have no real respect for their mothers (who are part of the female race) which pornography has been systematically debasing and destroying at a rapid pace."[84] In using the term "female race," Phillips aligned motherhood with a version of the citizen race grounded in civility, rationality, and whiteness. Calls for civic responsibility echoed the "cult of domesticity" or reproduction narratives from the early republic in which "white women were nonetheless constituted as the bearers of moral guidance and virtue, rendered responsible for cultivating their sons' investments in civic participation and state leadership."[85] Maternal calls made by those like Phillips invoked womanhood through white imaginaries that worked to sustain whiteness and erase the maternal histories and experiences of women of color and poor white women. Invoking the idea of "the human race" by nuancing a "female race" served to identify two perceived gender categories within that "race"—men and women—but also linked those genders to white civilization. This type of "discursive bordering," writes Ersula Ore, has always "render[ed] blackness the antithesis of citizenship, 'the people' synonymous with 'white,' and 'white' synonymous with the 'citizen race.'"[86] Linking "female" to "race" served to harness women's rights to a history of white supremacy, one deeply committed to patriarchy and misogyny. Advancing what was framed as a "feminist" agenda repositioned woman in relation to Man, recognized solely through this confined form of subjectivity, further erasing the rights and experiences of those imagined outside of it. Constructing women's rights through "the female race," in other words, was a project aimed to preserve the hierarchy of white masculinity.

Women's rights, as rhetorical scholars have shown, have always been tied to narratives of womanhood that ultimately constrain a legal capacity to be seen as equal.[87] But gender inequity is not simply a matter of the law; rights are always tied to the public sphere and its designation of private realms. The public sphere "exercise[s] decisive authority over the private world and over its female inhabitants in particular. [. . .] The public in this explicitly political and hierarchical apparition monitors the entire social continuum including the structural divisions between the genders."[88] Women who threaten the image of woman as "the helpmate of rational man" are seen as a hazard to the public sphere, a problem in which "her sexuality must be defeated."[89] In the case of the Meese Commission, women that admit to sexuality of any kind not used for the purposes of reproduction challenge this structure. That is, proper feminine roles complicate the options available to women who choose to disclose experiences with sexual violence because that sexuality is marked outside the purposes of reproduction, opening victims up to sexist and racist assumptions about who is seen as valuable in public life. The case of rape thus casts someone as outside the image of domestic motherhood, an image consumed by patriarchy and whiteness; their bodies have been used beyond the boundaries of conjugal bonds, constructed as a threat to proper citizen norms recognized for women.

When letter writers did invoke women who appear in pornography, blame often fell on behalf of the woman portrayed. One of the most curious accounts of this negotiation engaged the story of Adam and Eve in the Garden of Eden to illustrate this point. Invoking what he called his own "poetic license," Pastor Richard L. Dowhower wrote, "Once upon a time after Adam and Eve had been expelled from the Garden of Eden, Adam came upon a piece of slate. He soon discovered that with certain chalks and berries he could draw pictures on the slate. And before long, Adam was making pictures of trees, flowers, animals and sunsets. He particularly liked the pictures he drew of Eve, whose feminine attractiveness made him want to look at her all day long. The man liked the warm feeling that looking at her created in him."[90] During the opening scene, Dowhower refashioned the creation myth, a moment in which Adam looks lovingly and innocuously upon Eve, absorbed by her "feminine attractiveness," which created a "warm feeling" in his body. But this seemingly neutral depiction quickly changed: "Pretty soon Adam started drawing himself in the pictures with Eve, in scenes of them holding hands, kissing and other acts of lovemaking. [. . .] At first, Eve was flattered by his renditions of her, but when she got to the ones of their more intimate moments, she became concerned and embarrassed. 'Adam!' she exclaimed, 'What if the children should see those?' That's when the moral debate over pornography began."[91] Dowhower constructed an image of Adam tainted by sin that resulted from composing his own sexualized image of Eve. But Adam was not to blame. At first "flattered," Eve's shame ultimately provoked a "moral debate" after she expressed discomfort in seeing herself in more "intimate" ways, worried that her children may capture an image of her outside her identity as mother. Once her sexual identity seeped outside the boundaries of her maternal relationship, in other words, sexuality was seen as problematic.

While the images of each other naked initially provided the couple a shared sense of enjoyment and even arousal, they eventually established feelings of insecurity for Eve because of Adam's actions. Dowhower continued, "Adam liked the pictures of their sexual activity because he liked the warm feelings of arousal which they produced. But sometimes he felt guilty about the pictures and the effect they had on him, especially when Eve found him looking longingly at the other women who now populated their little world. Because, Eve said, the pictures did not do anything good to her; in fact, they made her embarrassed and ill at ease about herself."[92] Echoing the second frame analyzed in this chapter, Dowhower argued that pornographic images held the power to take hold over Adam's body, driving him to look at other women and produce a visceral reaction of arousal in his body. Such sensations were portrayed as an addiction—a stimulus that needed to be curtailed. However, according to Dowhower, it is Eve's status that was most threatened by his relationship to these images. In other words, Dowhower conceptualized a subjectivity for women decidedly nonsexual, docile, and on the verge of shame as a result of male sexual impulses. Importantly, Eve was the one who experienced guilt as a result of sex and sexuality.

Using iconography, Dowhower's letter reinterpreted original sin and the story of Adam and Eve to depict how marriages could presumably be ruined by sexuality presented in the form of pornography. In his recasting of the Garden of Eden, pornography alluded to sexually intimate acts that harm the marriage and disrupt normative depictions of women. He closed his letter calling for a control over sexuality and a return to it as "Godly [. . .] understood as *sacramental*," an objective of or obligation to procreation.[93] Dowhower's retelling of original sin suggests that the problem of pornography is really a problem of how we contain feminine sexuality, what Dowhower and others frame as the root cause of the problem. Importantly, shame was projected onto Eve, positioning her sexuality as a threat to the family, something that must be repressed, ultimately erasing a framework to understand sexuality in both positive and negative ways.

Recasting Eve's sexuality in the vein of original sin functioned to frame her as blameworthy, to associate feelings of shame with women's participation in sex in general. Framing women's sexuality in this way leads to a slippery slope in which women who engage with sexual activities outside the boundaries of reproduction that also count as rape or sexual assault are in effect blamed for what happened. That is, because feminine sexuality is always reduced to reproduction, specifically within the heteronuclear unit, disclosing an experience with rape or sexual assault evokes a form of sexuality unfit for the nation. Sex figured outside of marriage and outside the purposes of reproduction aligns sexuality with blame, an alignment that maps onto cases of rape and sexual assault and works to define proper womanhood. But it must be noted how prioritizing and idealizing this form of femininity is also distinctively racialized. Drawing from the work of Sandy Alexandre, Ore has foregrounded how feminine ideals are always tied to whiteness, linked back to slavery and the history of Jim Crow, in which fear of "the fair white maiden" subject to rape by black men "constructed the white female body as the physical embodiment of the nation," a figure deployed rhetorically to align docility with whiteness, one explored more deeply in the chapter that follows.[94] In other words, what these letters reveal is that limiting the options available to women to that of reproduction collapses the proper form of feminine sexuality with whiteness. Docility and motherhood—the only avenues available for apprehending the subjectivity of women—are uniquely yoked to the advancement of patriarchy and white supremacy. Any discussion of sexuality outside of marriage will ultimately always serve to blame women for any acts committed against them, to taint them with intersecting sexist and racist scripts, and ultimately to justify removal of them from the nation-state.

What About Victims?

In 1985, a growing awareness of rape cases motivated the government to investigate the presence of violence against women in the United States. From its inception, the Meese Commission grew from an initial concern for sexual violence. To respond to this problem, women were invited to testify during the hearings about their own experiences with sexual assault and/or rape. From that moment on, however, inquiry into sexual violence and its causes *from the perspectives of victims* faded into the background; victims' testimonies were "easily appropriated," used "to reinforce the existing structure," and consequently, actual experiences with rape and sexual assault slipped out of the frames that dominated public discourse about the Meese Commission.[95] Instead of responding to victims or the cultural prevalence of normalized, mundane, everyday violent attitudes toward women and minorities in the United States, the commission created a rhetorical problem surrounding pornography that called for persuasion of "proper" sex and sexuality and reaffirmed a white, male-dominated social hierarchy in the United States. In short, to recognize victims would require dealing with histories of misogyny, white supremacy, and violent masculinity, making the move to reaffirm normativity and blame society far easier.[96] Letter writers inherited this rhetorical problem and, in response, manufactured normative ideas about sex and sexuality that ultimately left disturbing consequences for how we talk about rape today.

While the majority of letter writers argued that pornography should be censored, some did acknowledge alternative arguments than the ones outlined in this chapter.[97] Among these, one woman who self-identified as an erotic dancer argued that the commission's focus on pornography miscalculated its core problems, overlooking the prevalence of sexist attitudes that circulated in society at this time. In her letter, Kellie Everts asserted that society "looks at women in pornography" who have been sexually assaulted and claims "that they deserve whatever happens to them because they chose to do what they are doing."[98] Her letter addresses how anti-pornography claims that associate actresses with "deluded" women or even "traitors" to those properly embodying womanhood serve to mark victims of abuse as personally responsible for what happened to them. In an attempt to uncover the underlying issues of gender inequality, she wrote, "I know of no instance in which a woman had the choice of being a doctor, a lawyer, an engineer or a porn actress and chose to be a porn actress. [. . .] [T]he women who get involved in pornography do so not because of a lack of morals, but because of economic necessity brought about by discrimination and a lack of opportunity."[99] In expressing concern over the misplaced judgment against women who act in pornography as opposed to interrogating the men who committed acts of aggression or engaged in sexual harassment or assault, she called for "an end to discrimination against women and an opening up of more opportunities for them."[100]

In many ways, Everts's letter invokes a classic problem facing many progressive politics today, a problem certainly obscured by the Meese Commission concerning identity politics and their relationship to political deliberation.

The role of identity politics, as illustrated by the 1980s and our current moment, is precarious, its position on the left's agenda always in flux. While academic, political, and public voices have long critiqued identity politics as a soft, infantile version of serious, leftist, critiques of issues like class or wealth distribution, reckoning with identity politics, as Duggan has argued, is not simply a question of diversity or discrimination spurred by radical fringe activists. Rather, these are questions of power, questions of identity and intersectionality in which the aspect of class mobility is intricately linked to gender, sexuality, race, and recognition of these overlapping identities. Rape culture will always be a problem that requires reckoning with identity—or perhaps identification, to be more specific—particularly the identities that are left unquestioned and unremarked.

To move forward politically, Duggan argues, "progressive social movements need deeper and broader analyses of the workings of neoliberalism" and, as this case study shows, specific interrogation of the subjectivities most protected by it.[101] At the core of gender and racial inequality remain questions of class, power, and opportunity that go unnoticed when wider rhetorics of risk and emergency seek to deflect attention away from inequality and toward normative (white and male) understandings of morality. The Meese Commission effectively limited any capacity to understand violence in relation to identity or inequity and operated with and through neoliberalism's dark grip on normativity and difference and who presumably counts within each of those categories. As a result, the Meese Commission formed a foundation to blame women and minorities for the violence committed against them in society while ignoring the aspects of identity and power central to the problem of rape in the first place. But "rather than admonish and advise," Duggan writes, "it would make more political sense to *locate, engage,* and *expand* productive political moments for future elaboration."[102] In the remainder of this conclusion, I hope to do just that.

What happened during the Meese Commission demonstrates a deep-seated commitment to protecting white supremacy, masculinity, and heteronormativity as guardians of the nation-state. It was women's sexuality, letter writers argued, that led to male arousal, a lack of control over the body, and ultimately, the potential for harm. The solutions for this "problem," they suggested, positioned women's sexuality—the very presence of their bodies—as a threat. To combat this threat, letter writers called for the bodies most prioritized in US society to return to a normative, heteronuclear state, one grounded in familial, hierarchical relations. Importantly, it was the visceral capacities of the body that served to spark fear and call for a politics of containment that ultimately justified belonging and cultural restoration through whiteness, masculinity, and a version of feminism tightly linked to both.

While second wavers attempted to dismantle troubling myths about rape victims and the normalized conditions under which sexual violence persists, neoliberalism reinstated individual responsibility, masking broader cultural factors that shaped and continue to shape the prevalence of gender-based violence. During the 1980s, those victim to sexual assault were once again to blame for violence committed against them, and the aims of anti-rape feminists were problematically folded into neoliberal policies of state regulation and laissez-faire economics, which, in turn, obscured alternative points of view. Beyond the case of the Meese Commission, we still see this trend of blaming victims in cases of rape or sexual assault while shielding perpetrators who are otherwise cast as normative, civic and economically minded individuals deemed "fit" for the nation-state from punishment. Put another way, what happened during the Meese Commission—aligning rape victims with deviance, ignoring the violence and toxicity of white masculinity, reinstating the patriarchy while blaming female sexuality—remain alive and well today.

The 2018 US Supreme Court Justice confirmation of Brett Kavanaugh is just one such example. In July 2018, once Kavanaugh was shortlisted to become the next nominee to the US Supreme Court, Dr. Christine Blasey Ford, a professor at Palo Alto University and research psychologist at Stanford University School of Medicine, issued a letter to her local and state congresswomen about a violent sexual assault that took place between her and Kavanaugh when they both were in high school.[103] Ford initially asked that her story be kept confidential, but as Kavanaugh advanced through the selection process, she came forward publicly in September 2018 to the media. She recounted the night when Kavanaugh and Mark Judge, a friend of Kavanaugh's from Georgetown Preparatory School, coerced Ford into a bedroom at a party, pinned her down on the bed, groped her, pulled her clothes off her, and covered her mouth when she attempted to scream. Fearful that Kavanaugh might rape and kill her, she eventually escaped their grip and both men fell to the floor. While Kavanaugh vehemently denied Ford's allegation, several other women came forward with similar accusations once Ford's story went public, one that included a time when Kavanaugh "thrust his penis in [a woman's] face, and caused her to touch it without her consent."[104]

As the whisper networks surrounding Kavanaugh's history with sexual assault became more public and Ford agreed to testify to the Senate Judiciary Committee, Kavanaugh released a statement prior to Ford's testimony claiming his innocence. In preparation for the hearing, Ford submitted therapy notes from several sessions recounting her history with sexual assault in addition to taking a polygraph test that concluded she was telling the truth. During her testimony she remained poised while she nervously but thoroughly responded to each question. When asked of the effect of what happened, she said, "Brett's assault on me drastically altered my life. For a very long time, I was too afraid and ashamed to tell anyone these details. I did not want to tell my parents that I, at age 15, was in a house without any parents present, drinking beer with boys. I convinced myself that because Brett did not rape me, I should just move on and just pretend that didn't happen."[105] To provide his own set of evidence, Kavanaugh submitted his childhood calendars and text messages from colleagues ostensibly attesting to his memory and character. During his testimony, he delivered an angry opening address, fumbled through a discussion of his own relationship to drinking, and demanded he was telling the truth. In his opening statements, he foregrounded how the delay to his hearing confirmation had been "harmful to [him] and [his] family" and that the accusations were ultimately efforts to "destroy [his] family."[106] The hearings, in addition to all the backlash he received from the public, he argued, "ha[d] destroyed [his] family and [his] good name. A good name built up through decades of very hard work and public service at the highest levels of American government."[107] At times he appeared belligerent, in tears, angry, and overcome with emotion—a body deeply in excess of its own feelings.

The public responded to Kavanaugh's testimony with reactions spanning from confusion to anger. Just before the final vote took place, the *New Yorker* commented, "At the time of this writing, composed in the eighth hour of the grotesque historic activity happening in the Capitol Hill chamber, it should be as plain as day that what we witnessed was the patriarchy testing how far its politics of resentment can go. And there is no limit."[108] In addition to critiques like this one, however, people also responded rehearsing familiar frameworks used during the Meese Commission, echoing claims that the accusation had been harder on him, that she was ruining his life for bringing up this history decades later, that her intoxicated account couldn't be trusted while his could. In short, several individuals grieved for Kavanaugh, framing his subjectivity in need of protection, positioning Ford's disclosure as a threat to *his* life and, furthermore, national politics. In a letter to the Judiciary Committee, sixty-five women who identified as having known Kavanaugh "for more than 35 years" attested to a version of Kavanaugh they understood as epitomizing "friendship, character, and integrity."[109] They urged the committee to view Kavanaugh as someone who "has always treated women with decency and respect."[110] President Trump went further, mocking Ford's testimony at a campaign rally shortly after the hearings, saying, "A man's life is shattered," that "his wife is shattered," that those who supported Ford were "really evil people."[111]

Responding in ways that seek to rehabilitate Kavanaugh and restore his "good name" while punishing Ford for disclosing what happened illustrate how deeply tied the question of sexual assault is to the nation-state and the imaginary it seeks to protect. Discourse about threats—threats that include sexual violence—will always be subject to scrutiny by state visions of the body politic veiled with white supremacy and toxic masculinity. Instead of interrogating Kavanaugh and his history with committing sexual violence, Ford became the problem, to blame for the actions committed against her along with ostensibly tarnishing his reputation. Ford was the disease, and, as a result, Kavanaugh and his supporters leveraged a visceral rhetoric of belonging that prioritized his heteronuclear family and sought to dispose of her and her disclosure of assault. Fixmer-Oraiz articulates this problem in relation to the project of feminism post 9/11: "In short, the only 'feminism' allowed to flourish [. . . is] decidedly post-feminist—not only a feminism stripped of its radical politics, but one retooled in the interests of patriarchy, capitalism, and US imperialism."[112] When threats to the state occur, the public largely reverts back to the normative, heteronuclear fictions viewed as most worthy of protection in an effort to rehabilitate the nation, debilitate unwanted bodies, and, ultimately in this case, erase that nation's darker reality of rape culture. Kavanaugh's whiteness and masculinity overshadowed his violence, marked him fit for the nation-state, and ultimately served not only to protect him but to advance him professionally and politically. On October 6, 2018, he was sworn in to the US Supreme Court, protected and contained by a nation more invested in preserving his subjectivity then interrogating his actions. Even someone with as much ethos and privilege as Ford couldn't disrupt the structure.

Ironically, adjudicating rape always operates through imaginative capacities. That is, to marshal evidence of rape—what happened and who committed it—invokes visual and sensory faculties that bring before the eyes of others what violence took place. But as the Meese Commission and the Kavanaugh cases show, the immediate testimony will always be shaped by a commitment to national security and its dominant frames of recognition. While women's testimonies of rape were coopted and reframed by the commission, they were also framed in the national imaginary as a consequence of pornography, as opposed to a consequence of gender-based violence, one that stems far back into this country's history, well beyond the 1980s. What images take hold in the national imaginary as grievable and losable influence how we understand existing realities of sexual violence today. The body is, thus, "always given over to others, to norms, to social and political organizations that have developed historically in order to maximize precariousness for some and minimize precariousness for others."[113] The letters analyzed in this chapter reveal how attempts to minimize precariousness for some while maximizing, thus casting out, precariousness for others deemed most risky functions in the service of ignoring a reality of sexual violence. In managing precarity, writers relied on affective images that served to associate particular visceral feelings of normativity or disgust with certain bodies marked as worthwhile and others as not. Disclosing an experience with sexual violence always runs this risk of clashing with the affective and embodied standards prioritized in the national image.

The Meese Commission and the Kavanaugh case are just two examples that demonstrate an unwillingness to interrogate perpetrators of sexual crimes who are white, heteronormative, male members deemed worthy of national protection. In the chapter that follows, I ask how we recognize and hail bodies that have been cast out of a national imaginary, or are at risk of being cast out, necessarily back into our purview. For Butler, "The derealization of the 'Other' means that it is neither alive nor dead, but interminably spectral."[114] Building on the case study examined here, I next investigate how the bodies of those who have experienced rape or sexual assault remain spectral due to a cultural desire to maintain whiteness, masculinity, ableism, and heteronormativity. Challenging these hierarchies, as this next chapter underscores, requires not only an interrogation into their discursive manifestations but rather certain affective claims for control, as well.

2

THE SPECTER OF PATRIARCHY:
IMAGINING VICTIMS IN BYSTANDER DISCOURSE

In November 2012, Jackson Katz—an educator and social theorist—gave a TED Talk in San Francisco addressing what he called "a paradigm-shifting perspective on the issues of gender violence."[1] Sexual violence, he maintained, has long been seen as something regarding "women's issues that some good men help out with," a framework he "[doesn't] accept" but rather views as one entirely entrenched in "men's issues, first and foremost."[2] His talk sought to illuminate potential confusion some from "the dominant group" may experience when adopting his approach surrounding "the key characteristics of power and privilege," characteristics "rendered invisible, in large measure, in the discourse about issues that are primarily about us."[3] That "us," Katz asserted, is men. In an attempt to cultivate renewed attention to the problem, Katz urged that conversations about gender-based violence must expose "how men have been largely erased from so much of the conversation about a subject that is entirely about men."[4]

To uproot the common victim-blaming refrains often projected onto those who disclose experiences with rape or sexual assault, Katz suggested that society probe a different set of questions. Instead of asking things like what was she wearing, was she drunk, or did she ask for it, he offered the following questions: "Why do so many men abuse [. . .] the women and girls, and the men and boys, that they claim to love? [. . .] Why do so many men rape women in our society and around the world? [. . .] What about all the boys who are profoundly affected in a negative way by what some adult man is doing against their mother, themselves, their sisters?"[5] Questions like these ground what Katz and others have termed a "bystander approach." Instead of interrogating women, calling them things like "man-hater" or "feminazi" (terms he cited) for speaking out against sexually violent conditions, Katz suggested expanding responsibility outward toward bystanders—those present for but ostensibly not involved in a violent act—encouraging them to speak up, challenge problematic behaviors, and, ultimately, refuse silence.[6] The ideas presented during Katz's talk derive from his cofounded international project, Mentors in Violence Prevention (MVP), one of the first programs to introduce the bystander approach specifically to sports, education, and military contexts. MVP states of its success, "When men (and women) were positioned as friends, family members, teammates, classmates, colleagues, and coworkers of women who were or might one day be abused, or of men who were abusive or perhaps going down that path, they fell into the virtually universal category of 'bystander.' This helped draw men into the conversation in a constructive fashion."[7] From MVP's perspective, teaching men about their own complicity in sexual violence and its ideologies, logics, and norms increases the potential that they might intervene in and mitigate sexist and violent transgressions that occur in their everyday surrounding contexts.

Katz's idea of the bystander approach has been deployed in national rape prevention advocacy efforts used today to address a specific site of rape culture this chapter takes up: the college campus. While the previous chapter analyzed how questions of sexual violence have historically been framed through male-centric lenses that serve to silence individual accounts of rape and sexual assault, this chapter extends those insights to analyze what happens when rape prevention discourses explicitly engage male voices. In other words, if chapter 1 examined the subtle ways masculinity has been invisibly naturalized as a subjectivity most worth protecting, this chapter looks at the not-so-subtle ways that positionality is invoked in new vehicles of response. Because contemporary deliberative frameworks often struggle to acknowledge how central male subjectivity is to the problem of gender-based violence, advocacy and prevention programs that focus on the bystander seek to include male voices in the conversation. In turning to "all of us," as these campaigns encourage, contemporary rape prevention efforts seek to reposition responsibility and blame away from victims and onto men, in particular.[8]

In shifting attention to bystanders, however, the dominant frames of recognition used in contemporary rape prevention efforts participate in constructing what has come to represent a quintessential "victim": a heterosexual, college-aged, cis, white, able-bodied, US American, middle-class, educated woman in need of protection from a male body and male gaze. In the process, bystander discourses affirm male speakers as the ideal agents of responsibility and define that responsibility through relationality: a victim could hypothetically be (or has been) a bystander's girlfriend, mother, sister, friend, and so on—all of which serve to generate activism through the presumption of a familial, or at the very least familiar, connection to a victim. Because the college campus has in many ways commanded public attention concerning rape culture today, those imagined within this context discursively, visually, and affectively contain how publics envision the majority of victims, perpetrators, and the act of rape. In naming the problem of rape culture today as one of bystanders—as opposed to violent masculinity, misogyny, or white male dominance—the solutions produced by bystander discourses sidestep a history of rape culture in the United States and masquerade as more palatable approaches to addressing the problem. Examining how bystander discourses reroute public attention, this chapter extends the work of chapter 1, locating how rhetorics of containment concerning the national imaginary appear in contemporary rape prevention discourses, limiting not only who is imagined as the victim but, more importantly, how such rhetorics foreclose an opportunity to unearth and name the more egregious roots of rape culture.

To understand the stakes of this new attention toward the bystander, this chapter analyzes two contemporary rape prevention campaigns—It's On Us and 1 is 2 Many—through a new methodological approach, what I term a "patriarchal spectrality." In the realm of anti-rape advocacy, bystanders remain highly visible in public discourse, wielding a new agency in larger, state-sponsored conversations about sexual violence. Their bodies occupy the scenes where public discourses form and circulate norms about rape culture, instructing the viewer of what counts as violence and the solutions for combatting such violence. But typifying the subjectivities of victims and bystanders, this chapter argues, is also saturated with a particular legacy of power and protection, one that haunts the project of intervention posed by contemporary rape prevention measures. That is, bystander discourses link a perception of rape culture with the historical tropes of "the black beast rapist, the innocent white maiden, and the chivalrous white hero," tropes that stem directly from a public memory of lynching in US culture, particularly during the era of Jim Crow laws.[9] Because images allow viewers to see themselves as public actors, the dominant frames used to recognize the problem of rape culture thus function to ignore its ideological underpinnings and preserve patriarchal systems that supported the proliferation of rape culture in the first place.

Methodologically, a patriarchal spectral approach to communication is necessary for interrogating discourses like the ones examined in this chapter because it illustrates how specters haunt the subjectivities made into spectacles in public discourse. It attends to the dominant optics used in public discourses that condition the visibility of certain bodies and forms of embodiment (men, feminine virtues of chastity, etc.) while illuminating the consequences for making invisible others (women of color, working-class women, people from queer and trans communities, etc.). Put simply, this approach demands that we contend not only with how normative discourses circulate and seek to contain certain definitions of rape culture but also (and more so) with "how panic resides in their inverse."[10] To do so, this approach draws from theories of visual rhetoric, public engagement, and hauntology to understand how a specter of patriarchy shapes the subjectivity of the bystander, one that serves to limit the scope of the problem of rape culture and obscure its historical roots.

In theory, specters or ghosts are present—*right there*—but invisible to the naked eye. Rape victims and perpetrators, too, are *absolutely there* but unable to be heard or seen as clearly due to the modes of vision that inform US rape prevention discourses today. In theorizing a patriarchal spectrality, I seek to "make space for the barely said whose traces must be excavated, necessarily from 'nothing,'" revealing how the work of oppression is masked by modes of intervention and prevention.[11] In the process, I build on the work of Ersula Ore, illustrating a connection between bystander discourses and a history of lynching in the United States, demonstrating how the archetypes imagined after Reconstruction emerge today, repackaged in new forms.[12] "The white female victim," as Ore has argued, "metonymically constructed the lynching audience as 'the people,' and the 'delicate virtue' of white womanhood as the body politic," a relationship that I argue undergirds bystander discourses used today.[13] While the archetypal victim is now positioned within the institutional space of higher education, the idea of her as white, innocent, and chaste still serves to cultivate public sympathy, support the image of the bystander as the necessary male hero, and position male protection of white feminine virtue as a restorative goal.

I begin situating these campaigns within a brief history of rape prevention discourses to identify the trajectory that prompted this new focus on the bystander. Next, I theorize the role and value of a patriarchal spectrality and then use that approach to analyze each contemporary rape prevention campaign. First, I examine the marketing tactics central to the It's On Us public service announcement (PSA) to explore how distributed responsibility functions to conceal actual material bodies who have experienced rape or sexual assault. Second, I complicate the work of the bystander presented in It's On Us, analyzing how the 1 is 2 Many PSA constituted men as both the problem of and the solution to rape culture—both perpetrator and bystander. This campaign, I suggest, problematically framed victims as both subject to and in need of protection from a male body and male gaze. Third, I investigate how these materials, together, rely on a figure of the rape victim that is heterosexual, cisgender, white, able-bodied, US American, middle class, and female—a figure that works to contain public awareness and ignore a range of bodies that experience sexual violence. I close connecting this analysis to the story of Recy Taylor and a brief history of sexual abuse against black women by white men in power. This dark underbelly of US history has remained largely spectral in public memory, overshadowed by the spectacles of rape constructed during Jim Crow that still circulate today. In dwelling momentarily on this historical moment through the lens of patriarchal spectrality, I hope to show how "to be haunted is to be tied to social and historical effects," effects that illuminate "endings that are not over."[14]

The Ghosts of Rape Prevention Discourses Past

It's On Us and 1 is 2 Many take an approach of collective responsibility in order to garner renewed attention to the problem of rape culture, one akin to what Iris Marion Young terms the "social connection model."[15] According to Young, this approach "does not isolate perpetrators," but rather "brings background conditions under evaluation" in order to cultivate collective attention toward the problem.[16] By examining these two campaigns, I demonstrate how a framework of collective responsibility—a framework with well-intended motivations that in many ways successfully drew vast public attention to the problem of sexual violence and created a new vocabulary to use in public deliberation—problematically obscures the optics for identifying those responsible for rape and sexual assault and those who experience it. Bystander discourses, I suggest, participate in making certain histories and legacies of sexual violence un/knowable and operate through forms of looking that affirm a normative conception of a rational, male speaker.

Before turning to my analysis of the It's On Us and 1 is 2 Many materials, this section briefly contextualizes these campaigns within a history of rape prevention discourses, demonstrating how the figure of the victim was once problematically present in anti-rape advocacy but now remains ghostly. Rape prevention emerged as a major public concern in the 1980s on the heels of second-wave feminist campaigns.[17] Activists worked to redefine rape as less so a crime committed by strangers but one more often inflicted by acquaintances and even partners. Several methods were implemented during this time that helped raise public attention to the problem of rape. For instance, researchers in the social sciences began addressing sexual violence, which led to the use of statistics when understanding the scope of the problem and the number of women affected—an approach still commonly used today. In addition, organizations such as the Bureau of Justice Assistance, the Center for Disease Control (CDC), and the American Medical Association (AMA) became key stakeholders in rape prevention efforts by developing materials for understanding this issue as one of public health and justice in the United States. Several activist and advocacy groups have since then developed such as the Rape, Abuse & Incest National Network (RAINN) and End Rape on Campus, among many other national and local organizations—all of which strive to educate the public and support victims immediately affected by sexually violent experiences.

At the core of these early efforts was an exigency of fear that sought to combat the problem of rape by encouraging self-defense strategies for women. In other words, responses to this problem centered around the assumption that heterosexual, cis women should remain vigilant of deviant men. Rape prevention campaigns, as Rachel Hall has argued, have largely relied on the idea that women's bodies are a risk factor for rape.[18] For instance, oft-cited statistics that estimate a percentage of women who have been sexually assaulted at least once in their lifetime permeated public discourse and continue today. These statistics function primarily by provoking public anxiety around the feminized body, suggesting that women need to be protective of their bodies in public, as opposed to efforts that would intervene in sexist, misogynist, and violent behavior. The core "problem" imagines the woman's body as a risk factor in which she is "reducible to her sex as violable space."[19] Instead of targeting sexually violent conditions, the through line that remains constant within the past three to four decades of rape prevention campaigns suggests that the space of a woman's body is at risk of danger because of its very capacity to be penetrated.

In contrast to these efforts, the campaigns analyzed in this chapter have sought to profile a body that had not yet been underscored in anti-rape public discourse: that of the college campus bystander. In 2014, President Obama and then Vice President Biden helped launch a series of public advocacy efforts aimed at educating broader public awareness of campus sexual assault as part of the White House Task Force to Protect Students from Sexual Assault, work that contributed to the 2013 reinstallment of the Violence Against Women Act and the 2009 creation of the White House Council on Women and Girls. The goal of the White House Task Force was clear: to reduce the rates of sexual assault on US college and university campuses. One of its more notable campaigns, It's On Us, began with a PSA on social media platforms such as Facebook, YouTube, and Twitter, and, along with President Obama and Vice

President Biden, public figures such as Kerry Washington, Lady Gaga, and Jon Hamm gathered together to join a public fight against sexual violence.[20] Within this campaign, responsibility for mitigating sexual crimes is now positioned on "all of us." In addition to It's On Us, Not Alone was launched in connection with the White House Task Force, releasing the first report that provided rape and sexual assault resources to higher education institutions.[21] As part of Not Alone's publicity materials, the program distributed a PSA, 1 is 2 Many, that followed the direction of It's On Us and included a number of celebrities who together argued that one case of sexual assault should be reason enough to generate public outrage toward the problem.[22] Unlike It's On Us, however, the PSA included only men and delved deeper into the causes of sexual violence by attempting to outline how men have been complicit in the problem of sexual violence in US society. Notably, these efforts, together, sought to spur public attention to the problem by including a broader range of voices in the conversation. In the process, they typified the spaces where rape and sexual assault are presumed to happen most frequently, making campus rape synonymous with rape culture more broadly.

In response to research that suggests college women are particularly at risk of rape, the federal government has mandated since the early 2000s that all higher education institutions that receive federal funding must provide safety programs to students specifically targeting rape prevention. These two campaigns are part of such efforts, providing programs linked to "bystander skill development sessions" that many higher education institutions have implemented.[23] The goal of bystander programs, as psychologist Victoria Banyard and her colleagues point out, is to focus on "interrupting situations that could lead to assault before it happens or during an incident, speaking out against social norms that support rape, and having skills to be an effective and supportive ally to survivors."[24] Social psychologists have examined bystander intervention programs, suggesting that while the promise they offer is well intended, these programs are still in need of further development. For instance, Sarah McMahon and her colleagues argue that bystander programs don't clearly define "what behaviors are considered forms of bystander behavior" or fail to address "the role of sexist language and its connection to creating a community that tolerates sexual violence."[25] In other words, while the goals and motivations remain rhetorically hopeful, the outcomes of bystander intervention programs are less so understood.

According to the campaigns analyzed in this chapter, the available responses to fighting rape culture involve engaging people not directly implicated in the attack, but rather, bystanders, those who know and walk among spaces where assaults ostensibly occur without intervening in the problem. While paying attention to bystanders doesn't alone erase victims' experiences, I argue that decentering those experiences helps preserve a particular identity in wider discourses of rape culture—that of the white fair maiden in need of public protection—at the expense of hearing from a range of people who experience rape or sexual assault. As *The Nation*'s 2018 Black on Campus Fellow Candace King wrote: "The national movement to address the college rape crisis seldom reflects the complexities of gender, race, and class black women face at both predominantly white institutions and historically black colleges."[26] Because college campuses are privileged spaces, they are undoubtedly connected to whiteness, yet this legacy goes uncontested by the discourse. The spectacle of a white, female victim permeates these promotional materials, and analyzing this spectacle exposes a heteronormative and misogynist desire grounded in white supremacy to sustain a hierarchy in which cis white men remain on top, norms "sacred" to US public culture.[27] The analysis that follows illustrates how, in James Bliss's words, "the limits of institutionalization are marked by a remainder, an excess that cannot be incorporated," one that profiles campus culture while denying an understanding of the range of bodies subject to rape.[28] In the process of imagining college women's bodies as vulnerable, these campaigns remove the experiences of trans women, femmes, people from nonbinary or gender nonconforming communities, working-class women, women of color, and even men from a conversation about the risk of rape.

While I remain critical of bystander discourses, I do not intend to dismiss them entirely. The logics of rape culture work to place blame and responsibility on women's bodies, "depict[ing] the female body as a surface of sexual signifiers," on which the male gaze can look and presumably find "a woman's unspoken yet visible consent."[29] Consequently, their bodies become sites of culpability outside of their own testimonies, constructing a rhetorical situation that always already works against women, a problem bystander discourses attempt to mitigate. But in shifting responsibility, such discourses risk participating in deflecting attention away from victims, their bodies, and the material, historically saturated conditions of rape culture, further marking victims' capacity to speak about their own experiences with their bodies as suspect. That is, within bystander discourse, the problem of believing victims still persists; the bystander serves as a Band-Aid to a much larger ideological issue regarding the gendering of testimony. While rape logics work to deny the agency of victims, bystander discourses—even in their attempt to disturb the imbalance in power—simultaneously contribute to displacing and removing victims' material experiences from conversation and instead reinstate more powerful voices as worthy of listening to. As a result, bystander discourses may inadvertently leave wider publics with inhospitable ideas about victims' own testimonies.

Put differently, I am not suggesting that distributed responsibility is unethical or altogether unhelpful for understanding the public problem of rape culture. By drawing attention to how contemporary advocacy materials are haunted by a privileged identity in the United States, my hope is that we may better address the scene of responsibility and acknowledge those who are included or excluded. I recognize that profiling bystanders is motivated by a feminist concern for taking blame off of victims, which can be viewed radically when compared to previous campaigns. Yet, we must bring the background conditions of sexism, racism, and patriarchy that condition sexual violence and its modes of recognition into focus when deliberating the problem. Most importantly, we must make room for victim accounts and avoid the centering of a male experience when attempting to combat the marginalization of victims, a centering that unfortunately plays out in these materials.

Constructing Victims and Their Protectors

History is consumed with ghosts, some of which represent those who have been forced to the fringes of public memory, influencing the norms and publics that support those memories. Meddling throughout our contemporary realities, ghosts and specters drift among us, at times imposing their presence, calling us to reckon with them and their histories. Following the spectral turn of the 1990s, which viewed ghosts and haunting as compelling methodological tools, scholars María del Pilar Blanco and Esther Peeren have suggested that spectrality can be a useful theoretical apparatus for understanding the elusiveness of presence, the disappearance of history, or the connection between the past and trauma because of its "link to visibility and vision, to that which is both *looked at* (as a feminist spectacle) and *looking* (in the sense of examining)."[30] Marshalled in largely by Derrida, this interdisciplinary approach helped scholars explore what many consider the unspeakable, ungraspable elements of human life and the bodies made absent throughout histories of colonization.[31] An uncanny removal of certain bodies, many have argued, mediates the normalized presence of other bodies made visible, and using this approach exposes how "the normative position (of masculinity, heterosexuality, whiteness) is ghostly in that it remains un(re)marked."[32] In other words, presenting certain bodies as most capable of response while obscuring others asserts a naturalized hierarchy of masculinity, heterosexuality, and whiteness, one deeply in need of interrogation regarding how such norms allow certain bodies to be seen and heard.

Tracing this relationship between what is seen and unseen, heard and unheard, illuminates how contemporary rape prevention materials help sustain white and male positionalities that motivate the goal of making the bystander most visible in this discourse. Spectrality, as a method, as Ayo Coly has argued, is "endow[ed] with a critical vision that brings to legibility some disguised repetitions and workings of oppression."[33] Thus, visual analysis is a critical component of examining specters and spectacles. "Careful, situated investigation of the social, cultural, and political work that visual communication is made to do," as Cara Finnegan has articulated, draws attention to how past legacies contribute to the unspoken and unseen elements that shape visual forms of engagement.[34] Considering an image's context helps illuminate "historical and social structures of feeling and ongoing ideological apparatuses" that cultivate forms of public empathy and drive modes of recognition.[35] Building on the last chapter, spectral analyses help establish who is constituted as most worthy of public grieving today.

My analysis extends this framework to examine what is made invisible through the visibility of others, how gazing at a visual marker operates as a mode of exclusion, exiling certain bodies and, furthermore, the material conditions of rape culture. While rhetoricians have leveraged an analytical lens of haunting and spectrality to examine questions of radical alterity, historiography, and public memory, I contribute to this body of scholarship by attending to the feminist concern of silencing in our present context.[36] In other words, patriarchal spectrality looks to the spectacles framed in dominant rape prevention discourse today and the specters that shape them, interrogating how silence percolates under the surface of such frames of recognition used to understand rape culture. In the process, I offer a methodological approach keenly oriented toward the visual and embodied elements of power. Tracking these elements uncovers how a normative male body and male gaze operates to silence nonwhite voices in particular but also nonnormative and marginalized voices from a conversation about rape culture. Because "the modern experience of communication is so often marked by felt impasses," a patriarchal spectrality compels us to trace the affective specter of silence, to pause at the visceral moments when subjectivity is imposed upon us.[37] Using this approach not only encourages an ethical orientation to how we engage with those who have been silenced, but it also lends itself to opportunities for change. Ghosts, in other words, don't only signal the uncomfortable erasures of our world but can be "comforting to us," as Jeffrey Weinstock observes, serving to "represent our desires for truth and justice."[38] Attending to their material presence gives hope for changing how we address past legacies of public problems such as sexual violence and make space for more equitable public engagements with such problems.

In what follows, I examine the It's On Us and 1 is 2 Many campaigns through the lens of patriarchal spectrality. I analyze how the specter of patriarchy haunts what is said and made visible within these efforts, drawing attention to the material bodies made absent through the presence of others. In the process, I seek "to 'listen to' rather than simply 'look at' images," which, as Tina Campt describes, "is a conscious decision to challenge the equation of vision with knowledge"—the perennial myth that seeing is believing—by investigating images "through a sensory register."[39] What is made known, who is marked as a potential solution to uprooting rape culture, is undergirded by an anxiety of patriarchy, one that works to obscure the voices and bodies of those who have experienced sexual violence and the roots of male dominance that promote the logics of rape culture. By turning instead to the identity of a bystander, these discourses attempt to frame a vision of intervention through heteronormative, white, male, and patriarchal frames, frames that Campt argues "can be felt," as an image "both touches and moves people."[40] Contemporary rape prevention campaigns cultivate public attention and public empathy through the preservation of certain raced, classed, and gendered hierarchies. But such hierarchies can be exposed, my analysis demonstrates, seen more clearly by deploying a lens of patriarchal spectrality, "attended to by way of the unspoken relations that structure them."[41]

The Problem of Bystander Silence: It's On Us

On the home page of its website, the It's On Us campaign describes itself as a "rallying cry, inviting everyone to step up and realize that the solution begins with us."[42] In expanding the purview of responsibility outward, the campaign affirms three core pillars regarding the project of uprooting rape culture—"consent education, increasing bystander intervention, and creating an environment that supports survivors."[43] In September 2014, the campaign launched a PSA including a number of celebrities who share the reading of different portions of the script, profiled through various shots of individual speakers' faces and bodies. At the end of the PSA, speakers encourage viewers to visit the It's On Us website and "take the pledge." The pledge involves reading a series of four statements, clicking "take the pledge," and then offering personal information, including an email address and institutional affiliation to which the campaign can publicize additional information.[44] While the campaign includes multiple videos by additional actors and multiple scripts that can be distributed to campus organizations who can then make their own videos, this analysis focuses specifically on the initial PSA in conjunction with the It's On Us pledge. Using a patriarchal spectrality, I examine how the identity of the bystander veils actual victims' experiences even though they remain present within this conversation. Expanding responsibility collectively to bystanders, I argue, is bolstered by masculine notions of responsibility that eclipse the capacity for a victim to be recognized. Actual victims' subjectivities are made barely there, in other words, but can be traced, found in what Avery Gordon identifies as "an animated state in which a repressed or unresolved social violence is making itself known, sometimes very directly, sometimes more obliquely."[45]

Initially released online and distributed through mainstream and social media, the It's On Us PSA aimed to shift how discourses of rape and sexual assault too often default to victim blaming in public conversations. In turning away from victims, the PSA assumes the discourse of collective responsibility communicated in the following script played throughout the thirty-two second clip: "It's on us to stop sexual assault. To get in the way before it happens. To get a friend home safe. To not blame the victim. It's on us to look out for each other. To not look the other way. It's on us to stand up, to step in, to take responsibility. It's on all of us to stop sexual assault. Learn how and take the pledge at itsonus.org."[46] The "us" deployed in the clip refers to bystanders, viewers who are ostensibly not perpetrators or victims of rape or sexual assault yet may have at some point been complicit in knowing sexual assault occurred but did nothing to stop it. Responsibility, in this vein, encourages bystanders to participate in ending sexual assault by acknowledging its presence and actively working to prevent it before it occurs. Put another way, intervention presumes known identification of violence and physical protection, framing sexually violent acts as those that begin in spaces that include congregation by others, possible spaces such as bars, dorms, or parties.

Throughout the PSA, a piano repeats a simple yet somber series of chords. The video opens in close proximity to actor Jon Hamm's face, where his forehead and chin are cut off by the top and bottom frames of the camera (see fig. 1 below). The background directly behind and surrounding Hamm's face appears faded as he takes up all but the corners of the frame. No other bodies are visible in this initial shot. Throughout, the PSA presents its subjects

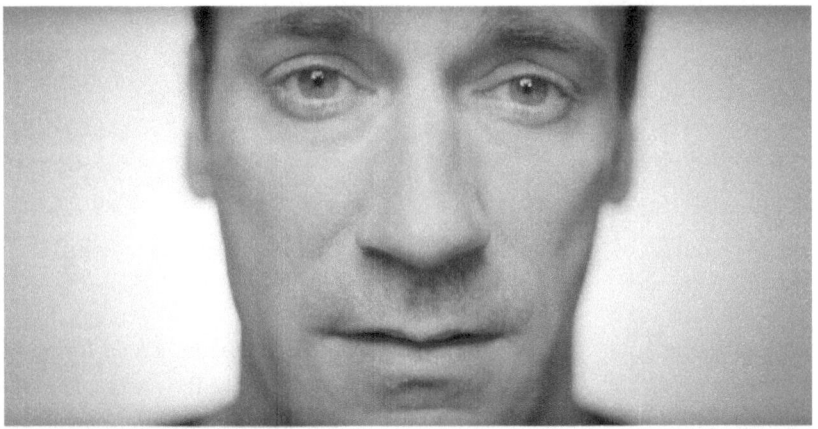

Figure 1 Image of Jon Hamm's face up close (personal screenshot of the It's On Us PSA).

in close proximity to viewers, so close that viewers can grasp the size of pores, the crevices of wrinkles, the crookedness of teeth, and the texture of lips. Encountering the bystander up close—sensing and feeling their bodily presence—creates a visceral connection between viewer and subject, constituting a viewer's connection to the actors through "impulses that register on our bodies."[47] Presenting the face of an actor who embodies the identity of the bystander creates a sense of intimacy with the viewer that serves to raise public attention to the problem of rape culture. In other words, the threat of violence is communicated through the presentation of an actor up close, registered through intimate visual contact with the bodies of bystanders. As Hamm speaks, viewers can hear the physical movement of words leaving his lips, the deep ringing of his vocal cords, and the sound of his tongue touching the roof of his mouth when emphasizing "it's" or "us." The clip works to establish peer-to-peer authority through the presentation and positioning of his face up close.

As the lines of the script change, different faces are profiled. Throughout the PSA, only faces and upper bodies are shown, and the frames rotate between profiling faces and then profiling upper body shots. At times, the frame is split into two, in which one side of the frame shows one person's face up close while the other side shows a larger portion of that same person's upper body or another person's upper body (see fig. 2 below). During these split frames, people's voices speak alone and in conjunction with one another, amplifying the message. Before closing, all voices speak together as one reading the lines "to stop sexual assault" while the PSA visually profiles

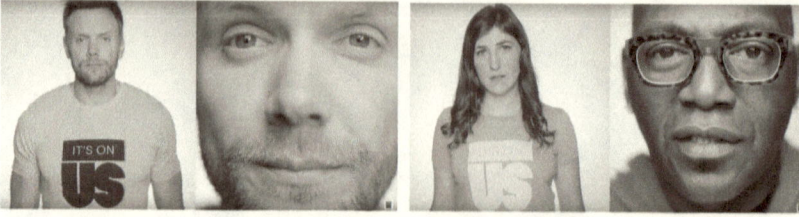

Figure 2 Images of Joel McHale, Mayim Bialik, and Randy Jackson (personal screenshots of the It's On Us PSA).

each face one after the other at an increasing pace. Finally, a solo frame of President Obama closes the PSA, inviting viewers to take the pledge. Rapidly moving from one face to another while halting with the president creates a sense of urgency, compelling viewers to view themselves in the context while actual known or self-identified victims remain visibly absent.

According to the central message, sexual assault begins in collective spaces and requires a form of embodiment capable of intervention. For instance, the PSA calls for bodily intervention by asking bystanders to "stand up" or "get in the way before it happens," presenting a version of violence that bystanders could disrupt. Safety for victims is facilitated through the bodies of bystanders, bodies ostensibly stronger than victims' bodies and bodies present during the scene of rape or sexual assault. In other words, an act of sexual violence is assumed to begin in public or semi-public spaces occupied by bystanders, as well as victims and perpetrators. Protection and the physical capacity desired in this form of advocacy assumes a more capable, more masculine body, one responsible for watching and protecting, identifying and gazing. Victims, in this vein, are assumed to be weak, less capable than bystanders, and are realized through their relationship to a more able person who can save them. In the process, the identified victim of sexual assault is positioned through a voyeuristic lens as a spectacle in need of intervention, a figure the bystander must grasp and mark as in need of help.

In the process of defining bystander silence as the problem, the PSA obscures how victims often do attempt to stand up and stop perpetrators, testifying to how their attackers may have assumed control or ignored pushback by victims. In other words, imagining a victim presence disrupts the idea that victims can't say no; rather, many perpetrators do assault victims even though consent has not been given or has been revoked. In positioning the idea of a victim through a construction of gendered helplessness—an innocent fair maiden trapped by uncontrollable male sexuality—the clip presumes that a bystander could not become a victim; the bystander is framed as capable of intervention but not at risk of physical violence themselves. Put differently, those that choose to "not look the other way" but instead "look after one another" could never be a victim themselves. Bystanders are too strong, assumed as saviors and in control, occupying an ideology akin to the white male hero.

Because victims are visibly excluded from the PSA—unable to be seen or heard—viewers are incapable of understanding the range of bodies who experience rape or sexual assault. Victims are defined through the spaces of college campuses, typified through the subjectivity of a young white woman innocently moving throughout university spaces. But within the close presentation of the bystander lurks a reality of victims. As Gordon reminds us, "Being haunted draws us affectively, sometimes against our will [...] into the structure of feeling."[48] This desire to speak for victims, to cultivate modes of address that serve to erase their voices, invokes a past history of rape, one laced with a felt residue of misogyny and racism. That is, suggesting that the end to sexual assault requires bystanders to intervene hails a scenario in which other male bodies become necessary for halting a sexually violent encounter. Haunted by a legacy of framing perpetrators as "out on the loose," racialized as criminals who prey on innocent white women moving throughout public spaces, the clip invites viewers into this scene of responsibility, marking white womanhood as that which needs to be saved.

To listen to ghosts and specters—to feel their presence—requires reckoning with the histories of trauma that seethe under the surface of public memory. Bystanders, or those given a platform to speak at the expense of not hearing victims, remain haunted by a history of white supremacy in this country. After the end of the American Civil War, it was not the rape of black women, who were far too often subject to sexual abuse, but rather "the rape of white women (whether real or imagined)," argues Ore, that "was deemed deplorable, unpardonable, and punishable by death."[49] Contemporary claims for civility and safety that shape rape prevention discourses like It's On Us are linked to this history and the drastic desire to protect whiteness and white womanhood. Examining how protection and response become intertwined with whiteness and masculinity—ideals of community engagement central to acts of lynching—foregrounds a much longer legacy of rape culture, the systematization of it, and the strategic modes of intervention that sought to rescue white female bodies while denying—and murdering—black bodies. This specter of patriarchy looms among bystander discourses, representing "the possibility of a return of the past in the future."[50] Yet, deciphering its encounter and listening to this felt history gives potential for exploring the "dense site where history and subjectivity make social life," including the physical, figural, and representational subjects that meddle among us.[51] The patriarchy haunts our everyday understandings of rape culture.

It's On Us suggests that sexual predators are always known, that they can be made legible and marked by bystanders. Thus, the clip leaves this racialization of rape unchallenged, haunted by a legacy of lynching that implicates viewers into a patriarchal vision of responsibility. In other words, the clip suggests that uprooting sexual violence can, in large part, be achieved if bystanders remain vigilant of potential attackers, constituting audiences as the people, bystanders as the patriarchy, and white female victims as at risk. Because this archetype of the victim is always already imagined as white, helpless, and chaste, this form of intervention may also serve to blame victims who aren't marked as cis, female, or white. That is, stopping an assault, according to It's On Us, requires a bystander to identify an encounter as an assault. However, a bystander may see an exchange and similarly view someone else as "wanting it," in her actions or clothing, participating in the problem of slut-shaming victims and blaming their actions, as opposed to interrogating the actions of perpetrators.

Dwelling on the experience of the silenced victim made into a spectacle in these materials illuminates how viewers are invited to participate in disrupting a very limited account of sexual violence. The limits of this account get amplified when viewers are directed to the website and encouraged to take the following pledge: "To RECOGNIZE that non-consensual sex is sexual assault. To IDENTIFY situations in which sexual assault may occur. To INTERVENE in situations where consent has not or cannot be given. To CREATE an environment in which sexual assault is unacceptable and survivors are supported."[52] The pledge's statements are intended for bystanders, presented as an agreement or promise to which bystanders will commit. Specifically, bystanders are asked to recognize what sexual assault is and vow, or rather, consent to embody such intervention tactics to prevent it. Acknowledging victim experiences, however, illuminates how rare it is for one to be in a position to analyze consent unless they were a perpetrator themselves. Victims are not invited to participate in this agreement, and those who attack victims are also not exposed in this exchange. Thus, the bystander pledge confirms consent outside of the victim's actual existence, outside of their perspective. Because everyone is imagined to inhabit a "bystander" role, no one is clearly identified as a victim or a perpetrator; their subjectivities loom in an imagined state. The bystander is the only subjectivity available for intervention, which forecloses serious conversation about who commits sexual assault, who experiences it, and how it proceeds.

After reading these statements, viewers are guided to click "take the pledge," led to a page that writes "saying things out loud makes them happen," then asked to submit personal contact information and a potential donation.[53] The pledge thus operates similarly to how J. L. Austin theorized the speech act.[54] The speech act here—uttering the pledge—plays out in what Austin viewed as the illocutionary act: "by saying something, we *do* something."[55] When considered alongside a legacy of lynching in US history, the perlocutionary effect, then, or the effect of this speech act, confirms a vision of whiteness and masculinity as the appropriate forms of intervention, a powerful subjectivity viewed as capable of ending rape culture. In other words, though not all bystanders within the clip are white or male, this form of responsibility is linked to patriarchy and therefore whiteness, conditioning responses to rape culture through this ideology. Because the pledge is intended for the bystander, ending sexual assault is fashioned through the bystander's spoken words, omitting perpetrators, interrogation into the conditions that foster rape culture, and the testimonies victims offer. Furthermore, because the It's On Us campaign functions by going viral—circulating among vast audiences—the repetition of this performative utterance serves to maintain and proliferate a hierarchical relationship between male protection of white female fragility.

Protecting Our Women: 1 is 2 Many

While the motivations that guided the work of It's On Us are paved with good intentions, attempts to redirect responsibility and disrupt the logics of rape culture by way of the bystander run the risk of reinstating men as the ideal solutions to mitigating rape culture, a problem that, as the opening of this chapter outlined, is one consumed by the actions of men. What makes this work even more precarious, however, deals with the modes through which these messages disseminate. The campaigns of It's On Us and 1 is 2 Many were intended to go viral, occupying the screens of televisions, computers, and handheld devices. The PSAs were produced so that colleges and universities across the country could replicate them easily, proliferating throughout individual campuses. This type of visual encounter, as Robert Hariman and John Lucaites have argued, "constitutes the viewer as a subject within that system," implicating viewers into the subjectivity constructed in the clips.[56] Thus, viewers are constituted through the subjectivity of the bystander, shaped by patriarchal notions of responsibility and intervention. Because visual analysis helps us understand "how publics come together, sustain themselves, and promote visions for the future," as Christa Olson puts it, analysis of bystander intervention materials unveils how visions of the future are grounded in patriarchy and sustained through the subjectivities most protected by it.[57]

Sponsored and produced by the Obama White House, the 1 is 2 Many PSA follows the approach of It's On Us and includes film and TV actors, comedians, and public figures.[58] Unlike It's On Us, however, the 1 is 2 Many PSA includes only men and identifies them as both the problem of and the solution to rape culture. While 1 is 2 Many follows It's On Us in advancing bystander intervention, the video clip also operates with the goal of consent education in mind. Thus, 1 is 2 Many attempts to go further than It's On Us, gesturing toward and punishing sexist behavior. In other words, these male actors and public figures call upon other men in public to recognize their own complicity in the problem of sexual violence, violence that is most frequently inflicted by men. But 1 is 2 Many poses an additional problem. While analysis of It's On Us illuminates how masculine forms of responsibility serve to cover over victims' voices, analyzing patriarchal spectrality in this case reveals the specter of the perpetrator, one who trickles out of the frames used throughout the PSA. In attempting to claim bystanders can be the solution to curtailing the prevalence of sexual violence, 1 is 2 Many remains haunted by the notion that male bystanders may also embody the positionality of perpetrator.

The 1 is 2 Many PSA uniquely positions a male speaker throughout the clip and imagines an audience comprising heteronormative men. Instead of focusing solely on responsibility, 1 is 2 Many opens up a discussion of blame, expanding a conversation about what exactly the problem of rape culture is. The one-minute clip unfolds through the following script:

> We have a big problem, and we need your help. It's happening on college campuses, at bars, at parties, even at high schools. It's happening to our sisters, and our daughters, our wives and our friends. It's called sexual assault, and it has to stop. We have to stop it. So listen up. If she doesn't consent or if she can't consent, it's rape. It's assault. It's a crime. It's wrong. If I saw it happening, I was taught you have to do something about it. If I saw it happening, I'd speak up. If I saw it happening, I'd never blame her. I'd help her. Because I don't want to be a part of the problem, I want to be a part of the solution. We need all of you to be part of the solution. This is about respect. It's about responsibility. It's up to all of us to put an end to sexual assault. And that starts with you. Because one is too many.[59]

Figure 3 Images of Dulé Hill, Steve Carell, then vice president Joe Biden, and then president Barack Obama (personal screenshots of the 1 is 2 Many PSA).

Each of the men are placed in traditionally male occupied spaces—in leather chairs, on neighborhood stoops, in wood-paneled offices, on stage, and in US government affiliated rooms (see fig. 3 above). The frames shift throughout the clip, profiling individual men in different locations, sitting at ease, clothed in suits, denim jackets, track jackets, and sport coats. Their bodies reside in masculine positions with their hands either crossed or pointing directly at the camera lens, knees relatively wide or placed under a desk, their bodies commanding attention within the spaces of their settings. Similar to the It's On Us PSA, 1 is 2 Many maintains a serious tone throughout but also asserts a more directive one by addressing the viewer specifically.

As one of its main goals, the PSA works to identify the places and people affected by sexual assault. The PSA opens, "We have a problem," and then rotates through a number of voices, identifying where that problem occurs: "It's happening on college campuses, at bars, at parties, even at high schools." While the idea that intervention can take place in public shaped the form of intervention in It's On Us, it is made more explicit in 1 is 2 Many. Here, schools and nightlife locations are directly called out as sites where sexually violent activity readily occurs. After identifying these extracurricular and educational spaces, the clip then identifies the target of that problem through the following lines shared by Steve Carrell and Daniel Craig: "It's happening to our sisters, and our daughters, our wives and our friends." By labeling victims "sisters, "daughters," "wives," or "friends," the clip draws a familial connection between viewers and victims, similar to the one posed by

MVP in the opening of this chapter: because I, as a hypothetical male viewer, might have a sister, wife, daughter, or even woman friend, I can better imagine violently inflicted crimes of sexual abuse. In other words, the legibility of the victim and responsibility for her is constituted through male recognition of and relation to that woman. Intervention occurs not because sexual violence is a problem on its own but because it is something that could happen to someone the viewer knows. But the victim invoked in relationship to these two white male speakers is also a particular imagined victim; state responsibility over sexual crimes is fashioned through patriarchy once again and the capacity for imagining those subject to sexual violence is limited to a particular set of known bodies.

Like It's On Us, those who have experienced sexual assault are visibly absent in this PSA, but in decentering their bodies in 1 is 2 Many, the clip poses an insecurity over the male subject. After the PSA opens asserting a problem, it names the issue in question: "It's called sexual assault, and it has to stop. We have to stop it." By moving from "It's called sexual assault, and it has to stop," directly to "we have to stop it," the PSA collapses the subjectivity of the male subject as both perpetrator and bystander. Put differently, that bystanders could also be perpetrators haunts this clip, constructing the future self of the viewer as a bystander while acknowledging briefly his potential past self as a perpetrator. Thus, while men are conjured as solutions, the PSA obscures whether the implied viewer (and speaker) is a perpetrator or a bystander. We know the subject in question is a male subject, yet the spectacle of the male speaker covertly vacillates between perpetrator and bystander.

It's reasonable to assume that the creators of the PSA may have intentionally decided not to call out men for fear that they may lose viewers. In other words, to accommodate the fragility of masculinity and avoid potential viewer defensiveness, creators may have strategically collapsed the identity of perpetrator with bystander to keep viewers watching. But wavering between the subjectivity of bystander and perpetrator allows the PSA to sidestep defining consent. That is, though the clip presumes to mark consent as a defining factor of assault, it puts very little emphasis on actually outlining it and instead jumps to the issue of blame. Following the line "we have to stop it," speakers explicitly call out male viewers and move to the issue of punishment: "So listen up. If she doesn't consent or if she can't consent, it's rape. It's assault. It's a crime. It's wrong." Immersed in a particular male anxiety, the following lines of the clip are layered with a fear of constantly being at risk of blame: "If I saw it happening, I was taught you have to do something about it. If I saw it happening, I'd speak up. If I saw it happening, I'd never blame her. I'd help her." Such lines seem to assimilate the past ("I was taught") with a projection of a future ideal self ("If I saw it happening"), serving to omit potential actions of wrongdoing. In moving rather quickly from the message that men are a part of the problem, the PSA avoids blame, blurring any recognition of one's potential individual history with rape or sexual assault. That is, the PSA presents a version of a bystander who might be haunted by their own complicity. In turning away from their own culpability, speakers frame themselves as protectors: "I'd never blame her. I'd help her." Even though men may have once been at fault for a crime, the PSA evades reckoning with culpability and blame by returning to a conversation of responsibility as intervention.

Throughout 1 is 2 Many, the specter of a perpetrator looms among discussion of bystander intervention. In prioritizing the role of the bystander, however, the clip forecloses any serious dialogue of interrogating perpetrators. They're let off the hook. The men close the clip sharing the last lines: "Because I don't want to be part of the problem, I want to be part of the solution. [. . .] It's up to all of us to put an end to sexual assault. And that starts with you." In these closing remarks, the pronouns further obscure whether the viewer is a perpetrator or bystander. Saying "I don't want to be part of the problem," could suggest that "I" to be a silent bystander, but it could also implicate the speaker as a perpetrator, one whose actions may have exacerbated the problem in the first place. Affirming that "it's up to all of us to put an end to sexual assault," may incite a collective action among viewers to intervene in a case of sexual assault. But suggesting "that starts with you," could simultaneously position the viewer as a bystander *and* a perpetrator, one who needs to stop assaulting women. In short, the PSA recognizes perpetrators without seriously calling them out. Bystander discourse leaves them unscathed.

By covering over actual discussions of blame and wrongdoing, the PSA hides behind a mission of collective responsibility. In struggling to confront the underlying roots of power, 1 is 2 Many ignores victims who could identify (and have identified) individual perpetrators while celebrating the future possibilities of male bystander intervention. The PSA acts as a pedagogical tool for men; however, it simultaneously protects perpetrators by encouraging them to change their behavior while failing to hold them accountable. But victims—those who are most certainly present in a context of sexual violence—do attempt to hold perpetrators accountable. They name perpetrators, describe their actions, and account for the harms that happened. In other words, in struggling to concretize an actual identity of perpetrator or bystander, the PSA bypasses the issue of punishment, an action that has long served to protect men and obscure possibilities for change.

While the problems of rape and sexual assault are entrenched in issues of male dominance, ironically, the solutions posed by this PSA are also imbricated in those same patriarchal norms. That is, the 1 is 2 Many PSA reinscribes the same male privilege that defines the problem of sexual assault by mobilizing and calling men to the table and maintaining that their voices will be heard over those who are silenced. In turning to a national platform to delineate the problems of sexual assault, men take center stage. The only subjectivity granted a voice within this PSA is that of a man and the victim is only imagined when they can be visualized as a woman in relation to that man. Invoking the spectacle of a victim while evading their actual material presence serves to deny the root causes of rape culture and ignore the individual perpetrators at fault. In short, masculinity remains unquestioned while it is leveraged as the solution.

Invitational Haunting: The Imagined Victim

In each of these marketing tools, the severity of rape crimes is made legible through bystanders who call upon society to protect "our" women—society's daughters, wives, sisters, granddaughters, and so on. In this last section, I extend this analysis to consider how these materials invite viewers to imagine a particular victim that problematically covers over other bodies subject to sexual abuse. Victim bodies—absent, invisible, yet invoked bodies—haunt the speeches of speakers within both of these campaigns. That is, the bodies imagined by speakers in both clips make a spectacle out of a particular body, one that can be conceptualized alongside each of these men, which is then distributed into the public repertoire. Victims remain a figment of imagination that can be called upon by speakers at their own choosing. The consequences of these constructed images, however, erase bodies that don't occupy the subjectivity of the archetype deployed, silence victims' feelings and attitudes toward sexual violence, and ultimately position future possibilities that ignore how central toxic masculinity and white male dominance are to the problem of rape culture.

The campaigns analyzed in this chapter resemble feminist attempts to protest sexism, what Annie Hill might call a "perifeminist response" to rape culture and its logics, responses trapped by the limits of their own ideological commitments.[60] To assess the effects of such attempts, I turn to Jacqueline Rhodes, who, in calling for a critical feminist rhetoric, argues that performance, virality, and intersectionality offer much-needed opportunities for analysis, opportunities that call us to examine where and how feminist intervention can take place.⁶¹ The two rape prevention campaigns analyzed in this chapter pose opportunities for thinking through how the aspects of performance, virality, and intersectionality manifest and shape public understandings of protest and intervention. But, as Rhodes insists, engaging any analysis of protest "needs to be rhetorical, in the sense that we need to understand both personal choice (to engage) and the power relations at work (who sets the terms of engagement?) in the act of choosing."⁶² Bystanders are given the choice to engage, but the terms of this type of engagement are set by a system of patriarchy entrenched in white supremacy. We should be haunted by the victim constructed in these materials, haunted by the limited terms set to protect a particular body while ignoring others. Put another way, the specter of patriarchy operates in the service of the protection of white womanhood, an eerie, subtle, yet powerful specter that shapes and influences how publics choose to engage and choose to view their own complicity and responsibility.

In imagining a victim, these materials locate college campuses as a main site where sexual assaults frequently occur. For instance, in order to "take the pledge" within the It's On Us campaign, people must affiliate themselves with a university or college. While acknowledging college campuses as a site where sexual assault happens can be productive and necessary, these materials risk marking a particular kind of victim that works to mask other people who have experienced sexual assault. When promoting the work of the White House Task Force to Protect Students from Sexual Assault, Biden asserted that the main goal should be to prioritize victims: "It's important that we keep the faces, and life-stories of our women and girls in mind as we continue this work."⁶³ Ironically, the campaigns analyzed in this chapter limit the opportunities for doing just so and focus instead on constituting a spectacle of the victim that serves to represent all victims.

During his remarks, Biden described the experience of a young woman, Lauren, who was raped during her sophomore year of college by an acquaintance at a party. He described the feelings of shame and self-doubt that inhibited her from speaking out about what happened, saying, "It was her inability to tell anyone [that] caused the most harm. She worried it was her fault. Had she drank too much? Did she lead him on? Did he not hear her say 'no'?"⁶⁴ This description of her experience with silence and shame positions Lauren as meek, weak, and in need of support, protection from others. But it also frames Lauren—a victim—in a particular context that epitomizes victimhood and the sites where sexual violence occurs, both of which are steeped in whiteness. That is, universities have long been critiqued for enacting gatekeeping mechanisms that secure them as elite, privileged spaces, serving to protect whiteness while casting out difference. Invoking the spectacle of a victim on a college campus will thus always be linked to whiteness. In his closing remarks, Biden affirmed, "Lauren's story is the story of millions of women, and one that we must never forget."[65] While I take seriously Lauren's story and the feelings that resulted from her experience with sexual assault, it is important to point out that too often stories like Lauren's profile particular kinds of narratives when drawing public attention to the problem. These narratives imagine a specific "victim" of sexual violence—a young, educated, white, cis woman—who is subject to a sexual assault that occurred in a specific privileged location—the college campus. Stories like Lauren's become the paradigm for imagining all sexual assaults, narrowing public attention to see such experiences as representative of all. But as Rhodes notes, "Critical imagination must be part of a vision of feminist rhetorics."[66] We must push back on these spectacles produced by mainstream, state-sponsored efforts. We must critically interrogate and imagine who is left out of the discourse.

Both sets of materials fall trap to identifying this imagined victim when raising public awareness. While neither campaign places direct boundaries on labeling certain identities as victim, they inadvertently do so through this imaginative, speculative work. As Robert Asen has argued, creating equitable public participation requires more than simply including voices previously excluded from debate: "Participation in public discussions does not proceed only through voice and body; inclusions and exclusions also occur in the perception of others—the imagining of others."[67] Put differently, asking the question of who is physically absent or present is not enough; rather, we must analyze who is discursively, symbolically, and affectively imagined as present or absent and for what reasons within public discourse. Contemporary rape prevention methods cultivate feelings of normativity that compel publics to sympathize with an identity portrayed as worth protecting. Safety is cultivated not only through masculinity but also through whiteness, class, gender comportment, ability, and so on. These PSAs are largely constructed with the intent to move audiences, in this case provoking audiences to confront their own complicity. But the feelings produced are problematic in that they are linked to a particular vision of victimhood, concealing the experiences of those who don't fit within this image. The experiences of those who fall outside of this constructed identity linger in the background of these materials, never called to the forefront of conversation.

In seeking to expose the powerful work of imagination, patriarchal spectrality as a method is in many ways akin to Debra Hawhee's concept of rhetorical vision with some important key considerations. Drawing together the ancient rhetorical concepts of *energeia* and *phantasia*, Hawhee's theory of rhetorical vision illuminates the central ways "words and the physical senses interact."[68] In theorizing her term, Hawhee importantly moves the field to see the "nonmetaphorical" work of vision, not simply how visual language aids comprehension (e.g., "I see what you mean"), but, more critically, "the visual work of rhetoric and language, the complex ways that words—oral or written—form perception."[69] Words tap into bodily faculties, interacting with how we see and imagine the world around us, resulting in "visualizable action" grounded in the body.[70] But one key consequence of the bystander is that the sensations produced by its discourses motivate visual faculties that may generate responses shaped by a masculine and normative subject. That is, the bystander serves to sustain patriarchal systems, and as a result, the sensations imagined and circulated in response are, too, subject to patriarchal norms. Because "language interacts with vision directly," the feelings that foster such engagement are never neutral; they are always layered within fields of power constituted by a speaker's or discourse's set of presumptions, commitments, and identities.[71] "Communicative interaction," as Greg Clark argues, "prompts individuals to choose with whom they will identify themselves and with whom they will not."[72] Consequently, imagining and feeling—interacting with—the bystander's normative positionality "constitutes much of what they experience as identity."[73] If the bystander hauntingly represents male dominance and individuals experience a form of felt perception based on the bystander, that perception risks constituting a sense of self tied to patriarchy. Bystander campaigns form a platform for viewers to see themselves, implicated in the sensations of patriarchy and all of its problematic forms of protection.

Using this method demonstrates how contemporary anxieties over normative sexual and political identities codify the available means for speaking of and responding to sexual violence. As the preceding chapter revealed, the US imaginary supports these ideals, subjecting nonnormative, nonwhite, and nonmale bodies to the threat of erasure in public discourse. To acknowledge other bodies requires us to use different modalities of apprehending that help bring to the fore these bodies. Patriarchal spectrality calls us to follow Rhodes and imagine and listen to what other bodies witness as sexual crimes that are made invisible by bystander discourses produced in contexts such as It's On Us and 1 is 2 Many. In other words, our inquiries cannot rely solely on examination of what is said and made visible. Rather, we must consider the abject and affective traces that lead us closer to understanding why certain bodies and experiences were excluded in the first place.

Historical Haunting

In 2018, Oprah Winfrey was awarded the Cecil B. DeMille Award for lifetime achievement by the Hollywood Foreign Press Association at the Golden Globes. The award was given in the wake of #MeToo and #TimesUp, and Oprah, who was the first black woman to receive the award, did not fail to recognize this moment. During her speech, she recounted the story of Recy Taylor. "A name I know," she said, "and I think you should, too."[74] In 1944, Taylor, a sharecropper and young mother, was abducted by car at gunpoint after leaving a church service in Abbeville, Alabama, by seven men. After six of the men stripped her clothes from her and brutally raped Taylor, she was left blindfolded by the side of the road. Before they left her, the men threatened to kill Taylor if she told anyone. What happened to Taylor was eventually reported to the NAACP, who sent their lead investigator and anti-rape activist Rosa Parks from Montgomery to Abbeville to examine the case. Though one of the men eventually confessed to what happened, two all-white, all-male grand juries refused to indict the seven men and the case never went to trial. Joe Culpepper, Robert Gamble, Billy Howerton, Luther Lee, Herbert Lovett, Hugo Wilson, and Dillard York dodged prison for their crimes.

After recalling this history, Oprah's speech prompted many, particularly white Americans, to research Taylor, and several headlines that followed days later led with Oprah's recognition of her. "She lived," Oprah said, "as we all have lived, too many in a culture broken by brutally powerful men."[75] Continuing on, "For too long, women have not been heard or believed if they dared to speak their truth to the power of those men. But their time is up."[76] For Oprah, Taylor represented a long history in which black women in particular were abused by white men in power and not believed when they spoke out, some punished even by death for doing so. Importantly, what happened to Taylor not only represents a history of not believing women; rather, invoking Taylor during the Golden Globes reckoned with a history of rape against black women *not remembered by mainstream white America*. Though Parks was linked to her story, Taylor's name is much less so remembered in the whitewashed histories written of Civil Rights and Jim Crow. While US public memory has widely archived the experience of a young black woman who refused to give up her seat on the bus to a white man, the legacy of black women sexually abused or beaten by white men in power remains spectral, on the fringes of cultural memory. Those shielded from this history fail to know their names:

> Celia
> Recy Taylor
> Gertrude Perkins
> Flossie Hardman
> Betty Jean Owens
> Fannie Lou Hamer
> Rosa Lee Coates
> Joan Little

And the list goes on. Taylor's story, like so many others, occupies a placeholder in history, representing a legacy of sexual abuse normalized by patriarchy and white male dominance. "Between 1940 and 1965," writes historian Danielle McGuire, "only ten white men were convicted of raping black women or girls in Mississippi despite the fact that it happened regularly."[77] These stories—commonplaces of abuse supported by logics of power that ignored them—have largely been erased from history books, haunting what has been made known. Their stories of private sexual abuse remain covered over by the presumption of violence that led to widespread lynching in America, spectacles of death made in the service of the protection of whiteness.

In *Frames of War*, Judith Butler writes, "What is this specter that gnaws at the norms of recognition, an intensified figure vacillating as its inside and its outside? As inside, it must be expelled to purify the norm; as outside, it threatens to undo the boundaries that limn the self."[78] Stories like Taylor's gnaw at recognition. Victims cast outside of the conversation constructed through the subjectivity of bystanders who take their place similarly gnaw at recognition and the norms that support them. A history of rape committed by white men in power has largely been forgotten, while black women who have been sexually abused have been expelled from memory, serving to purify the norm of white America and the archetypes it protects. Once outside, they haunt these archetypes, however, threatening to undo them. Part of the work of patriarchal spectrality involves exposing these norms and the signs they seek to cover over, illustrating, in this case, how the bystander as the site of response is haunted by the decision not to attend to victim bodies, victim experiences, or a history of rapes committed by those in positions of power against women of color, working-class women, and people from queer, nonbinary, or trans communities. Failing to reckon with this "haunting," as the case studies analyzed here attest, "enables the past to be kept alive in the present."[79] Not until we account for and question such specters "through interrogation of our reception of memory and history" will we be able to enact change.[80] Thus, to encounter the bystander and the subjectivities covered over by it requires excavating the past and the tropes that have supported and will continue to support an unchallenged legacy of rape culture. In examining the spectacles that drive our modes of vision—the felt residue of history at risk of erasure—we come closer to dealing with how this cultural memory of rape functions to protect and expel, to remember and forget, always animating our contemporary moment.

A patriarchal spectral approach to communication attends to multiple ways of understanding what is seen and felt, made known to vast public audiences. It aims to reorient analysis to what is made invisible through the visibility of others. The affective residue of silence forms an assemblage that shapes who or what is constituted, what is said in public discourse. "Affect is precisely the body's hopeful opening," writes Jasbir Puar, "a speculative opening not wedded to the dialectic of hope and hopelessness but rather a porous affirmation of what could or might be."[81] These visceral sites of feeling history's openings hold potential for change if we attend to that which seeps among what is seen and said. But these openings are consumed with vulnerability, at risk of violence themselves, as the next two chapters will show. Thus, to truly challenge rape culture—to attempt to change behavior and actions rooted in violence—requires attending to the visceral histories of trauma that took place for people like Recy Taylor. Protesting rape culture requires calling out the specters of patriarchy that so desperately seek to erase these histories.

3

THE PROOF IS IN THE BODY:
TRANSCENDING RHETORIC WITH RAPE KITS

In 2016, Melissa Souto was raped on campus during her junior year at Loyola University in Chicago. After struggling with the decision to share what happened to her with authorities, Souto eventually decided to report her rape after her father encouraged her to seek out a sexual assault forensic examination (what is commonly referred to as a "rape kit" or "rape kit exam") at their local hospital. Once there, she recounted the details of her rape to a sexual assault nurse examiner (SANE), endured a two-and-a-half-hour scrutiny of her body's insides and outsides, and submitted the details of her exam in the form of a report and contaminant-proof box for medical processing and a DNA check through the FBI's Combined DNA Index System (CODIS). She shares of that experience, "It's just so invasive and intrusive and it's the worst because you already feel so disgusted with other people touching you or looking at you after you've been raped, that that's the last thing you want to do."[1] Souto understood the nurse who conducted the exam to be gentle and caring, yet she ultimately claimed that "the testing felt like a nightmare."[2] While it took a year and a half to process the kit, Souto's story has a silver lining: her perpetrator was eventually found responsible for raping Souto by Loyola two years after the assault took place. Souto knew and named him from the beginning.

In 2014, President Obama announced for the first time that federal funding would be allocated toward a competitive grant program designed to help states process and eliminate their rape kit backlogs. Roughly five years before, a Human Rights Watch report was published that exposed a rape kit backlog of over 12,000 untested rape kits in Los Angeles County.[3] That report inspired local investigations by authorities and journalists across the nation, who similarly found that a significant backlog of untested and unprocessed rape kits had accumulated on law enforcement shelves over the past ten to fifteen years. While it is difficult to calculate a nationwide number on the backlog, *Time* magazine reported in 2013 that roughly 400,000 untested kits exist in the United States.[4] According to NPR, states such as Texas have totaled 20,000 untested kits, Ohio discovered 10,000, and the city of Detroit alone amassed 11,000 backlogged rape kits.[5] In addition to a number of state and local legislative attempts, the US Bureau of Justice Assistance responded to the problem by launching the national Sexual Assault Kit Initiative (SAKI) in 2015 to provide nearly $80 million in funding to states with large and/or growing backlogs.

Most certainly, backlogs of rape kits stall claims for justice in cases of rape or sexual assault. While legislative efforts assume the problems of the backlog to stem primarily from issues of faulty evidence collection or a lack of funding, mainstream news sources have suggested cultural and social reasons as also responsible for a growing disregard for rape kits. According to the *New York Times*, the backlog is "a dangerous gap in the nation's war against violent crime," or as stated by the *Washington Post*, "a symbol of the criminal justice system's failure to take rape seriously."[6] As one *Times* editorial suggested, "There is no doubt that we have often been lackadaisical about addressing sexual assault. The injustice of rape is compounded by the injustice of official indifference."[7] In short, media conversations have largely considered the backlog to be a result of widespread skepticism and doubt concerning the crime of rape and those who experience it. And yet, the rape kit—a medicolegal tool that functions to catalog the experience of violation with the hope of confirming and catching perpetrators—continues to serve powerful evidentiary functions, upheld by contemporary legislative efforts as an essential tool used in the reporting and prosecuting of sexual assault cases, including rape. That is, even though the backlog has been cited as a sign of systemic political and legal irresponsibility by the mainstream media, national programs like SAKI assemble a discourse of hope around rape kits, imbuing them with the potential to decrease the rates of rape and sexual assault cases more broadly.

In this chapter, I consider the rhetorical significance of the rape kit within wider public discourse by tracing the relationship between the materiality of the rape kit—a technology undergirded by a powerful discourse of science—and the legislative promises that shape the use and implementation of it. Recent public conversations about the rape kit backlog provide a springboard to explore the ideological underpinnings that support the use of biomedical tools used to make sense of the experience of rape. In Souto's story, for example, processing the rape kit helped her achieve justice, even though she had given testimony to what happened and who specifically attacked her nearly two years prior to receiving the results of the kit. Examination into stories like Souto's suggests that what the rape kit has come to symbolize participates in shifting the available means of disclosing, providing evidence for, and proving rape or sexual assault. While victims often testify to gruesome, harrowing, and deeply embodied details of their experiences and even name their perpetrators, as the next chapter will explore in greater detail, rape kits are implemented to process and suppress the sensory feelings expressed after rape, serving to manage the testimonies victims offer of their own experiences with their bodies. In privileging scientific modes of evidence collection over victims' personal accounts, however, efforts like SAKI consequently control the forms of storytelling available in cases of rape, replacing what I view as an anxiety about bodies and visceral testimonies with what is perceived as incontestable proof. In this way, rape kits are framed as hermetically sealed, portrayed with masculinized agency, seen as rational, logical, and empirical forms of evidence compared to victims' accounts, which are cast as irrational, hysterical, and emotional. Understanding the gendered implications rooted in the need to control sensation and contain their bodies exposes how victims' voices are devalued and discounted in the public sphere because they are tied to what many assume to be bodily, visceral, irrational excess.

In the quest to apply technological solutions to a cultural dilemma, however, a series of several problems emerges from public discourse about rape kits regarding who is responsible for rape, the tools available for proving it, and how society addresses it. As my analysis will show, discourses about rape kits that stem from efforts like SAKI produce medico-legal ideals that position the rape kit as a "technoscientific witness" better equipped to handle cases of sexual violence than actual testimonies.[8] In the process, rape is refigured as a problem involving "bad apples"—distant, criminal, social Others like those examined in chapter 1—that can be solved with science, as opposed to a cultural problem entrenched in deep-seated, insidious, everyday gendered notions of power. But worst of all, prioritizing rape kits over victims' voices, I argue, functions to increasingly push justice for rape outside the realm of the rhetorical. That is, turning to rape kits as a legislative solution for rape culture that manage the bodily trauma of rape through technologies buttressed by science repositions the public sphere as less of a place for arguments about the probable and more of a place for contestable facts. Put differently, this chapter argues that how the rape kit operates in a court of law negatively influences a public perception of the visceral and embodied—forms of communication so central to understanding the act of rape in the first place—contributing to a widespread silencing of women's voices that ultimately works to remove the role of rhetoric from the public sphere.

Even if they are deployed with the intent to bolster victims' voices, these material technologies tragically only serve to supplant them and transcend the rhetoricity of a feeling body, treated as arhetorical forms of evidence that ultimately work to shift the conversation about rape culture.

While the previous two chapters examined how perpetrators and victims are imagined in public discourse in ways that seek to contain the nation-state and the subjectivities deemed most worthy of protection, this chapter marks a shift in this book, one that turns to the intimate and vulnerable interactions bodies have with publics and larger discourses about rape. To conduct my analysis in this chapter, I take point from Jordynn Jack, who argues that feminist rhetorical studies of embodiment must consider the use of certain tools and technologies *"in practice,"* beyond the study of development or representation by interrogating "how use of those technologies depends on performances of status and gender, policy frameworks, space-time arrangements, and the material design of technologies themselves."[9] In the process, I draw from a number of texts—including news and research reports, opinion editorials, justice initiatives, medical protocols, and personal published accounts—to understand the interaction rape kits have with raped bodies, public perception of those bodies, and the tools used to assess them. In doing so, I hope to show how gender is embedded into the rape kit's technological design, use, and implementation alongside the spaces and interactions that engage with those technologies.

I begin outlining what the materials and procedures of sexual assault forensic exams are, contextualizing how this method of evidence collection circulates rhetorically within public conversations about the backlog while sketching an approach for reading how the rape kit interacts with bodies. Next, I turn to the recent legislative efforts of SAKI and the public conversations surrounding them, analyzing three central problems that emerge within public dialogues about rape kits and the rape kit backlog that together attempt to negate the role of rhetoric. The first problem illustrates how discourse about mitigating the backlog serves to resuscitate the idea of the stranger rapist, positioning rape as a crime that occurs primarily by racialized criminals unknown to victims. The second problem demonstrates a desire for science to work and an overstated optimism that shapes understanding the use of these tools. And finally, the third problem illuminates how rape kits are leveraged to contain the excess of a moving body and the feelings expressed after rape. In concluding this chapter, I draw a parallel connection to the contemporary use of police body cameras and explain the implications this case study has for how we treat technologies implemented to solve additional cultural problems of violence.

Taken as a whole, this chapter interrogates how medico-legal technologies and tools partake in conditioning publics not to believe victims. But the stakes of this case are high and deeply troubling for all members of publics if we, as rhetoricians, want to imagine the public sphere as a place for deliberation, a place to imagine a better future by opening up dialogues that help move us there. My intention in this chapter is not to suggest that scientific and medical tools central to rape kit technologies are inherently evil. On the contrary, tools like these have proved necessary for supplementing the testimonies of marginalized members of society who are often otherwise not believed. But in outlining the power granted to technology over actual voices and embodied accounts within legislative and public contexts, I hope to show how problematic instances of violence that are cultural and social are cast as scientific and legal. Such dangerous assumptions consequently reframe solutions to the problem through the idea of a "technocratic order," one that is devoid of the voices of and visceral rhetorics communicated by those so frequently subject to that exact violence.[10]

Reading the Rape Kit

According to the National Sexual Violence Resource Center, an overwhelming majority of women—eight out of ten—know their perpetrators and give testimony to that knowledge.[11] Yet, all people who experience rape or sexual assault and seek immediate medical care are encouraged to undergo a rape kit exam. Because rape victims have historically been discriminated against in the courtroom, often blamed for what happened and "revictimized" by procedures like cross examination, the rape kit can be viewed as a productive opportunity to challenge such discrimination.[12] According to Kimberlé Crenshaw, the law's relationship to women's sexuality marks it as "a central site of the oppression of women" where "rape and the rape trial are its dominant narrative trope."[13] Rape law "epitomizes," in Carol Smart's words, why justice for women and women's rights writ large struggle to achieve wider success.[14] Because of this reality, some view the rape kit as a tool that gives victims agency in a context that has so frequently worked to diminish it.[15] While well intended, legislative efforts that focus on the rape kit, I suggest, risk contributing to the problem of not listening to victims by calling upon a tool to speak for victims on their behalf, a tool presumed to hold more ethos and credibility. Most troubling though, is that in casting evidence for rape in particular terms, legislative efforts obfuscate how publics understand the everyday acts of rape culture that manifest in more insidious ways and overlook the necessity of deliberation in problems of this scale. Celebrating science overshadows what the broader roots of rape culture are and other modes that could be productive for apprehending and challenging it.

Rape kit exams, which can take up to six hours, are completed within seventy-two hours after the assault by a SANE or doctor and strive to preserve possible DNA evidence of the perpetrator, even when the offender is known. The kits include bags; combs; documentation forms; envelopes; instructions; sterile water and saline; a large sheet of paper that collects hairs and fibers while undressing; dental floss and/or wooden sticks for fingernail scrapings; and tubes and swabs for blood, urine, and semen samples. Prior to having an exam, one is encouraged to refrain from bathing, showering, using the restroom, changing, combing hair, and cleaning up the area of violation to preserve possible evidence. During the exam, one's clothes are taken and kept in a paper bag while a series of steps guide an examiner to assess any injuries, collect prior medical and sexual history, inquire into the details of the assault, and examine the body from head to toe with the approval of the victim at each step, including internal examinations of the mouth, vagina, and/or anus. In the process, the victim may be asked to lie on a gynecological table with stirrups while the examiner may scan the body with ultraviolet light, searching for semen and saliva. Photographs of the body may be taken, and digital cameras or colposcopes may be used to take pictures of the body's insides. Evidence from the kit may be submitted to the police for investigation, and any DNA found is entered into the FBI's national database for registering serial offenders.

While I do not intend to suggest that the technology of rape kits is intrinsically bad or wholly unproductive, it is important to acknowledge the many flawed ways these technologies have been implemented in medical and legal contexts. A wealth of research has been done on the use of rape kits and the rape kit backlog from scholars in disciplines such as legal studies, medical research, sociology, anthropology, criminology, and social work, among others.[16] Taken together, this body of research collectively cites the backlog as a gross disregard for rape crimes and rape victims, but it also tracks rape kit procedures and the precarious ways police and medical personnel interact with both victims and the evidence produced by the kits. Importantly, these scholars suggest that the expansion of SANE programs and rape kit technology is not the answer. Rose Corrigan, a well-known legal scholar on the topic of sexual violence, argues that rape kit procedures create "opportunities for police to discourage rape reporting, investigation, and prosecution by using the forensic evidence collection process as a way to intimidate victims, diminish the seriousness of the assault, and attack victims' credibility as witnesses."[17] In many cases, "negative, victim-blaming beliefs about sexual assault victims" held by law enforcement personnel shape whether or not victims undergo an exam at all.[18]

Even more troubling is that victims of rape or sexual assault face a unique response from medical and legal personnel when compared to victims of other crimes. "Unlike people who have been robbed, beaten, or defrauded," writes legal scholar Corey Rayburn Yung, "rape victims must bypass a series of gatekeepers that, beginning with the police, impede the criminal justice system from vindicating victims' allegations."[19] The rape kit is ideologically and symbolically saturated with a broader set of stigmas discursively projected onto someone who discloses rape or sexual assault and the belief that they are lying. The choice to process a case of rape with rape kit technology is layered with a set of rape myths that ultimately puts the victim on trial, having to defend themselves, and "obscures its [the rape kit's] political origins in patriarchal and racist legal histories of doubting and dismissing women's reports of rape."[20] In other words, the crime of rape—a crime in which the bodies subject to it are often other than straight, cis, white men—is met with a set of procedures that speak to a broader policing of certain bodies in public.

Because rape kits are viewed as providing more objective evidence, public discussions bypass the actual pain and suffering endured by the victim during the exam and narrowly focus on what the kit purports to prove. "The victim," writes Sameena Mulla, "is expected to facilitate this process by tolerating pain, discomfort, hunger, cold, and shame, and perhaps delaying her need to urinate or defecate."[21] Furthermore, to preserve what is perceived as "perfect evidence, a victim must be willing to offer herself up to the forensic nurse examiner's scrutiny and ministration."[22] Thus, while the exam itself is positioned as a source of care and immediate response for victims, both nurse examiners and victims alike describe the discomfort central to the exam. In offering herself up, as Mulla suggests, the victim's body is framed as an object of exchange, given over to the examiner who mines it for data, dissecting and prodding its parts. Because "contemporary forensic exams rarely live up to their promise of serving sexual assault victims' interests," they fall trap to the same revictimization that often takes place in court, subjecting victims to blaming mechanisms even as they attempt to bolster the testimonies victims offer of their own bodies.[23]

In the process of implementing these forms of bodily inspection, the law thus "build[s] legal truths about sexual assault and its perpetrators."[24]

That is, the legal standard of turning to such evidentiary forms as modes of proof discursively constructs perceptions of perpetrators and victims before they even walk into a courtroom, influencing wider beliefs about rape and producing topoi that legal experts, prosecutors, and defense attorneys may use to construct their arguments. For instance, during the *People of the State of California v. Brock Allen Turner*—a case I examine in the next chapter—Turner was initially indicted on five charges, two of which were rape.[25] The victim completed a rape kit exam almost immediately following the violent attack, which was then submitted to police personnel. Yet, once the deputy district attorney received the results of the kit, the two rape charges were dropped during a preliminary hearing, settling for lesser charges of sexual assault that challenged the initial testimony made by the victim.[26] In other words, even when implemented and processed in the best way, the rape kit is still subjected to and further circulates stereotypes of victims, perpetrators, and the act of rape that shape how it will be used in court.

Despite the challenges uncovered by scholars regarding the rape kit exam and the backlog, legislators continue to fight for solutions to help improve the experience for victims and mitigate backlogs across the nation. The 2015 SAKI provides a grounding point for my analysis, in large part because it is, at present, the most recent substantial legislation passed regarding rape kits. The initiative aimed to mitigate the growing number of untested or unsubmitted rape kits held in law enforcement custody by awarding money to local counties and cities. The first of several SAKI press conferences took place on September 10, 2015, and gathered key figures part of these efforts in New York City to announce that the first $38 million was awarded to over thirty jurisdictions in twenty states across the country. The press conference included then Vice President Joe Biden, US Attorney General Loretta Lynch, New York County District Attorney Cyrus Vance, and actress and advocate Mariska Hargitay, among many others, including victims of rape and sexual assault. My analysis builds from an archive including this press conference and the surrounding discursive landscape about rape kits and rape kit backlog legislation to understand the rhetorical significance of the rape kit today.[27]

The analysis that follows finds that how assumptions about evidence play out in public discourse can be understood through the idea of artistic or inartistic proofs. While artistic (or intrinsic) proofs are constructed or crafted and perceived as rhetorical, inartistic (extrinsic) proofs rely on preexisting data separate from the speaker and are perceived as arhetorical. Within public discourse, I argue that supporters of the use of rape kits frame DNA evidence collected from the exam as an inartistic proof, operating outside the realm of the rhetorical, whereas victims' visceral testimonies that communicate feelings of rape are framed as artistic proofs, which remain inside the scope of the rhetorical. While the materials and processes of these exams most certainly function rhetorically to claim what occurred and who participated, public conversations assume an arhetorical infallibility surrounding DNA. However, choosing to trust DNA and its assumed arhetorical character requires not trusting the rhetorical nature of victims' embodied accounts. And yet, the biggest problem surrounding rape adjudication is that confirming consent can never be proven; it can only be argued. Supporting the idea that DNA testing operates as an inartistic proof provides a safe haven for publics to continue not believing victims and casts rape kit processing as a foolproof system that can transcend the traumatized body, its sensations, and the rhetorical processes central to rape disclosure.

To understand how the forms of visceral rhetorics expressed by victims are taken up, interpreted, and challenged, I draw from Alexander Weheliye's biopolitical theory of the flesh, investigating how perceptions of the body's symbolic and material functions traffic in a larger capacity to be seen as human, one capable of speaking and being heard. For Weheliye, focusing on actual fleshiness draws attention to how violence is enacted epistemically to create categories of human. He maintains that biopolitical discourses do not operate merely in human or nonhuman ways; rather, attention to physical flesh helps account for the "not-quite humans" and the processes that participate in disciplining this form of humanity.[28] While cognizant of Elaine Scarry's well-cited theory of pain—a theory, no doubt, central to the concept of visceral rhetorics—Weheliye attends to the flesh to open up new ways of seeing and hearing: "What is at stake is not so much the lack of language per se [. . .] but the kinds of dialects available to the subjected and how these are seen and heard by those who bear witness to their plight."[29] When drawing from embodiment and feeling—modes of meaning making used to account for violation committed in and on the flesh—victims run the risk of being cast by legal or public audiences as using dialects or forms of discourse framed as outside the acceptable means of speaking in public. Their very fleshiness deems them unfit.

For one to expose these moments of marking one not-quite human, Weheliye calls for scholars to attend to a language of carnality. In the case of rape, these fleshy, corporeal moments take shape in how one describes the bloodiness and earthiness of violation, that which is assumed to be captured and controlled through the exam. In other words, my analysis tracks the moments where descriptions of the flesh are met with anxiety, the moments when rape kits are deployed to contain bodily excess, what is otherwise considered unspeakable at times: the physical lacerations of violation, the grit of a pavement or rug, scabs on one's skin, a gut empty of all but shame, blood in a body's parts, bruises blue with memories, crust left from tears. These are moments revealing of flesh, a flesh only given a narrative platform once translated, evaluated, and separated from testimony. The rape kit presumes these moments as in need of interpretation, as if rape kits are capable of revealing a "hidden truth of rape" unavailable under other discursive forms.[30] In the process of managing this flesh, the use of rape kits renders raped bodies as not-quite human, relegated to a dialect incomprehensible to authoritative powers, "a terrain of utter abjection outside the iron grip of humanity."[31] While the rape kit serves to uncover and reveal, the flesh is discarded, pushed outside normative order.

This biopolitical theory draws attention to how recognition is given only to some subjects in public; denying the visceral meaning communicated from a raped, fleshy body reveals this problem. "By making dumb flesh speak," as performance studies scholar and artist Aliza Shvarts describes, the tools of a rape kit serve to quell an anxiety about bodies but more broadly represent a desire to remove such forms of meaning making from public life.[32] That is, the rape kit "organizes inchoate flesh into a meaningful and legible form," demonstrating a mechanism for excluding visceral ways of making meaning in public.[33] As a result, "women lie outside the frame of justice from the beginning," and any attempts to testify by women or minorities are codified as less trustworthy, irrational, or excessive.[34] Thus, science is not simply leveraged to establish credibility for what is otherwise spoken. Rather, such biomedical meaning is marshalled in to eradicate the rhetorical forms and modes central to the body—meaning made in and constituted from one's internal organs and transpired through sensations that account for a robust sense of what it feels like to be raped. Understanding this approach foregrounds how I read the discursive landscape shaping public understandings of rape kits, which is where I turn now.

Translating Embodied Evidence from Rhetoric
to Science: Three Problems

In this analysis, I move through a series of three problems that emerge from contemporary discourse about rape kits and the rape kit backlog. First, the rhetorical environment surrounding rape kits and rape kit legislation works to redefine rape as not a cultural problem but rather a problem of violent criminals that can be solved with science, shifting how the act of rape is imagined and who it involves. Second, overprioritizing the use of biometric tools suggests them to be infallible and resonates with a history of not believing victims. Third, the interactions between rape kits and bodies found in a variety of medical, legislative, and testimonial sources indicate a perceived need for the law to suppress victims' bodies and control the messy experience of rape, which negates the value of visceral rhetorics. I maintain that these three problems operate at different levels that together increasingly serve to push justice for rape outside the realm of the rhetorical. In the process, the prevalence of rape is viewed not as a problem inflected by historical, cultural, and ideological underpinnings but rather a scientific one with scientific solutions.

Problem 1: Rapists as Violent Criminals

Understanding how publics decipher the purpose of rape kits requires turning to their legislative history and role in rape prosecution. The earliest legislation to attend to the issue of testing and processing forensic material gathered from a rape kit was named after a woman who was brutally raped and threatened at gunpoint just outside her home in Williamsburg, Virginia, in 1989. During the attack, Debbie Smith was blindfolded and dragged into the woods before she was raped repeatedly by an unidentifiable man wearing a ski mask. While Smith participated in DNA evidence collection, her kit remained untested for five years, until 1994, when it was finally submitted into a national database. One year later, after DNA analysis, her attacker was identified—a man already serving 161 years in prison for abducting and robbing two women.

For those somewhat well versed in violence against women legislation, Smith's story may sound familiar. It serves powerful rhetorical functions in public dialogues about rape kits. That is, what happened to Smith conditions how many in the public view the experiences of all victims who endure a rape kit exam and the kinds of sexual attacks for which rape kits become necessary, as was done during the 2015 SAKI press conference. There, Vice President Biden recalled the details of what happened to Smith and shared that before leaving, Smith's attacker told her, "If you say anything, I'll come back and I will kill you, which as [DA Cyrus Vance] can tell you is not an unusual refrain for a rapist."[35] In addition to telling Smith's story, Biden also recalled the story of another woman for whom the use of a rape kit was pivotal in tracking and targeting her assailant. She was the daughter of a friend Biden knew who "was raped on a Saturday night by [her] university. She lived in a garden apartment. They found her [huddled] in the apartment with the sliding glass doors open in the morning. Her brother found her, naked and shaking."[36] The similarities between each of these stories are noteworthy: both women were raped in similar places (in or near the privacy of their own homes), by similar perpetrators (unknown, male assailants), and were abused and threatened after their perpetrators broke in and attacked them. Together, these narratives—the only ones profiled during the press conference—function to intensify and heighten audiences' reactions by vividly illustrating a sexual attack.

While Biden's spoken words draw upon these similar stories, this archetypal narrative of rape and its victims extends far beyond the 2015 press conference. In the 2009 Human Rights Watch report conducted on Los Angeles County's rape kit backlog cited in the opening of this chapter, the authors position the need for stronger evidence collection around a similar narrative. The report profiles the story of a woman named Catherine, who "was in her forties, living with her young son. She was awakened at midnight by a stranger who raped her, sodomized her, and forced her to orally copulate him—repeatedly. Thankfully, her child remained asleep."[37] After initially told it would take over eight months to process her kit, the detective on Catherine's case pushed the kit through quicker and "when it [the rape kit] was processed, they got a 'cold hit.' Catherine's rapist was identified. He was in the offender database."[38] Following the same scripts deployed in the previous narratives, Catherine, too, is portrayed as a helpless woman at home, a mother, in this case. The report continues, "During the months Catherine's kit sat on a shelf, unopened, the same rapist attacked at least two other victims—one was a child."[39] Thus, the story of her attacker adheres to the same tropes of trespassing her home, attacking her, and repeating the same offense with multiple others. Together, these perpetrators are imagined as outcast offenders with a criminal history that should follow them if rape kits are properly processed.

In rehearsing a particular scene of rape, these narratives enact a scope of rape culture in which rapists are invoked through discourses reminiscent of political programs that sought to decrease violence or drugs, declared through a "war" against crime, which has ultimately served to align criminality with race and class and construct the rapist as a deviant Other. After citing statistics that more than half of all rapes are committed by serial rapists, Biden asserted that increasing the testing and processing of rape kits "does a couple things. It takes serial rapists off the street so every woman in every community is safer, because these serial rapists are not wandering the street. It reduces the total number of victims."⁴⁰ While serial rapists are not to be taken lightly given that individuals known to commit one assault are frequently found to have committed many, Biden's terms are slippery. Biden uses the term "serial" rapists to understand the majority of rape cases by perpetrators "wandering the street," invoking the idea of a *serial* rapist as the *stranger* rapist racialized through the idea of criminality, one lurking on "the street" who then trespasses a random woman's home. Yet, as advocacy organizations have argued, the vast majority of rapes occur by perpetrators known to the victim.⁴¹ Biden's imagined serial rapists are not the Harvey Weinsteins, the Jeffrey Epsteins, or the Larry Nassars, serial rapists otherwise found in workplaces, hotel rooms, churches, doctors' offices, classrooms, film sets, or other mundane contexts. These rapists are imagined through racist and classist frameworks that eclipse interrogation into a wider scope of rape culture. Yet legislation like SAKI, Biden suggests, "sets women free."⁴² In other words, rape kits are rhetorically instilled with the power to create a more just society by targeting and eliminating criminals while paving a process of healing for women.

Framing rape cases through this narrative creates the need for a solution that involves cracking down on crime, narrowing an account of rape culture that fails to represent most cases. As Biden described, a rapist found through DNA testing could be someone who has "also committed two murders or is responsible for six burglaries or three robberies."⁴³ Because the perpetrators profiled in these kinds of stories are framed through criminality, rapists are perceived as "bad apples"—offenders not commonplace in society but rather criminals in need of punishment. As one *Times* story put it, "Through mandatory sampling of prisoners and other known criminals, states are rapidly expanding their computer databases of DNA profiles, which allow investigators to compare tiny bits of biological evidence from crime scenes against pools of potential suspects."⁴⁴ Confirming the DNA of an attacker, however, relies on the fact that that DNA must already exist within the FBI's database. And yet, less than 1 percent of all perpetrators will ever spend a day in jail, their DNA thus unavailable in CODIS.⁴⁵ In these narratives, perpetrators become aligned with social outcasts unfit for normative society, making the problem of rape culture not an ideological and gendered issue of power but rather a gap in the criminal system's ability to catch and identify perpetual lawbreakers. In other words, the narratives do not allow for a broader, more nuanced conversation about the *cultural* problem of sexual violence—a pervasive problem shaped by normalized sexist and violent attitudes toward women and minorities.

While these stories productively generate public outcry and deserve national attention, their parallel generic structure conditions a conventional case of rape, linking perceptions of rape kits with a specific kind of perpetrator and a particular kind of attack within the audience's imaginary. These are violent encounters initiated by male strangers who trespassed the safe boundaries of a woman's home. These are disturbing sexual attacks in which innocent women were violated, threatened, and forced to endure their attacker's sexual demands. The effects of retelling narratives like these, however, sensationalize the experience of rape for public audiences and, as a result, condition a narrow definition of who experiences it and in what ways that serves to illustrate all rapes. My point is not to discount the experiences of these women or suggest that sexual attacks like these do not ever happen, but rather to demonstrate how, within discourse about the need for and use of rape kits, the national perception of rape reduces rape to an act committed by a stranger criminal assumed to have a troubled legal history. Such narrative vehicles traffic in the racialized and classed discursive landscape of stranger-danger, and an overreliance on these stories feeds a public perception that imagines that the majority of rapes occur by strangers, as opposed to cases of date rape, acquaintance rape, or even partner rape—cases where victim testimonies would deeply inform assessments of violence, cases like Souto's from the opening of this chapter.

The narratives constructed around the need for rape kits thus pose problems for people who have been raped or sexually assaulted by people they may know or in ways that don't fit the mold of the stories narrated above. Retelling these narratives as an exigency for stronger legislation creates a hierarchy of what counts as a "crime worth fighting" in the eyes of the state, the kind of gender-based violence that is deemed illegal and in need of rehabilitation. Stories like these work to produce a "foundational narrative of the state," one that complicates an opportunity to expand a broader notion of gender-based violence and unpack how gender and power work in tandem in everyday life.[46] "The forensic examination" thus "serves as another type of institutional interpellation in which its subjects, both victims and perpetrators, are interpellated into an idealized configuration of these roles," much like the archetypes examined in the previous two chapters.[47] Perpetrators are figured through racist ideas of a violent criminal unfit for society, and the laws surrounding the need for these tools neglect other kinds of attackers that don't fall under this image. Victims, on the other hand, are portrayed through a heteronuclear imaginary of docility including cis, middle-class, and presumably white women, who were safely and innocently minding their own business in the confines of their home. Stories like these hold power, and circulating this narrow conception of rape forecloses discussion of other cases of rape and sexual assault that don't include the prototypical woman at home or stranger criminal offenders—stories that also deserve national and public attention.

While rape kits can be productively used to confirm the identity of an accused attacker, narratives deployed to justify the use of rape kits prioritize the stranger criminal as the quintessential rapist—what second-wave feminists fought so hard to overturn. In other words, nowhere in this narrative are we able to grapple with everyday occurrences of sexual violence that take place between men who are otherwise deemed "normal" members of society. Nowhere in this image are we able to understand sexual assaults committed against people from trans communities or women of color or working-class women or any of these overlapping intersections who experience sexual assault at a high frequency but often remain silent because of fear of retaliation. Outlining this narrative vehicle importantly exposes how narrowly defined the problem of rape is within this conversation, not as an everyday occurrence of power, but rather, a problem that can be resolved with stronger surveillance and law enforcement techniques.

Problem 2: The Desire for Science to Work

To enhance the ability to catch criminal rapists, speakers during the press conference reassembled a symbol of hope around the rape kit, one that overlooked the value of hearing a variety of experiences that count as rape or sexual assault and instead favored technologies as the ideal solutions. While the shadow of the backlog remained, rape kits were repackaged anew through an optimistic promise of fighting the injustice of rape culture. One of the chief architects of SAKI, Cyrus Vance, echoed the sentiments of Biden that suggest rape to be a criminal problem. Vance reiterated that solving rape crimes requires "getting rapists off the streets," contributing to the idea that those who commit sexual assault are outliers, a few bad apples in need of restoration.[48] Testing rape kits, he stated, will "provide closure" and "restore faith and justice" to all victims who have been subject to these kinds of attacks as well as the public's confidence in the criminal justice system.[49] Such ideas of hope and restoration were echoed by Senator Dick Black, who said to the *Post* that bills such as SAKI will not only "protect many, many women from sexual assault" but "save lives."[50] Revamping these efforts, however, requires stronger technologies, or at the very least, *the appeal of stronger technologies*. In this section, I outline how science is leveraged rhetorically to project a level of confidence surrounding the rape kit, making conversations about rape evidence—what were once a matter of testimony by victims—into a matter of perceived, clear scientific evidence.

Testimonies of rape and sexual assault are often layered with feelings of pain and trauma, and while powerful when disclosed to public audiences, scholars have theorized how testimonies such as these are frequently met with skepticism.[51] While feelings and viscerality illuminate the experiences of force, constraint, and trespass characteristic of violation, I argue that these feelings are exactly what rape kits are employed to boil down into manageable data, providing a new avenue to delegitimize victims. Rape kits are projected through ideas of objectivity and certainty, "evoking 'rational' arguments, empirical evidence, and results that can be methodologically represented," creating a dichotomy between bodies and technology that shapes public understandings of rape and its evidence.[52] Within public discourse, rape kits masquerade as apolitical, cast under the veil of an expert, and as rhetorical scholars have shown, scientifically or medically framed ideas appear convincing, indisputable, and are quickly disseminated into the public register, complicating who has authority to speak of issues regarding one's own body.[53] In the case of rape kits, rhetorical power is granted to scientific technologies in public discourse, motivated by an anxiety about bodies and narratives of the visceral that then plays out in how publics evaluate and debate the problem of rape.

Because rape kits have been used for over three decades, speakers during the press conference reframed their troubled history by advancing the use of science and technology. Said Biden, "The CDC estimates that x number of women are going to be raped in their lifetime. The number is somewhere between a minimum of 20 to 25 million [. . .]. But in the last 15 years, we've had the technology that could help set them free in ways that we never talked about before."[54] Attorney General Loretta Lynch also expressed this hope of technology when she announced that $41 million will be solely allocated to investigating stronger forensic methods. She stated, "We will continue to search for new and innovative ways to bring important resources to bear in this vital cause."[55] Part of the SAKI legislation is dedicated to enhancing the tools and processes central to rape kit examination and administration. But framing these solutions through perceptions of shiny new technologies overshadows the ideological problems at the heart of this issue and suggests that mitigating rape crimes requires faster, smarter, and stronger technological solutions.

This desire for science to work emerges from popular understandings of DNA testing and the level of certainty it purports. During the press conference, Biden remarked, "DNA technology is a guilty person's worst enemy and the innocent person's greatest friend."[56] Within this discussion, DNA is granted a higher status than testimony and acts as a form of indisputable evidence. Because "these checks are increasingly simple and fairly infallible," as one *Times* story put it, "they also offer fresh hope for breakthroughs, especially in the huge backlog of rape investigations that have gone cold."[57] Their assumed power reaches across time and space, as Vance affirmed, "DNA evidence solves crimes across state lines and across decades."[58] Finally, DNA was fashioned through a savior light, as one *Post* article shared, "The certainty that evidence is going to be sent to a lab and analyzed is huge and helps to begin the process of restoring faith in a system that quite frankly has not worked really well for victims of sexual assault."[59] These rhetorical claims assume broader agency for rape kits, projecting DNA as ammunition for fighting sexual crimes.

In her book-length investigation of rape kits, *The Violence of Care: Rape Victims, Forensic Nurses, and Sexual Assault Intervention*, Mulla observed countless emergency room encounters with victims and spent time interviewing both nurses and patients who partook in the rape kit exam. Notably, she foregrounds how nurses adapted to the process, perceiving DNA as "the hand of God," as one nurse described it.[60] As a result, Mulla found that empathy and care operated, at times, in opposition to the goal of forensic collection and that its rhetorical value has perhaps overshadowed its legal value. That is, after four years of participatory observation and interviews, Mulla argues that the point of the exam—its main purpose of capturing and containing a perpetrator's DNA—is perhaps a moot one. "DNA," she writes, "rarely figures in the legal resolution of sexual assault, although it is often the focus of the sexual assault intervention."[61] In other words, because the majority of crimes don't occur by strangers, confirming the DNA of a known perpetrator isn't enough to claim rape or assault occurred in cases where perpetrators are named and known. Proof of consent or the lack of it is needed, which can only be argued through and by the evidence provided in a kit—a point largely overlooked in discourse about DNA. The symbolic power of DNA, however, is undeniably present in current deliberative efforts surrounding rape kits, shaping what audiences perceive to be effective solutions to the problem.

Why DNA acts so powerfully is important to note. As public and political claims make clear, DNA is portrayed as irrefutable, authoritative, and factual, "a legitimizing feature of victim narratives as well as material validation of the experience of sexual victimization."[62] Analyzing it as a form of evidence through the idea of an inartistic proof, however, reveals an unstated premise that victims' words and the embodied sensations they describe are unreliable, unempirical, and fallible—in other words, *rhetorical*. Even though the problem of the backlog remains a national stain, the power of DNA persists—an unflinching and ostensibly arhetorical form of evidence, granted with agency to change the status of rape culture. According to one *Times* story, because of more routine DNA testing in criminal investigations, "rape survivors and law enforcement experts are finding that in the realm of sex crimes, science has outpaced the law."[63] Along these lines, the problem of rape justice is portrayed as no longer a cultural problem that would involve deliberation but rather a problem solely of forensics—both in the tendency to pitch the problem of rape, rhetorically, as only a question of what happened in the past (as opposed to a deliberative problem that accounts for the conditions or forces that shape the probability that rape happened juxtaposed against potential future action) but also as a criminal problem with obvious scientific solutions.

In the process of turning away from victims' testimonies and toward science, bodies and rhetoric merge, seen as forms of evidence that are less persuasive than their technological counterparts. In casting aside these embodied forms of communicating, however, the rape kit is assumed to transcend rhetoric and the meaning-making processes central to disclosing how the body was violated. In this way, the flesh is granted outside of the law, it "constitutes a liminal zone comprising legal and extralegal subjection, violence, and torture."[64] Relegating victims and their bodies to a lesser status reveals, as Weheliye argues, the "lines of flight from the world of Man in the form of practices, existences, thoughts, desires, dreams, and sounds contemporaneously persisting in the law's spectral shadows."[65] The law—and the medico-legal tools supported by it—participate in castigating certain forms of flesh outside; the law lurks in the background dictating what is perceived as absolute and credible. As a result, rhetoric and its intricate connection to the body are exiled, cast as unfit for rape adjudication, and furthermore, the public's understanding of it. The rape kit and the scientific discourses that bolster it transcend that which is positioned as a weaker form of evidence or proof when the outcomes of a violent crime are open to interpretation.

In this case, the presumption of biological certainty works to naturalize gender differences and mark certain bodies and forms of embodiment as irrational, placing legislative calls for rape kits in a long history of invoking scientific objectivity for bodies perceived as unruly, in excess or outside the norm, a quest that has always been motivated by gendered assumptions.[66] As Robin Jensen has argued, for women who experienced infertility issues in the 1930s, the labeling of "sterile" came to identify women's bodies as "in need of technical-mechanical diagnosis and repair."[67] That is, scientific intervention has a "moralizing component," one that carries hope for advancing or even fixing women's health, often deployed when medical unknowns emerge.[68] But as this case study illustrates, implementing rape kits is not simply a matter of using science when the unknown exists. Implementing science by way of the kit and its surrounding discourses is entrenched with a deep distrust over victims' voices and their embodied experiences to the point that such feeling matters must be managed and removed from what is framed as "real" or "hard" evidence. Put another way, the feelings and sensations that result from the perceived "enigmatic darkness of the female body" cannot be told; rather, evidence of such violence "must be discovered."[69] In the process, the power granted to the tools of rape kit procedures are made invisible within public discourse, concealed through the ideologies of masculinity and rationality that support their use.

Showcasing DNA testing most prominently in these conversations helps deflect attention further away from victims' experiences and suggests that the problem of rape culture can be solved through objective and scientific means. "The credibility of one witness, the technoscientific witness," writes sociologist Andrea Quinlan, "was thus built on the lack of perceived credibility of another, the victim."[70] However, claiming that rape happened requires crafting an argument through multiple sources that suggest the probability that rape occurred. In other words, the rape kit cannot confirm consent, what has come to be the definitive factor of rape; rather, multiple perspectives are needed to assess an argument of whether or not rape occurred. Rhetorically framing solutions to cases of rape and sexual assault through science imagines bodiless technologies that can confirm or deny rape with absolute certainty. Thus, the discourses shaping the use of rape kits invoke longstanding assumptions about science as rational and objective, affirming that the power of what a rape kit can illuminate is more credible than victim accounts of their own experiences with their bodies.

Problem 3: The Problem with Fleshy Bodies

In what follows, I build on the analysis given in the previous two sections to demonstrate how rape kits complicate the role and value of visceral testimony. I argue that the function of the rape kit has become such that it testifies for a victim, a more convincing account that speaks on their behalf. "Unlike victims and other human witnesses," in other words, "the kit is trusted not to forget, never to lie, and to always provide the objective facts of sexual assault."[71] Instead of chastising victims' ways of making meaning, however, advancing the use of rape kits covertly silences their accounts and the kinds of stories deemed knowable in public in the service of celebrating science and the presumption of rationality. As Mariska Hargitay noted during the SAKI press conference, "The rape victim's body is a living, breathing, feeling crime scene."[72] This ability for the body to feel—to convulse, cringe, and essentially communicate feelings of pain and trauma—is met with anxiety by authorities. Reported by the *Times*, "there seems to be a broad distaste for rape cases as murky, ambiguous, and difficult to prosecute."[73] Examining these "enfleshed modalities of humanity," however, is critical in revealing the epistemic and hegemonic privileging of certain forms of embodiment, how power is harnessed to render certain bodies into rational, controlled, and contained states, bodies that were once subjugated by those with more power.[74] In this last section, I illustrate how rape kits are called upon because of this exact discomfort surrounding victims' fleshy bodies and deployed to convert a soft body into hard, measurable, seemingly nonhuman evidence, translating the body out of a rhetorical, sensory state and into a scientific one.

As part of the exam, victims testify to what happened, recalling the actual harm done to their bodies, often revealing piercing details of the actual act. One *Times* editorialist recounted the gripping details of her boss assaulting her at work. She wrote, "I remember being [. . .] pinned against metal filing cabinets, one of my arms behind me, bent the wrong way. I remember how the drawer pulls clawed into my back, how he squeezed his left hand tightly around my neck. Then he forced himself into my mouth. My jaws locked, wide, in spasm."[75] Her account is layered with sensations that document violation—transformative, visceral forces attempting to communicate meaning about the pain of rape. Descriptions such as these invite embodied reactions of pain in audiences, bringing us closer to the language of flesh and carnality that Weheliye cites—the hyperextension of her bent arm, the pinching of her skin, the choking of her neck, the locking of her jaw. Even as these descriptions powerfully capture the unsettling and harmful nature of assault, they are often deemed emotional, immeasurable in their narrative nature.

People who have experienced rape or sexual assault are encouraged by authorities to endure the rape kit exam because, as one woman interviewed by the *Times* was instructed, "what's in the box could [tell] a different story."[76] The assumption that the rape kit could describe a story differently enthymematically frames visceral testimonies as less reliable accounts of rape. These testimonies assemble anecdotal evidence that articulate how someone felt—how bodies suffer invasion and violation at each moment. While powerful, these narrative retellings are often challenged and categorized as incomprehensible, or worse, untrue because of their relationship to the flesh. Perceptions of the body as flinching or hysterical call to mind what many have demonstrated to be perennial ideas of rhetoric that subvert the role of emotion, and such perceptions further stigmatize the role of embodiment in persuasion as feminized or irrational.[77] Yet the experience of rape is never a rational experience; it is always overwhelmingly sensory. Nevertheless, an examiner is instructed to curate material evidence from the literal body, positioning accounts rooted in the body as soft and unstable.

For those who undergo rape kit exam procedures, the experience is repeatedly described with discomfort as the body is forced to interact with the materials of the kit. The process of collecting evidence from a victim's body is one that is "invasive and humiliating," a cumbersome procedure that "can take up to six hours," and can be considered a "re-victimization following a horrific experience," as some people described to a variety of news outlets.[78] One woman quoted in the *Times* shared of her experience, "I felt invaded, terrified and exposed during the rape kit. [. . .] After undressing in front of strangers, I was poked, prodded, scraped, swabbed, combed and photographed. I wouldn't wish it on anyone."[79] The experience of exposure and terror mixed with perceptions of being mined or scraped invoke a rhetoric of sterility and inspection that dehumanize and convert the messiness of her body. Another woman who reported her experience to MTV News echoed this account, describing how her clothes were taken from her as her body was scrutinized. She said, "I know it's procedure and the doctors were just doing their job, but at the time I felt so violated, like my body didn't belong to me anymore."[80] This woman's feeling of a loss of privacy, the feeling of her body no longer belonging to her, suggests an exchange process, a negotiation between the body and the kit where the body must give over its pieces. These accounts imagine a body horizontal in a sterile hospital room as it is excavated by medical, investigative tools that manipulate the body into hard evidence. One *Times* editorial similarly invoked this image, writing of the process, "DNA evidence is *harvested* from their bodies."[81] In attempting to quell the body's sensations, rape kits arrange the body's materials by processing, scraping, and extracting it, all in attempt to catalog the fleshy, feeling body.

Examining how rape kits are assumed to render concrete what might be considered abstract or nebulous adds to a growing body of rhetorical scholarship committed to attending to the ways women's bodies have been subject to controversy in public, policy, and medical communities.[82] Even with the onset of new reproductive technologies that gave rise to the "biological revolution" beginning in the mid-twentieth century, as Sally Kohlstedt and Helen Longino point out, "there has never been a shortage of experts ready to pronounce on women's nature and women's bodies."[83] We don't even have to turn too far into scholarly conversations to see this point. During the 2016 presidential debates, then presidential candidate Donald Trump criticized Fox News anchor Megyn Kelly, describing how, in his opinion, she bombed her job as a moderator and that "there was blood coming out of her eyes, blood coming out of her . . . wherever."[84] Public audiences far too frequently approach women's bodies as sexualized and feminized, projecting onto them abject feelings of disgust. As a result, "women's bodies are constructed as dark, unknown territory," writes Amy Koerber, positioned as a mystery, in need of technological, scientific discovery.[85] Much of this discomfort surrounding women's bodies is rooted in a persistent myth of hysteria that has long plagued women's abilities to talk about trauma.[86] From notions of the wandering womb to madness, "mental illness," as Jenell Johnson has argued, "has become the quintessential 'female malady,'" in which the discourse of hysteria consistently shapes the idea that women's embodied testimonies, especially in cases of sexual assault or rape, are unstable.[87]

When the actual exam takes place, examiners are directed to guide and support victims as they endure this difficult process. But as accounts by actual victims show, the exam doesn't always feel that way. In a study investigating victim perspectives of the exam, several women who had undergone a rape kit exam spoke to a mismatch between the goals of nurses and the goals of victims. While many sought out treatment to support their physical and emotional needs, the nurses focused attention toward forensic collection. One such account stated, "I got too much blood taken that's why I passed out. [They] had all my blood, they had to take my underwear, and I had this water thing done. It was really gross, I didn't like it all."[88] Examiners and other medical professionals, while they may be well intended, are acting on behalf of the state and its gaze over the law when it comes to rape kit exams. Their demeaner may be clinical, cool, or sterile, and, in the process, "the particular form of care that emerges from the interaction of legal and therapeutic practices imposes a particular violence on victims of sexual assault."[89] One other account shared, "She [the nurse examiner] tried about three times [to insert a speculum], and I really didn't want to do that at the time, 'cause I think I was reliving the whole experience and just wanted to put my clothes on after awhile."[90] The intentions of the exam are often at odds with the goals of victims, and as a result, victims are subject to an interrogation of their bodies, which may leave them feeling worse off than when they started. Yet, while suffering is enacted on already violated bodies, viewers are trained to look away, using the exam as a mode of deflecting away from the body. Looking at the flesh, however, exposes how forces of marginalization function epistemically. In other words, while the state masks its interactions with bodies to produce evidence separated from them, we must look toward the viscosity and viscerality of bodies to understand the processes of dehumanization, subtly operating under the presumption of care.

Since being raped, Souto, the young woman profiled in the opening of this chapter, has advocated for survivor support. As part of her quest to raise awareness about sexual violence and offer resources to those suffering Rape Trauma Syndrome, she started a GoFundMe page in March 2018. Her page details her experience of living in the aftermath of rape, living with panic and anxiety that shaped her everyday life in the days and months following what happened. In addition, she also narrated the experience of being in the hospital, undergoing a rape examination all in the service of confirming the person she already named to authorities. She writes,

> I waited in the hospital bed for three hours as the nurse examined me. I cannot remember her name or even the way she looked. All I can remember is her soothing voice as she guided me through the collection kit. There was only one box left, and only a physician had the ability to make the check mark. He walked in, not once acknowledging the person to be examined. He pulled on his gloves as if he were in a madhouse and pulled out swabs. The nurse continued to comfort me, allowing me to understand what this physician was obtaining from my body. Shortly after, the nurse was sealing my rape kit to be sent to the lab for testing.[91]

Likening the experience of being scrutinized by the physician to being "in a madhouse," Souto acknowledged the experience of being objectified, aligning it with antiquated notions of hysteria that mark women and their minds unfit to characterize their own experiences with their bodies. As the physician sought to obtain materials from her body, she described her body as if it were an object, one giving over its parts. The descriptions of the kit and its boxes—its relationship to labs and testing—all serve to associate the rape kit with sterile ideas of objectivity, an objectivity in which the actual feeling parts central to her body have no place. Though scholars have endeavored to reclaim the body in rhetoric, the relationship between the rape kit and the body is one relegated outside the place of the law, outside of means of proof deemed most effective.[92] In other words, when it comes to deliberation over rape kits and rape culture, the question becomes not *if the body matters for rhetoric*, but rather, in mining, managing, and containing the body, *is rhetoric even valued at all*.

While publics perceive value in the tools of the kit, women's actual experiences such as those shared here demonstrate how the violation of rape gets redoubled during the exam. As victims' bodies are mined by nurses or doctors, the exam invokes a sense of animality and impurity while capturing the idea that it is the mined pieces of victims' bodies, and not their voices, that make available evidence of rape. In addition to these descriptions of the rape kit exam, one nurse examiner reported to the *Chicago Tribune* that she "once heard a sexual assault victim tell a detective that her exam with an emergency-room doctor made her feel like she'd had an oil change."[93] These characterizations of the exam invoke euphemisms that reimagine the body away from its presumed messy, hysterical state and into something that can be excavated by tools. Framing the rape kit exam through the language of a mechanized process assembling parts casts the raped body as something that can be contained, tinkered with, managed. In describing the exam in such ways, the discourse about rape kits works to translate victims' accounts of their own experiences with their bodies into what is perceived as certifiable evidence. In the process, they bolster prevailing myths about the rape victim as untrustworthy, marking her sensory accounts as unstable, and assert that the feeling body poses a precarious problem that the rape kit must resolve. In short, little room is left for embodied testimonies of rape; rather, material evidence disentangled from that body is desired, in its place.

Shifting the Purposes of Rhetoric in the Public Sphere

In this chapter, I have argued that rape kits function to contain feeling bodies and reconcile the lived experience of trauma by transferring the body out of a sensory state and into a sterile one. I maintain that prioritizing the technology of a rape kit is motivated by an anxiety about the raped body and consequently functions to convert the issue of rape justice from a cultural problem to a technical one with scientific solutions. My intention is not to suggest that rape kits cannot be useful for those who have experienced rape or sexual assault. Rather, the rape kit does provide one avenue for apprehending how the body may have been injured and offers a glimpse into how such acts physically manifested. But they can't provide context, which is explicitly rhetorical and a vital part of accounting for harm.[94] Violence is never just violence as such; rather, histories, power dynamics, and cultural norms contribute to both a legal and public assessment of harm. Exiling narrative, thereby rhetoric, eliminates the possibility for personal and cultural healing and forecloses a broader treatment of the institutional and historical causes that influence an ideology of rape culture more broadly.

One major problem central to rape kits is that this shift to science implies a changing role for how publics understand the use and value of evidence and the role of deliberation in addressing public problems. Writes Johnson, "The realm of rhetoric is defined by contingency and probability, which is why certain topics are kept outside."[95] While conversations about rape kits grant a level of certainty to what the rape kit can illuminate, confirming rape is always dependent upon contingent sources of evidence that are marshalled together to assert a level of probability that rape occurred. Removing rape justice from the realm of the rhetorical puts the productive and democratic values of deliberation at risk and reveals a technophilic desire to contain the messiness of trauma and the forms of embodied communication central to it. Making justice for rape into a problem of perceived fact erases the multiple questions, ideological causes, and methods of analysis necessary to address problems of this scale.

The analysis provided in this chapter submits that we must be mindful of the kinds of rhetorical claims assumed of the rape kit and its ability to support rape adjudication. In a research review of over four hundred materials (including book-length studies, research reports, annual reports, and journal and news articles) jointly conducted by the Sexual Violence Research Initiative and the World Health Organization, scholars collectively found a "limited impact of medico-legal evidence on the legal resolution of sexual assault cases," which include rape.[96] In other words, the actual use of evidence deciphered during a rape kit exam rarely supports justice for victims. And yet, the law's insistence on credible witnesses shapes the desire for and continued use of such technologies. "As a privileged site and destination in the idealized sexual assault intervention," Mulla argues, "the courtroom is present in the emergency room not simply as a space, but as an agency that structures the examination."[97] As this case study shows, the legal realm figures into the examination site, constructing the agency of the victim and her body as outside the frame of justice from the beginning. As a result, the rape kit participates in increasingly removing testimonies and their corresponding visceral rhetorics from discussions about rape, contributing to the idea that women are unfit to speak about their own experiences with their bodies in public.

Incorporating material tools that suppress the rhetorical by suppressing sensation extends beyond the case study analyzed here and can be seen in more recent calls for police body cameras as a result of the shooting and murdering of young men and women of color in public. In September 2015, the same month in which the first SAKI press conference was held, the Justice Department announced that roughly $23 million would be allocated to seventy-three police agencies in thirty-two states to increase use of the body camera. Like rape kits, these technologies—technologies developed with good intentions when the crimes committed are cultural and bodily—are leveraged to assume certainty and transparency yet often fail to protect those actually victim to violence. That is, rarely does the footage produced by police body cameras actually work to convict murderers.[98] Similar to the issue of the rape kit, I see a danger in relying on these tools to uproot the cultural problem of racial violence and police brutality. In these cases, technologies are being hailed in crimes where bodies frequently subject to violence are those who have been subject to risk for centuries as a result of systemic, violent, and institutional racism. And yet, the camera, like the rape kit, purports a technological solution to a cultural problem once again, a solution implemented to supplant the voices of marginalized voices, compounding the burden of proof needed to adjudicate such crimes.

Just like rape kits, the technological hope shaping the legal implementation and reliance on police body cameras risks deflecting further away from the ideological and historical conditions that shape the act of violence in the first place, suggesting, once again, that only outlying "bad apples" are to blame for acts of police violence. Similar to the problem with "believing women," the call for more technology suggests a need to verify or validate marginalized speakers' accounts, presumed as more capable of revealing "the truth."[99] While we should acknowledge the impulse by federal efforts to intervene in such historically rooted cultural problems of violence, we must critique how a narrow focus on such solutions serves to mask those same exact historical roots and sidestep the need to reckon with the patriarchal and racist ideologies at the center of both rape culture and police brutality. We're fighting a shared fight. But, to be clear, I am not suggesting that we must do away with these technologies. We cannot simply halt the use of rape kits or police body cameras *because* they have participated in conditioning publics not to believe the experiences of those victim to violence—the idea that experiential testimony alone is not evidence enough—making the debate over a rape kit's findings or the camera footage alone one of the last tactics of arguing proof.[100] When we narrow our focus to the law and funding carceral technologies instead of interrogating the conditions that undergird repeated acts of violence and aggression, however, we're grossly miscalculating the problem and our means of response.

This research urges publics to come to grips with how discourses surrounding the technologies used for cases of embodied violence leave the courtroom and work to contain a sense of bodily excess. Regardless of their initial legal intent, these technologies are perceived in public discourse as all knowing, understood to control forms of embodiment and assert a level of certainty in conversation, glossing over the voices who could attest to such problems. Yet, changing the question of *what probably happened* to *what happened* denies the voices, testimonies, and communicative frameworks that help illuminate crimes against bodies most at risk of violence. Privileging science limits the available means and opportunities for some voices to speak of such crimes in public and risks reaffirming a public sphere in which those who do not conform to rational and disembodied standards of engagement are left outside. Put differently, celebrating the use of these scientific tools for fighting injustice not only asserts a particular kind of gendered agency relevant in the public sphere but deems a particular conception of embodiment most fit for public engagement.

Instead of trusting the kit to tell a more credible story, the implications of this research ask us to take seriously what it might mean to listen to an individual's account of what has been done to their flesh and the dialects communicated by that flesh, as opposed to a technology that claims to translate it, especially when that body is in pain. While Weheliye critically demonstrates how the flesh provides insight into who is marked as fully human in the law's spectral shadows, he also suggests that recognition of the not-quite human offers hope for change. "Freedom," he argues, "stands at the juncture of the flesh's privation and potentiality"; the flesh allows us to imagine alternative forms of communicating and being in the world if we let it.[101] Searching for tools and technologies that turn away from visceral modes of communicating denies certain bodies access to public life and deliberation, but it also denies in ourselves a reality of feeling and narrative that speaks to our very being in public and a capacity to understand our social and relational lives. "To have been touched by the flesh, then," Weheliye asserts, "this is part of the lesson of our world."[102] The task now becomes letting us learn it.

4

DISRUPTING SILENCE: THE LAW AND VISCERAL COUNTERPUBLICITY

"You don't know me, but you've been inside me, and that's why we're here today."[1] So reads the opening of the victim impact statement read by Chanel Miller, previously known under her pseudonym Emily Doe, during the trial of Brock Allen Turner.[2] In January 2015, Miller was raped by then first-year student Turner behind a dumpster at a party on the Stanford University campus. While Miller remained unconscious, Turner penetrated her body with his fingers until two male international students riding by on their bikes noticed Turner on top of an unconscious woman's body and suspected harm. Turner attempted to flee yet was chased, apprehended by the men, and eventually detained by campus police. Initially charged with two counts of rape and three counts of sexual assault, Turner was only convicted of the three counts of sexual assault, a lesser charge than rape.

In 2014, Emma Sulkowicz (who identifies as nonbinary and uses *they/them* pronouns) garnered widespread public attention for their performance art piece, *Mattress Performance (Carry That Weight)*, in which they carried a fifty-pound Columbia University dorm mattress with them around campus. The performance piece was a call to university officials to reprimand Paul Nungesser, whom Sulkowicz accused of raping them in their dorm room during a sexual act that began consensually but turned violently nonconsensual in August 2012.[3] Sulkowicz publicly acknowledged their previous consensual sexual history with Nungesser and reported what happened that night in August to the university. However, the university ultimately cleared Nungesser of any charges and found him not responsible for sexual misconduct.

These recent, high-profile rape cases of Miller and Sulkowicz, cases in which victims of rape responded with public performances, have already shaped public debate over what it means to be sexually assaulted on a US college campus.[4] These cases are indicative of a new moment in US public consciousness concerning what it means to experience rape and the available means for speaking out against sexually violent conditions. These cases also call attention to how bodies and their boundaries—despite how central they are to rape and sexual assault—fade from view in the process of adjudicating rape crimes. That is, together, the legal and institutional outcomes of both Miller's and Sulkowicz's cases demonstrate how the law works to negate victims' perspectives—perspectives feminized by legal and institutional codes and procedures—in the service of protecting an idealized male subjectivity. This chapter analyzes Miller's letter quoted above along with a second performance art piece by Sulkowicz, *Ceci N'est Pas Un Viol* (or *This Is Not A Rape*), to understand how these individuals push against that erasure, bringing their bodies to the forefront of public conversations about rape.[5] Thus, while the previous chapter investigated how evidentiary mechanisms prioritized by the law are implemented to quell and control the visceral nature of bodies, this chapter explores what happens when victims use their bodies to protest the law and its failure to assess what counts as rape. Examining how Miller and Sulkowicz use their bodies within public performances contributes to this book's investigation into visceral rhetorics by illustrating how affective tactics can engage participation from outside, non-counterpublic audiences through the jarring recognition of an existing counterpublic and inform public deliberation over crimes committed against marginalized bodies in ways that existing legal and institutional codes cannot. Consequently, this chapter paves a final direction for the remainder of this book, identifying the productive and rhetorical value bodies and feelings can have in disrupting public discourses by locating alternative modes of engagement.

In analyzing the role of the feeling body in relation to counterpublicity, I extend rhetorical theories of publicity and affect to consider how bodies at the limits of public engagement communicate when living in the aftermath of rape.[6] Intense feelings, as Jenell Johnson has argued, can play an essential role in the formation of publics, congealing publics together through a shared mood or affect.[7] "Visceral publics," writes Johnson, "emerge from discourse about boundaries" and "cohere by means of intense feeling," and her theory reveals the vital role bodies play in shaping how subjects connect to public life.[8] While Johnson shows "how individuals feel their way into publics," the case studies analyzed in this chapter identify how individuals feel their way *against* publics—how individuals use an embodied and affective form of publicity to challenge a widespread inability to apprehend violence committed against the body.[9] In other words, though intense feelings have the capacity to encourage public formation, Miller's and Sulkowicz's performances show they also have the potential to rupture it, to resist mainstream definitions and alter public opinion regarding rape.

The use of the body within Miller's and Sulkowicz's performances serves as a critique of how contemporary US legal and institutional definitions of rape and sexual assault assume a rational, male subject (in the traditional, Habermasian sense) and, in the process, assess violence through a male perspective, male body, and male gaze.[10] Specifically, their performances demonstrate how definitions of rape ignore a range of bodies that experience rape, focusing solely on male penetration and male perceptions of women's desires, and, as a result, continually fail to deliver justice to those who experience sexual violence.[11] Miller's and Sulkowicz's performances challenge this failure and aim to inspire public opposition to contemporary understandings of rape and the legal and institutional structures that shape them, and these performances are especially important because they document the experiences of individuals who identify with the categories of women of color and gender nonbinary, identities that are notably overlooked in wider public discourses of rape and frequently subject to intensified scrutiny because of the assumptions propagated by mainstream definitions of rape.[12] To illuminate the violence of rape from their perspectives, Miller and Sulkowicz draw upon modes of engagement rooted in the body and orient themselves toward a level of deep splanchnic (related to the viscera or the internal organs of the body) intensity. In cultivating an intensity of feeling at the boundaries of the body, they unveil a different, more visceral vantage point of rape, one frequently occluded by legal structures in US society. In short, instead of using adjudicatory frameworks to make an argument that rape occurred, their performances create conditions under which audiences might sense *what rape feels like*—seeking to produce a shift in public opinion over rape crimes.

Taken together, this chapter theorizes the use of visceral rhetorics in cases of protest, or what I call "visceral counterpublicity": modes of public engagement that proceed when discursive frameworks understood through liberal subjectivity fall short; expose the body's threatened boundaries to incite an affective response, or bodily intensity, in audiences; and illuminate a subjugated position within the public sphere. Previous theories of counterpublicity help underscore how visceral communicative tactics illustrate articulations of counterpublic activity oriented toward the state and constitute a discursive space of opposition grounded in the body and feeling.[13] While theories of counterpublicity typically consider tactics that unveil injustice within the state through reactive tactics, the tactics examined in this chapter react to the state but also expose proactive uses of counterpublicity, specifically in a context laced with pain and violence. That is, each performance draws upon the visceral to retrain public opinion of rape and rape culture, to disrupt its relationship to the law and inspire change. Sexual violence is (and should be) a public matter "of concern to everyone," and the performances analyzed here speak beyond their individual testimonies in an effort to demonstrate how definitions of rape are normalized by patriarchal discourses in ways that trouble victims' modes of explicating violence committed against them.[14] Miller and Sulkowicz respond to the limits of these definitions by moving beyond a disembodied discourse grounded in rationality and demonstrate how the norms and values presented by these definitions in fact do not represent the cultural and social realities of sexual violence. In using the body, visceral counterpublic tactics risk violence and uncover the messy, bloody, material aspects of violation to remind audiences of the physical, corporeal body at the center of the problem. Analyzing visceral rhetorics in this context demonstrates what role the body can have in shifting public opinion, motivating wider publics to understand embodied violence such as rape outside of the limits imposed by patriarchal frameworks.

I begin contextualizing each case study within its adjudicatory setting and draw from political theorists and experts in legal studies to show how these legal-institutional frameworks carry implications for how publics discuss and understand rape. Drawing from theories of counterpublics and affective publics, I then theorize the visceral in relation to counterpublicity and use that theory to analyze each individual's performance, exploring how the use of the visceral challenges mainstream definitions of rape. The differences in how each individual uses the visceral to bring audiences into the body and provide a bodily telling of rape show how the visceral defies the norms of public discourse, how these forms of protest seek to unpack contemporary constructions of rape by delegitimizing textual definitions of rape and legitimizing embodied experiences. Together, these case studies show how Miller and Sulkowicz use their bodies to demonstrate how mainstream discourses of rape often evade the body, isolate assessments of violence within a perceived contractual exchange of consent, and overlook the asymmetrical power dimensions imbued in the struggle to prove nonconsent. I conclude by offering several implications for visceral counterpublicity regarding its potential for changing how publics talk about rape and its use for rhetorical theorists interested in analyzing broader cases of embodied protest and the legal structures that shape public understandings of them. This theory, I suggest, provides utility for rhetorical theorists and critics aiming to understand various repoduluno of these tactics seen in instances of sexual violence, police brutality, and racial protest that use the body to challenge efforts by legal discourses to sanitize and contain it.

Assessing Rape Through a Male Body

Both Miller's and Sulkowicz's cases garnered widespread attention from the public almost immediately following their performances. Then Vice President Joe Biden responded to Miller's statement with an emotional public letter, and *Glamour* magazine named her the 2016 "Woman of the Year." Sulkowicz attended the 2015 State of the Union address as the guest of Senator Kirsten Gillibrand after attracting attention for their *Mattress Performance*. Amid these positive reactions, however, both cases were not without criticism. Turner's aspiring career as an Olympic swimmer inspired debate during the trial and led many to cite his crime against Miller as a one-time offense and reason to decrease his sentence. An unidentified Twitter account under the name of "Fake Rape" started a #RapeHoax hashtag targeting Sulkowicz, and, in addition, posters were hung around the Columbia campus with their picture and the phrase "Pretty Little Liar."[15] While audiences in the United States marveled at and contested each case, important legal and institutional factors shape this public uptake.

Miller met Turner the night of the assault when attending a party with her sister, who was home visiting from college for the weekend. At the time, Turner was a first-year student athlete at Stanford, enrolled on a swimming scholarship. While Turner admitted to sexual conduct, claimed verbal consent, and denied all rape allegations, in January 2015, he was indicted on the following five charges under the Santa Clara County Superior Court: "rape by an intoxicating, anesthetic or controlled substance," "rape of a victim unconscious of the nature of the act," "assault with intent to commit felony," "sexual penetration when the victim was intoxicated or anesthetized," and "sexual penetration where the victim was unconscious of the nature of the act."[16] While the first two charges of rape were dropped during a preliminary hearing, Turner was convicted of the latter three sexual assault felony counts in March 2016, even though he pled not guilty to all five charges. He was sentenced to six months in jail, of which he served three, and three years of probation. Turner's sentence met much backlash for being too lenient, and immediately following the sentencing, many called for the removal of Judge Aaron Persky, who oversaw the case.[17]

Sulkowicz and Nungesser previously engaged in consensual sex twice before the night Sulkowicz claimed they were raped, and at the time of the crime, Nungesser was a second-year German exchange student at Columbia. While the attack took place in August 2012, Sulkowicz waited until April 2013 to report it to the university's Office of Gender-Based and Sexual Misconduct after they corroborated their experience with two other individuals who later filed similar complaints against Nungesser to the university. Sulkowicz reported rape—specifically, a sexual encounter that began consensual and then turned nonconsensual—and that Nungesser slapped, choked, and restrained them before anally raping them. During the hearings, Nungesser admitted to having sex with Sulkowicz but denied all claims of violence and nonconsent. Ultimately, he was cleared of all three accounts. After, several students filed Title IX federal violations, leading the US Department of Education's Office for Civil Rights to open investigation in 2015 on both Columbia and Barnard College.

State laws around rape and sexual assault condition the public to focus on particular factors when discussing and assessing rape. For instance, at the time of the Turner trial, California Penal Code 261 broadly defined rape as nonconsensual sexual intercourse; however, nonconsensual sexual penetration by a foreign object fell under the category of sexual assault, receiving a lesser charge, as demonstrated in the Turner case.[18] As is the case in many state laws, the legal definition of *rape* is often centered on the role of a man's body during the sexual act; constituting *rape* is dependent upon penile violation, while other forms of penetration are constituted as less violating; the "objects" of a man's body—for instance, his fingers, fists, or penis—determine the degree of the crime. Defining rape in such a way obscures the victim's body and the experience of violation, and Miller's case suggests a flaw with this standard in that her body was most certainly violated but not by a penis.[19]

When victims file complaints to higher education institutions regarding nonconsensual sexual misconduct, instead of turning cases over to the police, university procedures like Columbia's assume a doctrine of *in loco parentis* in which the university acts as a sanctioning authority when privately investigating whether or not consent was granted. In response to calls by feminist circles for more legal protections for college rape victims, New York passed Senate Bill S5965, referred to as "Enough is Enough," in July 2015 requiring all New York colleges and universities, including Columbia, to adopt the following affirmative consent standard: "Affirmative consent is a knowing, voluntary and mutual decision among all participants to engage in the sexual activity. Consent can be given by words or actions, as long as those words or actions create clear permission regarding willingness to engage in the sexual activity. Silence or lack of resistance, in and of itself, does not demonstrate consent. The definition of consent does not vary based upon a participant's sex, sexual orientation, gender identity, or gender expression."[20] Despite celebration by some, legal experts suggest that these changes in the law—even in their well-intended efforts to bring agency to victims of rape—may not achieve justice and argue that the definition can still benefit the perpetrator and their assumptions of the victim's desires.[21] For example, according to legal scholar Allison Marciniak, the law risks "implementing a lower standard of proof for use in actual disciplinary proceedings," and fails to account for when a "yes" might turn into a "no"—the switch from consensual to nonconsensual—especially when an initial "yes" was granted, whether embodied or vocalized.[22] While Sulkowicz's case occurred prior to the passing of this bill, their experience illuminates how institutional codes failed to understand how sex with a man they previously engaged with could have begun consensually and still turned violently and abruptly into rape.

Feminist legal and political theorists have shown that one reason rape laws and institutional codes frequently fail to bring justice to victims of rape is because at their core, these definitions are rooted in liberal subjectivity. Consequently, these adjudicatory standards operate through a "heteromasculinist logic" and assume that sex is a matter of contractual exchange entered into by individuals possessing that particular kind of subjectivity.[23] For Carole Pateman and Catharine MacKinnon, consent will always be a problematic term used to determine rape because of its relationship to the state and an idealized rational, liberal subject (read male and white).[24] Women's sexuality has long been treated as property—something exchanged or taken from women. As a result, consent has been and continues to be understood through a male lens. Writes MacKinnon, "Man's perceptions of woman's desires determine whether she is deemed violated" where "the rape law affirmatively rewards men with acquittals for not comprehending women's point of view."[25] These legal conditions result negatively for those testifying to a nonconsensual encounter against a traditionally conceptualized heteronormative male perpetrator. For victims to argue violation, Pateman submits, they are forced to perform a virgin-like subjecthood that was met with violence and injury by a man: "A woman is unlikely to convince either the public, the police, or a judge and jury that she did not consent to sexual intercourse unless she is badly physically injured or unless she can prove that she resisted."[26] In other words, situations of rape that fall outside of this norm risk being perceived as *not* rape, echoing the narratives used to support bystander or rape kit legislation previously examined in this book.

As these scholars show, rape law writes particular bodies and particular cases of rape into and out of state recognition. Writing in 2016, MacKinnon asserts that "one reason rape law is so ineffective is its failure to define the legal reality in terms of the social reality."[27] This social and legal mismatch bears deep implications for public understandings of rape. Following the law, public deliberation over sexual violence is consumed with measuring the extent of violence, deciphering consent, and assessing the credibility of a victim. Because conviction for rape is framed in terms of the guilt or innocence of the perpetrator, public deliberation risks assuming that if a perpetrator is found not guilty, the rape did not happen and the accuser was lying, mistaken, or hysterical. This framework, I suggest, erases the bodily experiences of victims, even though these bodily experiences are the reason the case came to court in the first place. While feminist legal and rhetorical scholars have investigated legal discrimination on a range of women's rights issues, this chapter draws attention to the issue of bodily erasure within legal frameworks, hindering the range of experiences with sexual violence considered knowable in public discourse.[28] That is, the case studies analyzed here pinpoint a social reality of the violence of rape that falls outside of definitions constructed by the law and its influence over university procedures: Miller wasn't raped through penile penetration and Sulkowicz's prior consensual exchange marks their claim of rape untrustworthy.

Because adjudicatory systems are not constructed to understand the perspectives of women, femmes, or people from queer, trans, or gender nonbinary communities, the public performances of Miller and Sulkowicz deliberately turn away from the institutions that failed to bring them justice. Instead, they ask public conversations to understand rape not in terms of what consent sounds like but *what rape feels like* through the use of embodied and visceral frameworks. Doing so shifts deliberation over rape away from a debate about the legal or institutional assertion that rape did or did not occur and redefines rape through a perspective that mimics the messy, physical, and painful sensations endured when a body is violated by another. In what follows, I theorize this perspective through an analysis of their performances, which, together, offer new resources for discussing rape that productively trouble the use of legal frameworks within public deliberation.

Feeling Harm, Sensing Violence: Two Case Studies of Visceral Counterpublicity

People have long struggled to achieve justice in the face of sexual violence, and feminist scholars have examined the injustice of such violence through intersecting lenses of discourse, agency, and gender. Scholars have analyzed how rape is portrayed, exploring how dominant discourses and popular media representations emphasize prevention and, in the process, reinforce discourses of fear or vulnerability as a response to the problem instead of uprooting a larger system of gender inequity.[29] Other critics have investigated how disparaging understandings of rape and sexuality result in public, personal, and legal discourses that limit the options and experiences of individual people testifying to rape.[30] Consistently, these scholars have pointed out how women are imagined as "monolithic" and subjected to standards of womanhood and purity that often result negatively for victims.[31] That preexisting work critically informs this book and further illuminates how mainstream understandings of rape circulate in public discourse and trouble victims' capacities to disclose sexual violence. However, the analysis that follows interrogates an element not yet examined by studies of sexual violence: the capacity to use the body to protest a legal and institutional understanding of what counts as an act of rape or sexual assault, a capacity motivated by the goal of inspiring wider change.

As scholars have shown, dominant institutions pervade publics and often reject or make abject marginalized bodies. For instance, Cindy Griffin points out that the public sphere is not just a place but also "an ideology—a reified pattern of explanations, a hierarchical ordering of locations" that manages, sanctions, and prohibits "access to this realm."[32] Counterpublicity, then, becomes crucial when marginalized voices have no other recourse or access to the public sphere and must instead create "counterdiscourses" that help oppose "interpretations of their identities, interests, and needs" thrust upon them by the mainstream.[33] To examine embodiment as a rhetorical strategy, I draw from Phaedra Pezzullo, who argues that "technical, political, and popular discourses have historically tended to relegate women to bodies in a derogatory sense (as non-intellectual, utilitarian extensions of heterosexual men's desires and reproductive needs)," and helps illustrate how a "politics of the body and embodiment" can serve as powerful resistance to the oppression of rape culture.[34] The use of the body, I maintain, opens a public space aimed at emboldening and inspiring opposition to dominant public opinion regarding sexual violence, expanding the tactics through which counterpublicity is understood to happen.[35]

As a form of counterpublicity, then, viscerality strategically provokes feeling to redraw public attention back to the body, at the fleshy, physical, and material sites of pain and violence, working to incite a felt sense of that pain among audiences.[36] Attending to viscerality, Johnson reminds us, "concerns the surfaces and orifices," reveals the fluid links that "bring the body and world into relation," and exposes the dual role the body holds as both subject and object.[37] The visceral accounts for bodily parts such as the skin, the vagina, the mouth, and the anus and bodily processes such as digestion, breathing, and sex—all of which reveal the connections between the body's insides and its outsides. The act of rape violates bodily boundaries, draws attention to these fluid links, and positions the body in a deeply vulnerable relationship to the world. Drawing upon Johnson and other cultural theorists, I foreground how the visceral invokes animalistic and sense-oriented faculties that disentangle understandings of rape from their strictly discursive and disembodied frameworks and reveal what it means for a body to be vulnerable to the outside world.[38] Such tactics encourage audiences to dwell in a feeling of risk to understand rape as a problem of bodily harm, one that has the power to overwhelm one's intricately linked internal and external sense of self and security. Thus, visceral counterpublicity can be understood as forms of engagement that transpire through "feelings, moods, and sensibilities" in order to demonstrate how some bodies are subject to more violence than others in public, attesting to an embodied vulnerability central to public participation more broadly.[39]

Using this theory, I analyze two public performances composed by Miller and Sulkowicz. In the first case study, I examine Miller's letter, which was first read aloud in court and shortly after published on *BuzzFeed* and by other news organizations in June 2016, instantly amassing vast audiences. I suggest that Miller reorients audiences toward her body to understand violence from a perspective rooted in touch, sight, and smell, and, in doing so, identifies the limits of measuring rape from a male perpetrator's perspective. In the second case study, I analyze Sulkowicz's performance, *Ceci N'est Pas Un Viol*, which was released online in June 2015. The performance art piece was published on the heels of their more recognized piece *Mattress Performance*, which was profiled by several prominent news and cultural outlets that led to its broad public circulation. In this case study, I maintain that Sulkowicz crosses traditional modes of communicating rape in order to make viewers sense the experience of rape. In doing so, their performance illustrates that an argument about rape cannot be contained within liberal discourse; rather, audiences must watch, sense, and feel the body's boundaries violated to understand a range of experiences that constitute rape. Together, these individuals expose threatened bodily boundaries and encourage affective responses in an effort to shift public deliberation over sexual violence to account for rape by sensing the effects of violence felt on and in one's body.

"My Brain Was Talking My Gut into Not Collapsing": A Case Study of Chanel Miller

From the time he was indicted, Turner argued Miller consented, and during the actual trial, his legal team focused on Miller's memory loss due to alcohol consumption in order to deflect blame away from Turner and claim that the sexual act was consensual, desirable, and even pleasurable. Even though Miller could have reimagined the scene of assault to assert nonconsent, at no point in her letter does she attempt to reclaim the memory of what happened behind the dumpster. Her statement does something different. While Turner's attorneys capitalized off her memory loss and positioned her as willingly and eagerly consenting, Miller evokes her memories of coming to know the consequences playing out in her body due to that night, from the morning when she woke up in the hospital all the way through to Turner's conviction. I argue that in doing so Miller asks audiences not to see things from her perspective but *to feel her perspective, to feel what her body felt* in the aftermath of rape.

Because Turner's defense team positioned Miller as an untrustworthy source, they consequently disempowered her ability to speak about her experience from that night during the trial, subjecting Miller to compounding racist and gendered scripts that worked to objectify and sexualize her Asian American identity and ultimately discredit her. She writes, "I was not only told that I was assaulted, I was told that because I couldn't remember, I technically could not prove it was unwanted. And that distorted me, damaged me, almost broke me. It is the saddest type of confusion to be told I was assaulted and nearly raped, blatantly out in the open, but we don't know if it counts as assault yet."[40] Her letter speaks from a marginalized perspective and positions her body prominently in the text to underscore the consequences of sexual violence from her embodied perspective. In drawing upon her body, Miller invokes "non-verbal activities that are involved in negotiating public life, including physical, emotional, and aural dimensions," and constitutes a new discursive space in which the body acts as a central agent to shed light on the affective consequences of rape that evade mainstream definitions.[41]

Beginning her account of the assault at the scene of coming to consciousness at the hospital, Miller assesses the state of her body. She takes a mental scan of her physical body, vacillating between the physical landmarks on her body, which signal harm, and the sensations of fear flooding her perceptions. She writes:

> I had dried blood and bandages on the backs of my hands and elbow. I thought maybe I had fallen and was in an admin office on campus. I was very calm and wondering where my sister was. A deputy explained I had been assaulted. [. . .] When I was finally allowed to use the restroom, I pulled down the hospital pants they had given me, went to pull down my underwear, and felt nothing. I still remember the feeling of my hands touching my skin and grabbing nothing. I looked down and there was nothing. The thin piece of fabric, the only thing between my vagina and anything else, was missing and everything inside me was silenced. I still don't have words for that feeling.[42]

The blood and bandages signal to her that an accident of some kind occurred, yet the absence of underwear—underwear taken from her without her permission—catalyze her certainty of being violated. Miller acknowledges the boundary of her vagina exposed through a viscerality of shock, one that "silenced" her inside as she slowly comes to grips with her body's various wounds. While Turner claimed that Miller "orgasmed," she recalls how medical professionals found "abrasions, lacerations, and dirt in [her] genitalia."[43] Miller elicits the experience in the hospital through her sense of touch as she brushes with her body and remembers the feeling of "nothing" in the place where underwear should be, moving audiences toward the embodied boundary separating the most intimate parts of her body from the outside world.

Throughout the letter, Miller remarks on the impossibility of communicating out loud, feeling "too empty to continue to speak," unable to "digest or accept any of this information."[44] In describing herself as without words, she orients herself inward, provoking audiences to grapple with her internal experience. While waiting for the hospital staff to inform her why she was in fact sitting in a hospital bed with not even underwear on, she writes, "My brain was talking my gut into not collapsing. Because my gut was saying, help me, help me."[45] Here, Miller invokes an embodied sense of communication where her organs speak to one another while in a state of distress and reveal a positionality of total defeat. This depiction of her organs speaking on behalf of her takes audiences into her body, encouraging them to understand the consequences endured deep within the body's surfaces, and the force of interlocution between her brain and gut underscore the role the body can play in elucidating sexual violence. Audiences don't witness an argument of penile violation; however, they do witness a body struggling to keep itself alive. Later she addresses Turner specifically, stating, "If you are hoping that one of my organs will implode from anger and I will die, I'm almost there. You are very close."[46] In these moments, her attunement to the body's internal functioning moves beyond the technical definitions of rape and sexual assault and identifies an explanation of violence powerfully communicated by way of her body.

Communicating through such visceral tactics exposes an orientation to violence felt within the body's deep insides—at the level of the body's organs—and instills a bodily intensity in audiences, as Miller's letter helps illuminate. That is, instead of arguing consent was lost or not initially granted, Miller invites audiences to sense sites of harm and trespass, which asserts a level of certainty that rape occurred, echoing how Elaine Scarry has theorized pain.[47] "Having pain," Scarry argues, compels someone to feel certain, whereas "hearing about pain" may lead some to feel doubt or suspicion.[48] Scarry's theory is especially powerful for understanding the need for viscerality in deliberating rape crimes—crimes in which victims' claims of pain caused by the violence of rape have been historically doubted. Thus, for Miller, using the feeling body as a tactic of protest aims to incite affective reactions of pain in audiences in order to achieve a level of certainty that is impossible under available liberal subject models. Put simply, if audiences feel discomfort while listening, reading, or watching, then such tactics are rhetorically successful.

Miller was able to use evidence from a rape kit completed at the hospital to confirm the physical markings left by Turner on and in her body. As the last chapter argued, evidence found in these kits is typically perceived as factual, inarguable, and arhetorical; however, Miller contrasts the rape kit's sterility with bloody, earthy, and messy depictions of the collection process. In recalling such evidence, Miller recounts the experience of the exam, documenting the tampering of her body. She writes:

> My clothes were confiscated and I stood naked while the nurses held a ruler to various abrasions on my body and photographed them. The three of us worked to comb the pine needles out of my hair, six hands to fill one paper bag. To calm me down, they said it's just the flora and fauna, flora and fauna. I had multiple swabs inserted into my vagina and anus, needles for shots, pills, had a Nikon pointed right into my spread legs. I had long, pointed beaks inside me and had my vagina smeared with cold, blue paint to check for abrasions.[49]

In remembering her body naked, measured, and photographed, Miller moves audiences toward the violated surfaces and orifices of her body. Within this description, Miller distills her senses to the smell and point of pine needles, the smear of cold paint touching her vagina, and the poking of swabs as they searched for his DNA. Directed by nurses to understand this process as "just the flora and fauna, flora and fauna," her body is reduced to its mere biology. Arguably, the rape kit induces a dual violation for rape victims; however, the feelings surrounding the experience contextualize its purpose. As she reimagines her experience through "the flora and fauna," she frames the scene through a discourse of impurity and uncleanliness—a body tampered, ravaged, and prodded—demonstrating that the violation of rape is not an isolated event. As her body is mined by nurses, she invokes a sense of gritty biology to capture how it is her body, and not her voice, that makes available evidence of rape. These embodied ways of sensing rape's consequences foreground how much the visceral matters for understanding the experience of rape.

To counter Turner's claim that Miller orgasmed and felt pleasure during the night of the attack, Miller recounts the experience of coming to learn how her body was found by the international students and later the police. Importantly, she reiterates the details through an encounter with the physical context in which her body lies naked on ground: "I learned that my ass and vagina were completely exposed outside, my breasts had been groped, fingers had been jabbed inside me along with pine needles and debris, my bare skin and head had been rubbing against the ground behind a dumpster, while an erect freshman was humping my half naked, unconscious body. But I don't remember, so how do I prove I didn't like it."[50] This portrayal of her body jars with Turner's assertion that Miller consented. She writes of being found with a "long necklace wrapped around my neck, bra pulled out of my dress, dress pulled off over my shoulders and pulled above my waist" while identified as "breathing, unresponsive with her underwear six inches away from her bare stomach curled in fetal position."[51] Audiences envision a body naked, like a doll brushing on the ground as it is stuffed with dirt and penetrated by Turner's fingers. Audiences are encouraged to sense her bare skin rubbing on pavement and pine needles, which complicates Turner's claim of Miller's pleasure.

Along with documented descriptions of her body submitted to medical personnel, Miller also explains her perceptions of her own body at this time. In particular, she comments on her relationship with her body: "After a few hours of [the rape kit examination], they let me shower. I stood there examining my body beneath the stream of water and decided, I don't want my body anymore. I was terrified of it, I didn't know what had been in it, if it had been contaminated, who had touched it. I wanted to take off my body like a jacket and leave it at the hospital with everything else."[52] Particularly evocative, Miller's description of wishing her body was something she could remove or disown, something no longer belonging to her, invites audiences to consider the body and the person as distinct entities—a separation between body-as-subject and body-as-object. In this description, Miller speaks of her body as an object now polluted, something unwanted. As Miller conceptualizes her body through contamination, she identifies an abject quality of her body, a body improperly belonging to her, and her experience of loss is explicated through the feeling of being bound by her body, trapped. Such attention to the body-as-object captures what legal frameworks cannot—that the consequences of physical trespass felt from the perspective of the victim can be those of disgust and dejection.

Miller's description of her relationship with her body elucidates how aspects of her body were once taken from her. Miller closes her letter directly addressing Turner and the power imbalance of what they each endured: "Your damage was concrete; stripped of titles, degrees, enrollment. My damage was internal, unseen, I carry it with me. You took away my worth, my privacy, my energy, my time, my safety, my intimacy, my confidence, my own voice, until today."[53] While Turner's sentencing was centered on the use of his body within hers, Miller notes the intensity of feeling experienced *on and inside her body*, an intensity that opposes the liberal frameworks used to adjudicate Turner. Her mode of engagement rejects the consistent focus on memory as a point of contradiction pitted against women who have been raped, and she demonstrates how her case "gives the message that a stranger can be inside you without proper consent and he will receive less than what has been defined as the minimum sentence."[54] Turner's body—regardless of which parts—trespassed and invaded Miller's body. While these bodily parts were used to measure violence in the eyes of the law, her letter illustrates what violation by a stranger in public *feels* like, asking audiences to prioritize the feelings of the victim over the perceptions of the perpetrator.

Miller's attention to viscerality complicates prior theories of publicity grounded in a "normative stranger sociality" and the idea that public engagement is constituted through circulation among other bodies in public.[55] While Michael Warner argues that public subjects require an orientation to others in public where "strangers can be treated as already belonging to our world," Miller's letter draws attention to how certain bodies are subjected to risk in the public sphere and reveals how a stranger was not made normal but *made violent* to her.[56] Though Warner's theory opened new possibilities for conceptualizing embodiment among public subjects, Miller's letter illustrates how his idea of the stranger is grounded in a male, homosocial sociality that can overlook gendered assumptions when applied to other case studies. For example, rhetorical scholars such as Robert Hariman and John Lucaites draw from Warner to assert that "publics by their nature require [. . .] embodied forms of sociality (or they will not be effective)."[57] Miller's visceral counterpublic tactics illuminate how idealizing the stranger presumes a level of safety that inadequately captures the experiences of some embodied forms of sociality in public. Miller's letter makes visible how the feminized and racialized body does not have the same access to public space, which suggests that effective inclusion in a public extends mainly to bodies not subject to risk or harm from strangers. Revealing this subjugated positionality harkens back to Judith Butler's idea of a socially and politically constituted body that is always "attached to others, at risk of losing those attachments, exposed to others, at risk of violence by virtue of that exposure."[58] Most certainly, the public sphere is not only a place where meaning is made but also a place where meaning is felt, a place saturated with emotion and affect in which our attachments to the bodies, surfaces, and materials around us constitute political life. But, these attachments, as Miller documents, can also place public subjects in vulnerable positions. Visceral counterpublic performances like Miller's adhere to these ideas of attachment, risk, and exposure in ways that unsettle the assumptions within a stranger sociality and acknowledge an important component of publicity that recognizes how public attachments can turn violent, tracing public attention toward an inequity among bodies that move throughout public space.

"What Are You Looking For?": A Case Study of Emma Sulkowicz

While Miller calls audiences to attend to her body's internal experience, in contrast, Sulkowicz's form of visceral counterpublicity externalizes the use of the body and aims to amplify a bodily intensity in viewers. Sulkowicz's performance piece *Ceci N'est Pas Un Viol* functions in two parts: a brief introduction followed by an eight-minute video. In the introduction, Sulkowicz offers a set of textual directions for viewers to follow while watching the video, and this section uses written language to direct viewers *not* to view the contents of the video as rape. In the video, Sulkowicz paradoxically portrays what seems like rape and draws upon nonverbal modalities such as physical, visual, and aural dimensions. Taken together, I argue that the performance uses viscerality to accomplish two goals: to undo public assumptions about the experience of a rape by redirecting the discomfort of boundary crossing away from Sulkowicz as "rape victim" and onto audiences, and to reverse the standard used for deliberating rape by delegitimizing the text and legitimizing the use of the body.

When Sulkowicz's video stages the violent act of rape and viewers witness skin on skin contact, physical restraint, and nonconsensual penetration, Sulkowicz crosses the traditional norms of public discourse about rape. That is, their performance intends to overwhelm viewers and shock them into seeing and feeling rape. While it is nearly impossible not to have a visceral response to the video given its sheer physicality, it is possible for viewers to experience a range of visceral responses, as demonstrated in the commenting section in which viewers' reactions span from support to extreme hostility. This analysis focuses on how Sulkowicz uses viscerality to elicit a tension between what they tell viewers and what they show them. By positioning viewers in a state of dislocation, Sulkowicz asks viewers to reflect on what they are feeling while they are viewing and how those feelings contradict their own stated desires. This tension between telling and feeling produces a disruption that urges viewers to reflect on their own state of embodiment—or as Sara Ahmed argues, sensations that ask audiences to "*attend* to [their] embodied existence."[59] In what follows, I first examine the framing text of the project before moving to the contents of the video.

Publicly available online, the performance begins with written instructions for the video embedded in the project, which directly hail viewers into a relationship with the text.[60] Sulkowicz provides important direction for both the topic of the performance and the conditions under which viewers should watch the video. They write, "The following text contains allusions to rape. Everything that takes place in the following video is consensual but may resemble rape. It is not a reenactment but may seem like one."[61] Immediately, Sulkowicz places viewers in a vulnerable relationship with the text. Their directions eliminate distance between viewer and text as they write, "*Ceci N'est Pas Un Viol* is not about one night in August, 2012. It's about your decisions, starting now. It's only a reenactment if you disregard my words. It's about you, not him."[62] These initial framing questions generate feelings of uncertainty and even paranoia as Sulkowicz maintains that the video contents do not represent rape and viewers would only see otherwise if they neglect Sulkowicz's *words*.

The textual introduction lists questions under the categories of "Searching," "Desiring," and "Me." While the categories of "Desiring" and "Me" pose questions about Sulkowicz's identity of victim, the category of "Searching" asks, "Are you searching for proof? Proof of what? Are you searching for ways to either hurt or help me? What are you *looking* for?"[63] Questions like these call to mind questions immediately asked of someone who claims to have experienced rape. These questions aimed at gathering proof appear procedural, yet by placing viewers in close proximity to the text where viewers struggle to discern whether or not the video represents an actual experience, Sulkowicz shows how these questions are always guided by public motivation and are never value neutral. When Sulkowicz questions what one *looks* for, their performance suggests that public opinion trains audiences to identify qualities that would serve to doubt or deny the possibility of rape. In other words, they illuminate how such practices of looking are so conditioned by a public impulse to search for consent or blame the victim that audiences risk missing the larger landscape of violence.

After setting up the viewer's relationship to the text, Sulkowicz outlines an agreement of consent to watch. They write, "Do not watch this video if your motives would upset me, my desires are unclear to you, or my nuances are indecipherable."[64] Sulkowicz's consensual agreement summons viewers to inhabit the body of a rapist, producing a moment of fraught consubstantiality.[65] As Sulkowicz directs, viewers are to watch with an understanding of *their* desires, under the direction of *their* intentions: "If you watch this video without my consent, then I hope you reflect on your reasons for objectifying me and participating in my rape, for, in that case, you were the one who couldn't resist the urge to make *Ceci N'est Pas Un Viol* about what you wanted to make it about: rape."[66] These viewing conditions metaphorically blur the lines between consent to watch and sexual consent: if viewers watch on Sulkowicz's terms, then the viewing is consensual; however, if viewers watch on terms guided by public perceptions of rape, then the viewing is nonconsensual. Such textual framing mimics how publics are informed of rape—through linguistic direction of what it is and isn't. In doing so, Sulkowicz mocks the legal system's perceived power to dictate discursively what counts as rape, and furthermore, how their own experience was devalued and mistrusted.

The viewing begins after clicking agreement to the following consent statement: "I have read the above text and understand what it means for me to click PLAY."[67] The video itself is shot in four panels from four different angles—from the bed level, from the door and above, and the remaining two from angled opposing sides of the room. Viewers see all four frames at once, which emulates the format of a security feed. The video begins with Sulkowicz and an unidentifiable man entering Sulkowicz's dorm room while kissing. They each begin to take off their own and each other's clothes, move closer to Sulkowicz's bed, and engage in oral sex. The video has no background music; instead, the viewer can acutely hear movement in the room such as a leg brushing against a bare dorm mattress, wet lips, the crinkle of a condom wrapper opening, and breath released from the mouth. Sulkowicz and the other actor engage in vaginal sex embracing one another while Sulkowicz remains on top of the man. After a few seconds, the man switches positions and places Sulkowicz under him.

At this moment, Sulkowicz's body begins to go limp as he restrains their arms behind their head, and his bodily movement quickens. He slaps Sulkowicz across their face, and their voice whimpers. He hits them across the face harder again, causing them to shout "ow." He begins to choke them, they plead "stop," and their knees begin to curl less around his body and closer to their own head. Viewers hear Sulkowicz's shortness of breath as they weep and pull their legs closer. He pauses motion for a moment, pulls off the condom, and throws it to the ground. He then pushes Sulkowicz's legs against their own body forcefully and penetrates their body anally, while they proceed to yell "ow" several times and push the top of his bare thigh away from their body. He begins to restrain Sulkowicz more directly, and they moan as their voice clenches. They loosen one foot from his grip and kick it against the wall to fight back, yet he pins both their arms and legs down. They cry, "stop," and he thrusts his body more quickly into theirs. With one hand, Sulkowicz covers their face, hiding their eyes, begins to cry, and then covers their whole face with both hands. He eventually releases himself from Sulkowicz's body, and they immediately curl into the fetal position away from him and toward the wall, still covering their face and moaning quietly.

After getting off the bed, he grabs his clothes and walks naked out the door, as Sulkowicz remains curled. Once he leaves, they slowly begin to unfurrow their body, still placing one hand on their forehead and eyes, tenting their fingertips in a contemplative position. They take a deep breath and viewers hear its release. They rest like this for almost a minute before proceeding to get up slowly. They cover their body with a bath towel and leave the room. After a few seconds, they reenter and let down the towel. They place bed sheets on the bed, get into the bed naked, and turn over toward the wall. The video ends.

The scale of bodily intensity builds as viewers are encouraged to watch a man seemingly violate Sulkowicz. While viewers have been directly instructed not to identify rape, Sulkowicz's video encourages viewers to see and feel rape happen on the screen. By staging the rape in a video that requires a consent agreement prior to viewing, Sulkowicz highlights a shortcoming to affirmative consent laws. Even though consent was granted in the initial and isolated click—just as consent was initially exchanged during the beginning moments of sex—viewers' reactions while watching might cause them to feel otherwise; just because you consent once does not necessarily mean you consent to everything. The video illuminates how consent is not an isolated moment exchanged once as viewers are made to feel something change while watching the contents of the video play out.

Discerning rape from this point of view allows viewers the chance to grapple with the experience of rape beyond the discursive assertion that violation did not occur. Viewers are suspended into the action of the performance and encouraged to dwell in their own discomfort. Viewing aims to induce vulnerability, anxiety, and even the desire to look away or break viewing consent. Shot like a hidden security camera, viewing the four angles at once encourages a sense of voyeurism, and during various moments, viewers are presented with the genitalia of both actors up close. Performing rape in such a way invites viewers to grasp violation through embodied dimensions where viewers hear and see the condom snap on a body, bodies brush with an industrialized dorm room mattress, skin flap with other skin from a body's thrust, and Sulkowicz gasp for air. They see one body dominate another body, restrain it, press it, and slap it. They sense resistance on Sulkowicz's part that turns into eventual defeat as their body recoils. In the process, viewers may feel awkward peering into this intimate moment of violence, possibly clenching in their own reactions. Even though viewers experience discontinuity in that Sulkowicz (and the public) directs viewers not to identify rape, the performance creates conditions under which viewers can attest to rape, emulating the connection Scarry theorizes between feeling pain and having certainty. That is, whether or not Sulkowicz intends viewers to actually see rape through their opening directions, feelings generated while watching produce a certainty that defies that intention. As intensity builds, the video trains viewers to apprehend rape from the level of feeling.

The title of Sulkowicz's project quite obviously plays on the famous painting *The Treachery of Images* by René Magritte. Magritte's piece presents a challenge to a visual's representative power and a didactic lesson for viewers' individual relationships to symbols. Displaying both a pipe and the actual text, "Ceci n'est pas une pipe" ("This is not a pipe"), the piece forces viewers to see the text and image together while simultaneously destabilizing the meanings of both. That is, the visual image calls the linguistic interpretation into question. Similarly, while Sulkowicz's performance suggests rape, the project textually claims otherwise. Sulkowicz, thus, acts exactly as Magritte's pipe: the performance is both absolutely an act of rape but also not because it is a performance. However, Sulkowicz's deeper point suggests that viewers need little to no text to feel with certainty that rape occurred. By staging a performance of rape that jars with a set of directions, Sulkowicz demonstrates that the experience of rape is often managed through text, and their performance contends that arguments about rape should not stall in a place of language over consent. Determining rape requires sensing and feeling, which are made available through visceral counterpublic tactics.

Ultimately, *Ceci N'est Pas Un Viol* suggests the need to understand violence committed against marginalized bodies from an experiential, visceral level, bringing audiences to the body—its edges, its surfaces, and its insides—illustrating the violation of a body in ways that contemporary public discourses fail to address. The performance offers a visceral hermeneutic for viewers to turn toward, not away from, their sense faculties when they interact with the performance to understand the embodied existence of violence. This form of visceral counterpublicity aims to provoke a bodily intensity with the goal of shattering the debilitating definitions of rape that plagued Sulkowicz and many others. Sulkowicz's call is not for incremental change but rather for large-scale reorienting of the public practices of looking used to understand and determine what counts as rape.

Corporeal Vulnerability in Public Life

Public performances that attest to contemporary rape culture, especially in cases when institutional forces failed to bring justice to victims of rape, should not be ignored. Miller's and Sulkowicz's performances feature counterpublic activity that emboldens opposition to contemporary public opinion regarding rape. In feeling their way against publics, these individuals draw attention to the limits of legal and institutional frameworks, frameworks that discounted their experiences and, consequently, inhibit a wider public from understanding a broad range of experiences that count as rape. As I have shown, their forms of engagement seek to shift public opinion by opening a new discursive arena that conceptualizes the violence of rape through visceral frameworks, and their efforts call attention to the ways language alone has proved inadequate for capturing how marginalized bodies are subject to sexual violence in the United States. These tactics hold potential for moving audiences to apprehend the violence of rape at the level of feeling, shifting how public conversations understand and define rape and those who experience it.

While people in the United States have long witnessed and experienced what more recent conversations have coined a "rape culture," the performances analyzed in this chapter offer some of the most provocative stances to date against the insidious and normalized sexual attitudes that lead to violence against women and minorities. I view these performances as "moments of interruption," as Davide Panagia calls them, that "invite occasions and actions for reconfiguring our associational lives."[68] Visceral counterpublic tactics seek to expand public access for marginalized voices, especially when available liberal frameworks are not designed to hear or acknowledge them, and demand legal recognition for bodies that fall outside the idea of a (white) rational, male body. Acts like Miller's and Sulkowicz's call publics to reconsider how particular bodies subject to violence get elided from legal frameworks and inspire public conversations to achieve a more just and equitable society. And to some degree, they've demonstrated some success. Shortly after Turner completed his sentencing, California Governor Jerry Brown signed legislation that would expand the legal definition of rape to include nonconsensual sexual assault (AB 701) and the mandatory minimum sentencing guidelines for sexual assault offenders (AB 2888).[69] Many cited Miller's letter as a key source of motivation for legislators across the country, particularly in California.[70] Even with this incremental yet necessary change, however, both performances demonstrate an ultimate call for radical, robust, and widespread change. That is, in challenging the legal status quo, these forms of publicity ask not for legal accommodation but rather for a transformation of the public sphere.

What this chapter terms visceral counterpublicity extends beyond the case studies examined here and can be seen in other contemporary forms of public engagement that put the body at the center of protest. For instance, when people stand at the front lines of marches with their hands up to symbolize "Don't shoot," wear shirts or masks donning the phrase "I can't breathe," kneel during the national anthem, or collect in public areas to stage a die-in, these are visceral counterpublic tactics used to highlight embodied violence that has been otherwise negated by legal decisions. These forms of engagement use the body to reveal a subjugated positionality in the public sphere, constitute a discursive space grounded in the body and feeling, and most importantly, critique the state's inability to account for the bodies of marginalized groups. Similar to perpetrators within rape cases who are found not guilty, when a police officer is acquitted for shooting and killing a young man or woman of color, mainstream conversations risk adopting legal outcomes and treating these scenarios not as murder—grounded in deep rooted cultural, institutional, and ideological inequity—but rather as a societal outlier, an accident, or even a regrettable outcome of historic inequity. When legal outcomes circulate public discourse, social reality becomes subject to the law insofar as the innocence or guilt found in court determines whether or not violence happened.

Despite cases where the law says violence did not happen, performances drawing upon viscerality make audiences feel the echoes of the violence that did happen. Ahmed writes, "Injustice is a question of how bodies come into contact with other bodies" and suggests that our response to injustice must avoid erasing the complex "relation between violence, power and emotion."[71] In cases when the law says murder or rape did not happen, visceral counterpublic tactics become necessary for revealing injustice among bodies moving in public. Such tactics use feeling to generate opposition and demonstrate a mismatch between the law and a cultural, institutional, and ideological problem of violence circulating within our society. These performances help prevent erasure of the complex relation Ahmed cites and shed light on a corporeal vulnerability that is a constitutive element of the public sphere. As Butler encourages, "We cannot [. . .] will away this vulnerability. We must attend to it."[72] Visceral counterpublic tactics call attention to the power that embodiment holds for theorizing public life and, more importantly, illustrate the risk of violence endured by some bodies over others.

This theory helps rhetorical theorists understand how forms of embodied protest are both a reaction to the state and a proactive call to public audiences to shift mainstream dialogues. While contemporary cases of sexual violence, police brutality, and racial protest document the use of such tactics, this chapter also encourages rhetorical critics more broadly to be mindful of how patriarchal structures (and the subjects they imagine) shape public understandings of the body. Once disseminated into public dialogues, legal outcomes assume certainty in conversation, influence how publics discuss cultural problems and, in the process, constrain discourses and the available means for speaking about the body. When visceral counterpublic tactics are employed, however, audiences are jolted by their own visceral responses and exposed to a disturbing reality of violence in US society, one that comes close to the messy, bloody materiality of embodied violence. Audiences that choose not to grapple with their own visceral experiences demonstrate a profound privileging of patriarchal frameworks and their attempts to contain discourses about the body. Nonetheless, confronting both the interiority and exteriority of pain endured by another body in public guides audiences toward a discomfort that challenges the use of those structures in public dialogues, encouraging publics to assert a level of certainty by way of our shared, corporeal vulnerability among one another in public. Attending to this corporeal vulnerability gives hope for opening broader public dialogues concerning violence against marginalized bodies by prioritizing the body when deliberating these problems.

5

TAKING IT ALL IN: #METOO, FEMINIST *MEGETHOS*, AND LIST MAKING

In 1997, Tarana Burke worked at a youth camp in Alabama. One night, she listened to the story of a thirteen-year-old girl she publicly calls Heaven, who struggled to tell Burke the gruesome details of how her mother's boyfriend sexually abused her. Horrified by her account, Burke cut Heaven's story short and guided her to the help of another counselor who could, as Burke describes, "help her better."[1] Heaven's story haunted Burke, and she recalls that night, writing, "I could not muster the energy to tell her that I understood, that I connected, that I could feel her pain . . . I could not find the strength to say out loud the words that were ringing in my head over and over again as she tried to tell me what she had endured . . . I couldn't even bring myself to whisper . . . me too."[2] That night stuck with Burke, and in 2006, she founded the Me Too movement as part of her organization, Just Be Inc., an organization committed to supporting the health and wellness of young women of color and raising public awareness about the quiet pervasiveness of sexual abuse.

Over ten years later in October 2017, Alyssa Milano tweeted a screenshot of a friend's text that said: "Suggested by a friend: 'If all the women who have been sexually harassed or assaulted wrote 'Me too' as a status, we might give people a sense of the magnitude of the problem.'" She sent it out, went to bed, and woke up to a flood of responses linked to the hashtag #MeToo. Quite literally thousands of people responded almost immediately in solidarity, many of whom offered testimonies of personal experiences with sexual harassment or assault. That Sunday night in October, Milano—initially unaware of Burke's movement—assembled a digital space of protest in which "for the moment, the world [was] listening."[3]

Why Milano was able to generate a firestorm of public response that vastly outpaced that of Burke's original movement requires understanding how aspects of race, gender, technology, and testimony shaped this specific cultural moment in 2017. Feminist scholars have long been concerned with how and why women's testimonies are largely met with distrust and doubt in public.[4] As this book has argued, women and those feminized by US cultural and sexual norms regarding rape are frequently cast as unreliable witnesses to their own bodies, and, consequently, their claims for justice are tainted by voices who, according to Leigh Gilmore, aim "to contaminate by doubt, stigmatize through association with gender and race, and dishonor through shame, such that not only the testimony but the person herself is smeared."[5] But what marks #MeToo as different is how it transcended the limits of testimony that victims of sexual assault frequently face in the movement's efforts to affect audiences. Using the hashtag afforded what Meredith Loken refers to as "the potential to reimagine narratives for demanding agency, autonomy, and institutional inclusion," expanding the scenes available for discussion about rape culture.[6] #MeToo, as a term and assemblage, has changed how we talk about sexual violence and constituted its own vocabulary, embedded into mainstream discourse and deployed to account for acts of sexual misconduct that occur in a range of professional, personal, and public contexts. Many use the term, for instance, to mark solidarity with others or to reframe their interactions and experiences (e.g., "in our current #MeToo moment" or "he has a #MeToo history"). In particular, #MeToo catalyzed a collective anger online that disseminated widely through Twitter feeds and other social media platforms beginning in October 2017, which, at present, has offered one of the most recognized and ongoing protests against sexual violence.

While feminist communication scholars have traced how online platforms can be a productive space for narrating feminist issues, this chapter maintains that #MeToo unleashed a shifting testimonial landscape available to victims of rape and sexual assault.[7] Instead of disclosing long-form stories about personal experiences with sexual violence, #MeToo users collaboratively testified to their experiences by linking them to one another. They described in deliberately confined forms what happened to their bodies in addition to offering critiques of those who fail to hear the experiences of victims. Taken together, the collection of tweets formed a massive and daunting list that invited audiences to understand rape culture through matters of scale, revealing a new mode of online activism with potential to facilitate powerful feminist protest. As a result, the magnitude of this feminist list created a sense of collective believability through numerous tweets *intended to be read together one after the other*, which served as evidence audiences were hard pressed to challenge, much like the magnitude amassed by the testimonies given during the Nassar case. Specifically, while Twitter offered a space of solidarity and empowerment for victims, #MeToo promoted awareness and action among passive sympathizers and, more importantly, those who either know very little about or fail to take seriously the ubiquity of sexual assault and those affected by it.

This chapter argues that analyzing the rhetorical power of the list generated by #MeToo reveals a feminist utility of an old strategy. Central to Aristotle's epideictic forms of rhetoric, *megethos*—or magnitude—fosters the justification of "what should be made to matter," as Thomas Farrell has argued.[8] While scholars such as Debra Hawhee, Christa Olson, and Jenny Rice have theorized how constituting magnitude illuminates the rhetorical work of sensation, I extend these ideas by illustrating the affective work of disruption that can occur when *megethos* takes the form of a feminist list.[9] Generating magnitude, I maintain, serves "not only to engage viewers, but also to overwhelm them"—specifically, in this case, with feelings that encourage a level of belief in victims' testimonies and a commonplace reality of rape culture.[10] Theorizing the magnitude generated by #MeToo through this list-making function resonates with scholars who have identified the instructive function of a list: "It [the list] tells us how to act with regard to a particular goal."[11] Thus, examining how #MeToo operates as a list moves theories of magnitude beyond ideas of "piling on excessive details," cultivating coherence, or amounting greatness or beauty.[12] That is, #MeToo reveals quite the opposite: within their confined form, #MeToo tweets often provide little to no detail, which, when listed one after the other, employ *megethos* in an effort to replace problematic assumptions of victimhood or apathetic opinions of rape culture with visceral feelings of pain and outrage, feelings that aim to provoke viewers into action. In other words, what I term feminist *megethos* can be thought of as a strategy for puncturing—even if only slightly—pervasive yet normalized attitudes that constrain efforts for justice by instilling a bone-deep, felt assurance in audiences through the accumulation of a list.

Investigating how feminist *megethos* functions through listing expands the groundwork laid in the previous chapter, offering another tactic of visceral rhetorics useful for changing the conversation about rape when certain groups, individuals, or institutions fail to capture and account for its scale. Like visceral counterpublicity, feminist *megethos* underscores a performative and embodied role of protest but differs from visceral counterpublicity in the collective, viral form it takes, contributing to rhetorical theories invested in understanding the relationship among gender, injustice, and testimony in addition to the modes and forms through which testimonies can be made. Listing personal accounts and commentaries on the status of rape culture over and again functioned to immerse audiences in the mundane, naturalized, and everyday experiences of sexual violence that so many face in their day-to-day lives yet evade the law's gaze. Cultivating such "affective states," as Deborah Gould argues, "can shake one out of deeply grooved patterns of thinking and feeling and allow for new imaginings."[13] #MeToo deliberately invoked such an affective state by way of listing in an effort to jar audiences into seeing and believing a reality of rape culture by coming to grips with their own felt attachments to the robust set of evidence generated through the list.

In what follows, I situate this chapter in the broader network of rape culture that shaped #MeToo and describe the contours of the movement as a list. Then, I theorize #MeToo as a feminist form of *megethos* that calls upon the tools of list making in order to shift public perception of victims' testimonies through an archive of both tweets published during the #MeToo movement and public discussion of them. Communication scholar Jennifer Ziegler argues that "the meaning of a list exists less in the items on its face and more in the discourses surrounding it. Thus a search for the true meaning of a list requires a search for the story behind it."[14] To understand #MeToo as well as the discourses that shaped its uptake, I employ a critical reading of dozens of tweets, newspaper and magazine articles, and opinion editorials about #MeToo.[15] In doing so, I seek to understand the story of #MeToo as the tweets unfolded as well as how #MeToo was interpreted by mainstream news sources and public audiences. I close this chapter highlighting some additional instances of feminist *megethos* while outlining some implications this concept has for future forms of activism.

The Click Moment

In October 2017—the same month that Milano's tweet would ignite the #MeToo movement—the *New Yorker* and the *New York Times* reported on over a dozen cases of women who had accused Harvey Weinstein of sexual harassment, sexual assault, and rape over the course of the last decade.[16] Ashley Judd and Rose McGowan were some of the first to accuse him but were joined by many others as the aftermath unfolded. Weinstein, who initially denied all accusations, was fired from his production company, removed from the Academy of Motion Picture Arts and Sciences, and criminally charged with rape. Weinstein's allegations led to what many have called "the Weinstein effect," a trend in which powerful, famous men—including Matt Lauer, Charlie Rose, Kevin Spacey, and many others—were accused of sexual assault and quickly fired as a result. This trend of swift institutional action catalyzed what many in public viewed as a shift in mainstream responses to rape.

While prior, high-profile cases of sexual assault provided a foundation for #MeToo to gain force (e.g., Bill Cosby, Larry Nassar), #MeToo is largely attributed to the Weinstein case and the subsequent public conversations that ensued afterward. It inspired additional hashtag campaigns such as #TimesUp and #WhyWeWearBlack that occurred during and after the 2018 Golden Globes and aimed to expand the initial interest in raising awareness about sexual assault to the gender pay gap, harassment in the workplace, and, furthermore, an intersectional view of rape culture. The *Times* called what happened in October 2017, "The 'Click' Moment," citing a new "army of voices" used for the social movement of rape prevention.[17] Just ten days after Milano's initial tweet, Twitter reported that the hashtag spanned over eighty-five countries and 1.7 million users.[18] As conversations grew on Twitter, many took to additional platforms (e.g., Facebook, Instagram, news media, podcasts, etc.) to offer longer testimonies of their own experiences with sexual abuse or comment on the movement's participation in challenging rape culture more broadly.[19] Thus, even if audiences didn't engage with #MeToo explicitly through Twitter, the general US public was presented with several other outlets consumed by it. Avoiding a conversation about #MeToo was nearly impossible.

Those who did engage specifically with #MeToo on Twitter encountered tweets (brief messages using 280 characters or less), retweets (messages circulating a message published by another user), and replies to re/tweets that were arranged on one's Twitter feed—an ongoing stream of messages presented on one's home timeline by users one "follows." In addition to this variety of options, users could also engage with the movement by clicking the hashtag if it was presented on one's timeline or clicking the hashtag as it appeared under trending topics, a set of hashtags popular in real time among vast users displayed on the social media platform. By clicking #MeToo, users were presented with a feed of re/tweets—what this chapter views as a list—using that hashtag by any user, not only users one follows. While users could choose to skim through the magnitude of tweets listed together through the trending hashtag, because the movement reached tremendous popularity, many home timelines were, too, extensively populated with a list of #MeToo tweets.

The content of individual tweets, while varied, can be broadly categorized by the following three groups: (1) tweets by victims disclosing individual accounts of sexual assault; (2) tweets by sympathizers supportive of the movement and/or critical of rape culture; and (3) tweets that simply wrote

#MeToo, or what I view as an echo to the movement or a reference to an experience with sexual violence that the user does not want to disclose publicly. While the specific audiences of individual tweets are many (e.g., other victims, perpetrators, institutional or workplace administrators, wider mainstream publics), overall, #MeToo imagined a collective type of audience: those apathetic about the prevalence of rape culture or unwilling to acknowledge it. For instance, in retweeting a *Sports Illustrated* article documenting a USA gymnast's sexual assault by Dr. Nassar, actress Gabrielle Union tweeted, "You know us. We are your family members. Your friends. Your coworkers. Your neighbors. And yes, even your heroes. We are everywhere. #MeToo."[20] Using the pronouns "you" and "us," Union's tweet invokes this audience, drawing a more personal connection to how everyday people are affected by sexual assault. Some tweets were more deliberate in addressing this audience: "If #MeToo is 'making you uncomfortable,' you're the one it's meant to reach. Silencing sexual assault victims doesn't make it any less real."[21] Conjuring a similar "you" as Union, this user calls out indifferent or stubborn audiences, asking them to dwell in their own discomfort as opposed to foreclosing it, a discomfort unparalleled to that of actual victims but one useful for persuading doubtful audiences of the realities of rape culture.

When analyzing the meaning of a list, Ziegler argues that it's important to investigate why "a particular list made 'perfect sense' as a solution at the time it was adopted."[22] Because testimony as a genre has not typically worked well for victims, users of #MeToo repackaged their experiences in list form, linked together and amassed through broad solidarity, demonstrating what scholars have shown to be the power of lists, the ability to move beyond the constraints of narrative.[23] Lists take up space, such as that of a newsfeed, functioning like what literary theorist Brian Richardson refers to as "disruptive elements" to more traditional forms of narrative.[24] While lists may seem to be at odds with the function of narrative, I suggest that lists *do* tell stories, even in their confined form. Modes of social media like Twitter, I argue, orient themselves around the idea of lists in order to capture the attention of a reader that a longform narrative might not. For instance, lists crop up in internet posts on *BuzzFeed* and *Vox* as well as platforms like Hootsuite and Storify, intervening in what is perceived as a more traditional narrative arc, acting as interruptions that can be both intrusive and quickly consumable. In other words, #MeToo made "perfect sense" because of its disruptive emotional form, a form rooted in outrage about the doubt victims have faced when telling their individual stories that alternatively aimed to demonstrate the robust scale of experiences currently held by individuals across the globe.

It sought not to follow adjudicatory frameworks in narrating a lack of consent but rather to define violence through notions of ubiquity and the mundane. In the process, it crossed borders, identity categories, age groups, religious affiliations, and so on.

While #MeToo was by no means the first time feminists took to Twitter to protest anti-feminist events and ideologies (e.g., #EverydaySexism, #NotOkay, or #BlackGirlMagic), what marks it as distinct is that the list *did* intervene in the public sphere to a degree unlike other prior hashtag movements.[25] That is, while it followed other movements by acting as "a space intended both to hail and constitute a virtual audience of like-minded individuals for conversation" as Tamika Carey puts it, the massive list it generated targeted audiences outside of actual #MeToo users and was picked up and talked about in everyday vernacular beyond its digital space.[26] But #MeToo's association with celebrity—particularly white and wealthy women celebrities—cannot be ignored. Unlike Burke's earlier movement, #MeToo grew out of deep privilege that made it easier for some voices to speak and be heard, mobilizing a form of anger "rhetorically rendered available for some [. . .] while simultaneously limiting the emotional expression—and thus political potential—of others."[27] Put bluntly, the list of tweets was able to capture vast public attention because its initiators were grounded in white privilege and less at risk of retribution by their abusers or public, personal, and/or professional reprimand. While non-US, working-class, nonwhite, male, queer, and trans voices most certainly joined the movement, these early voices undeniably helped the list stand out and formed a platform for public audiences to listen.

Knowing this context—that #MeToo is most certainly flawed, that it largely overlooked Burke's initial movement and a broad history of rape culture in the United States, that it fell trap to a legacy of whiteness tied to the patriarchy it sought to protest—absolutely informs this analysis. I do not intend to call for postfeminist tactics that fail to engage intersectional lenses when calling for change. While provocative, protests like #MeToo are not enough, similar, in many ways, to how Jacqueline Rhodes has analyzed the SlutWalk protests that emerged in 2011, protests filled with "blind spots" regarding their inability to recognize privilege.[28] Like #MeToo, "SlutWalk," Rhodes argues, "shows us the well-intentioned but also complicitous rhetoric of mainstream (read white) feminism at the same time as it engages in some of the unruliness needed to change US patriarchal culture."[29] In other words, protests like SlutWalk and #MeToo, while flawed, employ unruly tactics that have led to change and thus offer us a place to start—to inspire future progress and shift the conversation—and for that reason, we don't have to throw the baby out with the bathwater. We must, however, strive to reckon with these flaws and think through conspiratorial lenses in order to cultivate solidarity across difference. Promoting real change requires risking retribution and acknowledging how privilege shapes the kinds of claims able to be made, the forms those claims take, and the effects they have. As Rhodes reminds us, we must be intersectional and willing to acknowledge when certain voices are given platforms that have so frequently worked to deny others. With this in mind, I hope this chapter likewise offers an opportunity to nuance our tactics while sustaining the motivation needed for change, encouraging feminists and activists to identify the effective and disruptive capacities garnered through the list-making efforts that surfaced in 2017 while grappling with Burke's initial movement that started over a decade earlier.

In what follows, I analyze the #MeToo movement as a list through the idea of feminist *megethos*. I draw from both individual tweets and surrounding public reactions to understand how #MeToo was indexed by public audiences. This approach helps capture the feelings or what Ralph Cintrón calls the "storehouses of social energy" that are distributed across publics and culminate in meaning making about #MeToo.[30] Approaching #MeToo in this way serves to archive the energies that circulated throughout the movement—the feelings that called publics to respond—and understand what effect they had on public perceptions of rape culture.

Entering the Lists

Many victims find themselves silenced after they disclose an experience with sexual violence. They may receive a variety of reactions from audiences, many of which can be grounded in doubt or seek to shame the victim. Silence circulated throughout several tweets and was categorized by the media as an exigency for the movement. For instance, actress Marlee Matlin joined the movement tweeting, "#MeToo. I was 14, he was 36. I may be Deaf, but silence is the last thing you will ever hear from me."[31] As #MeToo unfolded, one woman described how her prior attempt to disclose was unexpectedly met with pain and guilt caused by people in her life who doubted her. In an editorial published in the *Washington Post*, she detailed what happened after she publicly shared her experience:

> Almost immediately after my essay was published, I was attacked online and off. People, extremely well-meaning and loving people I know in real

life, to my utter shock, took the mess of what happened to me, wrapped it in a neat little bow, handed it back to me and said, "Oh, is that all?" It happened, they said, because I did not read the situation properly. They said: It happened because I was too nice and accommodating to the person who assaulted me. They said: It happened because I was not forceful enough. Or maybe it didn't happen at all.[32]

Laura Gianino shares that her story was not written during #MeToo but rather at a time when "the media was not, in turn, surrounding these women like a protective fortress from the trolls who might try to scare them away from revealing what happened to them."[33] To challenge the stigmas often applied to those who disclose their stories, Gianino hopes "that #MeToo never stops trending."[34]

What happened to Gianino illustrates how individual stories risk being perceived as false and, as a result, fail to create a changed future for victims. As one user wrote, "What's worse? the amount of women posting #MeToo or the amount of women who feel their story isn't 'bad enough' to be shared or talked about."[35] On its own, the individual story may garner empathy among audiences and provide a testimony of what happened. But as Gianino's story illustrates, individual accounts are often stigmatized and discounted by audiences. As a response to this failure, #MeToo spoke unapologetically to audiences, provoking them to engage with a multiplicity of experiences, not just one or two.

For Aristotle, *megethos* was central to his definition of rhetoric in that persuading audiences of shared goals or opinions requires a sense of magnitude or amplification and its role in invoking "greatness."[36] As Farrell has pointed out, producing "largess, degree, quantity" constitutes the subject of discourse apart from its counterparts in terms of size or worth.[37] More simply, *megethos* can be thought of as "the weight of rhetoric."[38] Given its nature in understanding amplification, rhetorical scholars have used *megethos* to consider questions of aesthetics, weight, scale, and the sublime.[39] In her study of the mid-nineteenth-century US influence within South America, Olson argues that magnitude is "absolutely fundamental to US rhetorics."[40] Drawing from this same history of *megethos* as Olson and Farrell, Rice suggests that magnitude is not purely rhetorical in its capacity to aggregate evidence but also carries an aesthetic quality, specifically in the context of conspiracy theory and big data archives and the marking of what she calls "a kind of coherence."[41] While Rice and Olson theorize *megethos* with different goals in mind, they align in considering the capacity of *megethos* to capture grandeur or quantify large amounts of data—what it means to "take in" meaning, whether it be evidence or a visual impression. In other words, we can understand *megethos* as the speechless moments when we are presented with things like the Grand Canyon or even a hoarded mess. We are confronted with the need to consume and cohere greatness—whether positive or negative.

As a strategy, then, *megethos* offers rhetors a way to reach audiences, audiences who may need more convincing through the presentation of something consequential. "Magnitude," writes Farrell, is "essential to the most important concerns of traditional rhetoric: namely, whether an audience may care about any topic sufficiently to attend to it, to engage it, and to act upon it; what consequences will weigh most heavily upon their prospective deliberation; what priorities will finally tip the balance in their judgment; and what appetitive attachments will need to be overcome for rational reflection to be feasible."[42] In other words, generating the felt weight of an argument is a process central to rhetoric because it's a process central to the work of persuading an audience to respond a certain way. That is, if the object carries a sense of magnitude, audiences are more prone to connect to the topic and even engage it if they can grasp a sense of weightiness. Olson is keen to point out that engaging *megethos*, however, doesn't "simply allow rhetors to parse an audience's commitments and arrange reasoned discourse to sway it."[43] Rather, magnitude has the capacity to "lift audiences beyond reason."[44] It can be impressed upon an audience visually or viscerally.

In generating a space for deliberation about rape culture, users of the hashtag sought to redefine—and thus visualize—what it means to be at risk of rape through the idea of an argument's felt sense, its weightiness. To challenge victim blaming, one user tweeted, "She is not asking for attention. She is asking to be heard. #MeToo."[45] Users targeted apathetic or disbelieving audiences by exposing commonplace experiences of rape culture in an effort to stun them into paying attention. Users tweeted things like, "Hey women: retweet if you've ever been shown a penis you did not want or expect to see," a message that was retweeted over 210,000 times.[46] They tweeted about everyday work experiences: "My supervisor asked me to step into the bathroom so he could show me how to do the inventory. He pinned me against a wall. #MeToo."[47] Or even moving throughout public space: "#MeToo Watch a young girl walk home at night with her keys in between her fingers and fear in her eyes and tell me that this isn't a problem."[48] On their own, tweets like these may register with an unwilling or doubtful audience, but when linked together and read one after another after another, the list of tweets aimed to disturb readers, to "tip the balance in their judgment," by making them feel uncomfortable, demonstrating the tweets' unified potential for making readers cringe, listen, and believe. In generating magnitude, #MeToo desired an "imaginative reconstruction at the collective level" by constituting a rhetorical environment grounded in *feeling the fear, disgust, and pain* central to rape culture.[49]

Thus, unlike previous deployments of *megethos*, users of the hashtag did not work from the presumption of establishing a grand or coherent picture of beauty for rational persuasion to happen. While users did respond from the mutual objective of protesting rape culture, the motivations for using the hashtag were grounded in the need to alter audiences' opinions by rupturing them. Because victims and sympathizers have long been protesting the conditions of rape culture, #MeToo took an unrulier, seething approach. Users most certainly aimed to "lift audiences beyond reason," as Olson suggests, and engage in a shared affect intended to disrupt the logics of rape culture. In the process, they employed what Emily Winderman describes as the "circulation of emotions as a diffuse economy of rhetorical forces" to ground the experience of what it means to live in a rape culture.[50] #MeToo demonstrated how encountering magnitude involves "matters of embodied encounter," matters that help *move* an audience to believe something.[51] The goal of "rational reflection," as Farrell suggests, did not motivate their actions because, quite frankly, there is nothing reasonable or rational about the persistence of rape culture and, furthermore, a public failure to view it as such. Rather, the goal was to encourage audiences to *sense* the greatness of the problem, to *feel* the weight of rape culture and the scale of its effects on victims.

What helped shape this potential, I argue, is the form that #MeToo took. Viewers of the movement were confronted with the need to "take it all in at once," as Rice describes of magnitude, having to embrace the totality of the movement and its many responses.[52] Scrolling through the feed of tweets generated a vast number of testimonies viewers were invited to consume but also couldn't possibly do at once. Cultivating magnitude was particularly useful in this context given its ability to "overcome a paradoxical exigency"—that being the need to shift public perception about the frequency of sexual assault or harassment after centuries of struggling to do so.[53] The media, no doubt, recognized its force. One *Globe* reporter wrote, "The floodgates have opened and the deluge won't stop. Across various social-media platforms, women are coming out in droves to divulge the day (or days) they 'got Harveyed.'"[54] Or, as one reporter for the *Capital Times* described, "'[It was] almost like it was a ticker tape rolling in' . . . women were getting to voice something that they'd never been able to say before."[55] In addition to the metaphors of outpouring and flooding used to describe #MeToo, depicting the movement through the idea of a ticker tape alludes to a sense of consistency, repetition, and continuity. As one user noted, "Every single woman has a #MeToo story. If that doesn't terrify you then you're the problem."[56] #MeToo's use of numbers engaged in sentiments of data collection that aimed to confirm the realities of rape culture unlike other approaches before it (e.g., one in four women will be raped or sexually assaulted in their lifetime). That is, instead of sampling, descriptively illustrating, and summarizing the nature and extent of sexual assault, #MeToo cataloged the ongoing numbers of victims in raw form. Audiences were not simply invited to take in meaning; rather, they were inundated with experience after experience.

Queer theorist Ramzi Fawaz views a similar effect of lists as capable of shocking audiences into a state of believability. He argues that "lists can shake us out of our complacency" and invite us to account for existences previously excluded from normative meaning-making or public life.[57] Examining Eve Sedgwick's use of multiplicity throughout her career, Fawaz maintains that while they are creative, "lists are one way to reparatively confer plentitude on an event of mass diminishment."[58] That is, lists can shed light on the multiplicitous as the universal, as they did for Sedgwick in the *Epistemology of the Closet*, which, Fawaz writes, sought to avoid "the flattening abyss that mainstream culture simply calls 'AIDS deaths'" by acknowledging the magnitude of individuals who suffered throughout the AIDS epidemic.[59] In other words, we might understand the role of list making as an ethical mode of communicating. The list has potential for making visible the enormity of individuals who suffered AIDS and were, as a result, disregarded, or in the current case, were sexually assaulted and then ignored or not believed. As a form and structure, the list performs mourning and asks audiences to engage with a public problem by feeling a sense of pain shared by the many who suffered without editorializing their experiences. In the process, the list, I argue, reveals a feminist undertaking of generating magnitude: lists like the ones Fawaz points to and those examined in this chapter seek not to create a coherent narrative legible to the law but rather aim to interject and illustrate the incongruous nature of state protection that occurs in crimes of queer and gendered violence.

Most certainly, based on the numbers identified by Twitter along with numerous public reactions in support of #MeToo, the movement can be identified by its undeniable sense of visceral magnitude—a bone-deep certainty, a *felt* assurance of the veracity of these linked accounts of rape culture. The embodied nature of the list encouraged what Judith Butler describes as a "primary affective responsiveness" that informs how we interpret, judge, and critique.[60] That is, #MeToo was layered with rage and anger that inspired interpretation to "take hold" and challenge the assumptions of nonbelievers or bystanders by generating reactions to a multitude of visceral accounts.[61] Wrote one user, "Most men will never understand the primal fear all women have felt when out alone. It's weird to always feel vulnerable to attack. #MeToo."[62] Another tweet that appeared the first night read, "My entire twitter & facebook feeds are full of women i [sic] know saying #metoo. Men, no matter what your history—just let this sink in."[63] In constituting this digital space, users of the hashtag encouraged an engagement with the body's own gut reactions. Reading through the tweets urged audiences to understand rape culture by letting the list "sink in," as this user described. The list held the potential to trigger a form of judgment felt deep within the body, saturating audiences with bodily intensity and vulnerability to "magnify conviction in their truth."[64] Engaging the feeling body in this way placed viewers in the position of being "overwhelmed and re-shaped by magnitude" in order to establish believability and shift the dialogue about victimhood.[65] Laced with pain, the list created a new discourse and space available for understanding rape culture beyond those previously deployed to do so.

As scholars of lists have revealed, lists are always layered with motivations for using them but point out the role audiences play in assessing a list's value. Writes Larry Browning, "The success of a list depends on the scrutiny of a community; they have to accept that the list is the right one."[66] Thus, there is a collective aspect to list making; to approve or accept the list, communities must establish it as relative. For victims of sexual assault, many tweeted in celebration of the movement, acknowledging a feeling of relief in identifying a shared experience among others. One tweet heavily circulated wrote: "Best Thing: Finding out we are not alone and have all dealt with this. Worst Thing: Finding out we have all dealt with this#MeToo [sic]."[67] Thus, the list of tweets created an opportunity for solidarity among victims while also serving to speak back to dominant public opinion.

But the specific audience users sought reaction from were those unwilling to view their own complicity in rape culture. Unlike many other movements before it, #MeToo demonstrated some (however little) success in achieving this goal. For instance, one journalist in British Columbia reacted to #MeToo by starting the hashtag #HowIWillChange after seeing a friend write on Twitter, "It's time for all men, me included, to listen to what is being said and try not to defend ourselves or other men, try not to color what is being said with our own experiences, our own suffering, our fear of ****ing up or being called out."⁶⁸ Echoing this sentiment, a journalist from Australia tweeted, "#HowIWillChange: Acknowledge that if all women I know have been sexually harassed, abused or assaulted, then I know perpetrators. Or am one."⁶⁹ Finally, actor Mark Ruffalo helped generate usage of the hashtag after he wrote on Twitter, "I will never Cat call a woman again. Growing up we were taught from watching movies that a cat call was a compliment. I would do it to friends and girlfriends. Sunrise clued me in that it was totally inappropriate. Not cool. Not a compliment. Gross. #HowIWillChange."⁷⁰ While I do not intend to suggest we should merely champion men for making statements such as these, what draws me to the use of #HowIWillChange is its effort to "transport the audience away from the familiar," a central goal of *megethos*.⁷¹ Viewing certain behaviors as "gross" suggests a gut reaction, an internal, bodily form of judgment that led to seeing certain commonplace behaviors as problematic. Though #HowIWillChange reached relatively small audiences compared to #MeToo, tweeting things like, "I know perpetrators. Or am one," suggests not only the ability for #MeToo to reach male audiences but its ability to change male behavior.

#MeToo overwhelmed US and international publics with feelings about actual violent experiences of rape culture that occur in everyday people's lives. While intentionally short, the tweets served to accumulate feelings about the pain of violence, illustrating how "*megethos* operates through the human body as an excitable entity, an entity aroused by the sensation of more."⁷² On their own, each tweet might have held the potential to provoke embodied reactions, yet seeing them listed together over and again intensified the experience, accruing in the form of a "visceral encounter" used to encourage recognition of the realities of rape culture.⁷³ "Feeling discomfort (prickly sensations, cramps)," writes Sara Ahmed, "become transformed into pain through an act of reading," an act, in this case, bubbling with outrage.⁷⁴ In the process, the magnitude formed through the list of tweets attempted to generate a bodily intensity that functioned to disturb and unsettle problematic assumptions about sexual violence, assumptions that view sexual assault as "not that bad," her fault, or simply an unavoidable byproduct of, say, "locker room talk." While generating magnitude drew attention to the problem of rape culture, the enormity of tweets served to jolt audiences into recognizing their own bodily vulnerability and, ultimately, inspire change, reminding audiences that pain is central to living in a world where sexual violence persists, particularly in the banal and routine occasions of many people's day-to-day lives. Taken together, it argued that demonstrating empathy or rational forms of argumentation are not enough. Rather, audiences need to grapple with what it means to *feel overwhelmed by an intensity of risk* in order to grasp the realities of rape culture.

A Methodology for Change

I want to conclude on a point Rice leaves open-ended in her essay "The Rhetorical Aesthetics of More: On Archival Magnitude." She writes, "Could we imagine [. . .] a methodology that approaches activist rhetorics through a vocabulary of sensation?"[75] #MeToo (and rape culture more broadly) gives us a context to understand a potential response to this question—the work of approaching activism through the lens of our felt sense of embodied attachment to others, how knowledge forms in the moments when our skin crawls or we start to sweat. #MeToo offers us the chance to see value in our visceral responses, our gut instincts, our knee-jerk reactions, our bone-deep senses as driving forces for meaning-making and judgment. It demonstrates that disruptive forms of narrative—like lists—can be valuable and even necessary when cultivating broader public attention to issues of injustice. #MeToo sought to jar audiences' reactions—specifically audiences who might doubt the testimonies of women or minorities when presented in isolation but who could no longer entertain such disbelief when confronted with these experiences en masse. In the process, #MeToo created core attachments among some—those most in need of solidarity—but intended to foreground the vulnerabilities central to attachments in others who stubbornly fail to see their own complicity in the problem.

I do not want to suggest, however, that we can simply employ forms of feminist *megethos* to their logical end each time we are presented with questions of injustice or moments when the law fails to capture everyday, normalized acts of violation. That is, we cannot simply ask people to list their most painful or humiliating experiences with violence in order to garner public attention. While #MeToo engaged with audiences by overwhelming them with a list that expanded the whisper networks that motivated both Burke's and Milano's initial actions, some users were more critical of having to disclose their experiences publicly. For instance, NARAL retweeted a quote from author Lindy West, who wrote: "I wish women didn't have to rip our pasts open & let you ogle our pain for you to believe us."[76] Beyond the critique of sentimentalizing pain, West draws attention to how participating in the #MeToo movement involves risk, especially for those most marginalized in society. At its best, #MeToo offered a vocabulary for shifting how public audiences understand what it means to *feel at risk*, what Kyla Schuller calls "affective security," or the kinds of attachments that help foster or endanger our very being in public.[77] We cannot, however, simply ask victims to expose themselves and their pasts because of this exact risk of further endangerment.

Which means, we must again answer the question: Why were some people—particularly white and wealthy women—who participated in #MeToo the ones who were heard and celebrated the most? In other words, to return to Rice's question, calling upon sensation or this book's interest in visceral rhetorics can offer us a methodology for change for those invested in activist rhetorics with some important key considerations regarding embodied or emotional expression and how that expression is inflected by one's subjectivity and thus received and represented in public. Documenting a visceral account, particularly one grounded in a sense of anger, "waxes and wanes through public life along raced, gendered, and classed lines," as Winderman notes often in ways that bolster the accounts of those already with privilege while obscuring, denying, or even challenging the expressions of those at the margins.[78]

Examining events that surround #MeToo help illustrate this point. Nearly a year after the digital movement materialized, Brett Kavanaugh faced his Supreme Court Justice hearing, and many may recall the CNN coverage of Latinx activists Ana Maria Archila and Maria Gallagher, who emotionally and forcefully confronted Arizona Senator Jeff Flake in an elevator prior to Kavanaugh's confirmation vote.[79] With her voice cracking, Archila addressed Flake, "What you are doing is allowing someone who actually violated a woman to sit on the Supreme Court. This is not tolerable."[80] When Flake tried to look down or deflect attention, Gallagher stubbornly forced his gaze, saying, "Don't look away from me."[81] She went on, "Look at me and tell me that it doesn't matter what happened to me, that you will let people like that go into the highest court of the land."[82] Archila later reflected on the moment saying, "I wanted him to feel my rage," and that while she considered participating in the #MeToo movement when it first emerged, she ultimately chose not to at the time but that what happened during the Kavanaugh hearings "forced [her] to think about it again."[83] The movement, most certainly, unleashed an emotional response among many in public, but the mainstream celebration of it during and immediately after that October 2017 night undoubtedly covered over the complexities some face when attempting to nuance or share their accounts in public. While the form of feminist *megethos* #MeToo cultivated compelled a shift in public life—one that helped nonbelievers feel the rage of victims as Archila suggests—it was one grounded in whiteness and privilege that served to prioritize the rage given in testimonies by those who fit those same archetypes examined earlier in this book. During its initial moments, it overwhelmingly embraced the anger of white and wealthy women while obscuring the opportunity to understand experiences of those like Archila or Gallagher, whose anger was most certainly more at risk of public condemnation than someone like Milano, who was falsely credited by many for starting the Me Too movement.

But feminist *megethos* as a tactic is not alone tied to this patriarchal history. Black feminists, in particular, have long been employing forms of feminist *megethos* after consistently being overlooked or disregarded by the law's—thus the state's—failure to protect them. During the late nineteenth and early twentieth centuries, Ida B. Wells-Barnett dedicated much of her time to investigating, accounting for, and distributing the long list of individuals lynched, many of whom were wrongly accused of raping white women. She published decades of this research in pamphlets like *Southern Horrors: Lynch Law in All Its Phases* and *The Red Record*, pamphlets that spread widely during their time of publication. In 2015, Janelle Monáe released what NPR called a "visceral protest song" titled "Hell You Talmbout."[84] The song, performed with members of her Wondaland Arts Society collective, vacillates between singing and deliberately and emphatically listing the names of black men and women killed by the police. The song mimics the work of #SayHerName, a social movement that similarly employs feminist *megethos* to raise awareness of black women and femmes who have been disproportionately subject to acts of racial injustice and police brutality in the United States. These mere few examples illustrate the productive and provocative value of feminist *megethos*, but they also call attention to a legacy of this form of protest implemented by black feminists in particular. Listing injustice committed against black bodies—black flesh, to recall Spillers—provokes me to respond to Rice's question by positioning an intersectional lens first and foremost when addressing sensation for the purposes of activism.

The anger that mobilized Archila and Gallagher, but also Wells-Barnett and Monáe, is subject not only to gendered assumptions but also to comingling racist, sexist, and classed ones that serve to qualify "whose speech can be interpreted as justifiably angry."[85] Giving testimony through listing, whether spoken or written, is not only about arranging and structuring the right words and actions in a particular order; rather, the emotions and flesh that buttress that testimony shape what kinds of victims are deemed acceptable in public and, as a result, the kinds of feelings deemed commendable, worthy of a public audience and even public outrage. The anger assembled by powerful white women who helped catalyze a widespread movement that eventually included many other diverse voices was nonetheless sheltered by "white, middle-class respectability."[86]

With this said, however, the movement itself doesn't seem to be going away, and frankly, it shouldn't. After Weinstein was convicted of sexual assault and rape in New York in February 2020, Me Too founder Burke shared that she was both "shocked" and "relieved," acknowledging that while many victims will not see a courtroom, Weinstein's conviction sends a message to mainstream publics of the realities of serial rapists who obtain positions of power and then abuse that power.[87] At this critical moment, Burke suggests that we need the movement now more than ever in order to "keep amplifying the voice of survivors who don't often get spotlight, who don't often get attention and don't see any recourse for the harm they experience."[88] To keep with this momentum, we must refuse to let outside commentary surrounding lists like #MeToo drown out difference. When considering what methodologies for change we need to disrupt the insidious nature of rape culture, we must acknowledge how rape culture is not only a problem of sexual violation but one that is imbricated in the multifaceted and historically rooted problems of gendered, sexist, ableist, classist, and racial oppression. Isolating a felt sense of sexual violence crimes from these other factors ignores how, following Lisa Flores, all "rhetorical meanings," especially embodied ones, "are already raced" and risks celebrating a type of visceral rhetoric devoid of these critical intersections, a project I am certainly not invested in promoting.[89] Alternatively, I follow the efforts of activists and feminists before me who have suggested that real action takes place not when we act as allies but rather as coconspirators, particularly when we might inhabit positions with more power. In other words, acting as a coconspirator recognizes and takes seriously the pervasive power of white supremacy, confronts how that power has served to protect and conceal certain identities, and ultimately works across lines of difference to change it. Activist efforts that draw upon tactics of visceral rhetorics can and should adopt this same perspective, a perspective that remains aware of how subjectivity and expression are inextricably tied to one's flesh and, furthermore, the assumptions people make of that flesh. As Jo Hsu reminds us, we must grapple with how power is "a resource that can be shared rather than hoarded," and that "those who benefit from presumed masculine authority," just like those powerful white and wealthy women who spearheaded the digital movement, "will need to shoulder responsibility for reforming gendered behavior and values."[90]

Though the movement is not without criticism, I believe scholars and activists can learn from #MeToo the value in the forms used for interrupting apathy, an apathy influenced by a long history of failing to respond to the subtle yet pervasive ways people have been subject to violence in this country. Listing doesn't seek to summarize or qualify the experience of violence but rather illustrates an enormity to a problem felt viscerally. By encouraging audiences to see a list of tweets about the current status of rape culture, #MeToo inspired publics to understand vulnerability and fear from an embodied perspective, inviting audiences to understand the public problem of sexual violence deep within their gut. In other words, to answer Rice's question, #MeToo reveals a kind of methodological hope in the sensations generated throughout the movement, a hope that must not be hastily or uncritically idealized but constantly interrogated in order to better reflect the realities many experience in everyday life when they move throughout publics. At its core, this form of feminist *megethos* holds potential for impressing upon audiences the commonplace nature of violence in the United States, a critical step because "regimes of perception confer what counts as common sense."[91] The reactions felt in one's skin and bones that result from viewing the magnitude of #MeToo provide a starting point for changing how we live, walk, and work among one another in public.

CONCLUSION: "I WAS TRAPPED IN MY BODY": WRITING AND LIVING AFTER RAPE

In July 2019, Jeffrey Epstein, a former teacher and wealthy financier, was arrested for sex trafficking of minors in Florida and New York. In addition to a federal indictment that alleged Epstein solicited sex from, exploited, and sexually abused minors, federal prosecutors found thousands of lewd photographs of girls as young as fourteen in a safe in his Manhattan mansion. While Epstein pled not guilty to the July 2019 charges, his history with pedophilia and sexual abuse dates back to 2008 when he was convicted of soliciting prostitution from a seventeen-year-old girl. During that time, federal officials identified thirty-six of Epstein's victims stemming back to cases that took place as early as 2002. Yet Epstein was sentenced to only thirteen months in custody and allowed work release out of his office six days a week. Alexander Acosta, then US Attorney for the Southern District of Florida, brokered the deal with the help of a team of federal lawyers who secretly negotiated with Epstein's lawyers and agreed to grant Epstein immunity from all federal sex trafficking charges. Nearly a decade later, Acosta would go on to become President Trump's labor secretary, and investigative journalist Julie Brown of the *Miami Herald* would unveil that the number of Epstein's victims was over eighty.[1]

That Epstein was able to evade a stiffer sentence in 2008—protected by individuals employed to uphold the law—is reminiscent of the controversial 2018 Supreme Court Justice nomination hearings when Dr. Christine Blasey Ford, a psychologist and professor at Palo Alto University, accused then US Supreme Court Justice nominee Brett Kavanaugh of a violent sexual assault that occurred in 1982 when they both were in high school. Kavanaugh, who was accused of sexual misconduct by multiple women after Ford came forward, vehemently denied all allegations and was eventually sworn in as the 114th justice to serve the nation's highest court. Appearing as a disturbing foil to what happened nearly thirty years prior when Anita Hill testified against then US Supreme Court Justice nominee Clarence Thomas, Kavanaugh's hearing—which put the very topic of sexual assault on television screens across the country—fueled several of rape culture's central tropes, including "boys will be boys," "she was drunk," and "why should we let what happened so long ago ruin his career?"

At present, Kavanaugh serves as the Supreme Court's third-youngest justice, Acosta remains unpunished though has since resigned from his post as US Labor Secretary, and Epstein, after he was denied a $77 million bail proposal and incarcerated for just over a month, died in his jail cell in August 2019 of what many considered to be his second attempt at suicide while in federal custody, dismissed of all criminal charges as a result of his death, denying dozens of women their opportunity for justice. During a televised news conference days before Acosta resigned, he defended his 2008 plea agreement decision, claiming that going to trial would have been "a roll of the dice," that prosecutors would have framed Epstein's victims as opportunists out for his money and, furthermore, would have discredited their accounts—a similar form of disbelief to which Ford was subjected in the aftermath of both her and Kavanaugh's hearings.[2] But what happened to Epstein in 2008 and Kavanaugh in 2018 is perhaps unsurprising. For it bears repeating that in 2016, the US Electoral College elected a known sexual predator to its highest-ranking political office in the country. Well into his first term, President Trump, who once publicly socialized with Epstein, was accused, yet again, of rape by E. Jean Carroll, this one occurring in a luxury department fitting room in 1996.[3] As he has done with every other sexual misconduct allegation, Trump denied Carroll's claims and responded to an interview with *The Hill* saying, "she's not my type."[4] Rape culture, in other words, is unfortunately alive and well in the United States.

While Epstein, Acosta, Kavanaugh, and Trump were each able to essentially evade criminal punishment for their crimes, former film producer Harvey Weinstein was not. After Weinstein was arrested in May 2018 by New York police for five felonies, he was found guilty in February 2020 of two counts, including sexual assault in the first degree and rape in the third degree. As I write this conclusion, he still awaits a criminal trial in Los Angeles on four felony counts despite the fact that over one hundred women have come forward with allegations of sexual harassment or assault to date.[5] Though Weinstein's conviction in New York deserves celebration, citing his sentencing of twenty-three years in prison as a mark of real progress coincides with a form of carceral feminism that has worked to criminalize those most marginalized in society through a system that simultaneously shields those with privilege from the law, individuals like Epstein, Acosta, Kavanaugh, and even Trump. In other words, while Weinstein's conviction is and should be thought of as a win, justice for rape culture cannot be left to the legal system. For one, praising Weinstein's criminal outcome as a sign of hope may lead people to understand his case as unprecedented. But the problem with rape culture is that the insidious nature of its acts and repeated offenses are most certainly precedented, normalized patterns of behavior that proliferate public life in ways that continue to go unchallenged and even unnoticed. Rarely do such mundane yet egregious offenses even make it to trial. What's worse, "the procedural norms that govern a criminal trial," writes legal scholar Lawrence Douglas, "render it a flawed tool for comprehending traumatic history."[6] When people give testimony to crimes of sexual abuse, they "bear witness to inconvenient truths" about our worlds and publics around us, truths that haunt the histories told in this country and the legacies of power and privilege this country continues to promote.[7] Putting faith in the law to apprehend the broad scope of a cultural problem such as sexual violence overlooks the need to reckon with a living history of pain and trauma that pervades US cultural life, naturalized into US society. For every Weinstein remain hundreds of other Epsteins, Acostas, Kavanaughs, and Trumps, individuals who will most certainly continue to subject people to sexual misconduct and abet offenders without punishment, reprimand, or even a glimmer of judgment. "The state will not save us," as Ashley Mack and Bryan McCann urgently caution.[8]

Knowing the shortcomings of the legal system, this book has sought to chart a different path to progress. *What It Feels Like* argues that debates about rape culture often fall trap to strategies of containment, strategies that seek to protect the subjectivities deemed most desirable in the public imaginary while negating and even expelling the affective experiences of those who have been subject to acts of sexual violence. *What It Feels Like* argues that rape culture's commonplaces—its norms, practices, and scripts—are intertwined with patriarchal and misogynist ideals linked to a vision of the nation consumed with whiteness, masculinity, ableism, and heteronormativity, one that a legal perspective alone cannot unravel. The effects of rape culture, as this book has endeavored to show, are rhetorical, lived and felt every day by vast swaths of the population. Coming to grips with its influence over public life, *What It Feels Like* has thus attempted to argue that rape culture can be challenged through the exact embodied sources of knowing it seeks to contain. Because the law is bound by norms of rationality and the roots of individual (read white and male) responsibility, inviting change requires an unrulier approach. "Having a sense of things as palpable," as Sara Ahmed has argued, "is [. . .] not unrelated to having a sense of injustice."⁹ In other words, seeking a change in how we live and move among this world requires a radical revisioning of the public sphere and the forms of communication deemed acceptable in public life. What I advocate for in the remainder of this conclusion is not a call to revise the law or its applications but rather a call to shift public consideration of rape culture by exploring visceral modes of deliberation that underscore its robust and throbbing ubiquity.

Visceral tactics, as the last two chapters outlined, hold potential for shifting public opinion, for disrupting mainstream understandings of rape and inviting audiences to apprehend the pain and risk of violence at a gut level. Encountering visceral rhetorics that seek to jolt audiences back into a bodily state, to inspire a bodily form of judgment deployed to shift public perception, moves audiences closer to the palpable understanding of the injustice Ahmed cites. While women and those subject to gendered and sexist discrimination have long been criticized for being too emotional, discredited as a result of their seemingly unruly bodies, weaponizing those bodies—and more specifically, the felt sense of simmering shame, pain, and rage—in response to the everyday, mundane, insidious nature of rape culture may be just the kind of tactic needed to disrupt what has long plagued US life.¹⁰

The work of Roxane Gay, I suggest, gives us yet another approach. In 2017, Gay released her book *Hunger: A Memoir of (My) Body* that details Gay's gripping narrative of being raped as a young girl of color, keeping what happened to herself, and then striving to make her body safe in the aftermath of rape.¹¹ She writes of her body as "unruly," detailing "the ugliest, weakest, barest parts of [her]," how "stories like [hers] are ignored or dismissed or derided."¹² In working through her trauma, body fat served a new purpose, one she frames at times as "a cage" but elsewhere describes as what "made [her] feel safe," like that of "a fortress, impermeable."¹³ As she gained weight, this form of protection—physical, visceral boundedness rooted deep within her body's insides well within the surface of her skin—began to jar with her sense of self: "I was trapped in my body, one I made but barely recognized or understood. I was miserable, but I was safe."¹⁴

Gay's memoir teaches us yet one more aspect of visceral rhetorics I want to impart upon readers in these last words: that justice is about reckoning with the fear of rape, a matter of visceral safety that can only be sensed, grasped deep within the body, reflective of the day-to-day feelings victims of rape and sexual assault witness of their own embodied being in the world. When a person experiences rape or sexual assault, that felt safety is threatened—the visceral boundaries of the body violated—but that embodied, affective risk doesn't end with the physical act of rape. "Feeling comfortable," writes Gay, "is not entirely about ideals. It's about how I feel in my skin and bones, from one day to the next."[15] Grappling with rape culture is not simply a matter of counting the number of victims who have been subject to such crimes or turning to a prejudiced legal system in order to prove sexual assault occurs at such a pervasive scale; rather, it's about coming to grips with the ongoing triggers of past memories, the anxiety of wondering if you will experience violence (again), the affective dread that conditions how some bodies walk and move among public space with fear and pain clenched within their bodies, clutched to their organs. Living in a rape culture is undeniably visceral.

Patriarchal frameworks have conditioned publics to interrogate victims, to metaphorically put them on trial, to grant a perpetrator's perception as a more realistic portrayal of "what happened." Writes Gay, "He said/she said is why so many victims [. . .] don't come forward. All too often, what 'he said' matters more, so we just swallow the truth. We swallow it, and more often than not, that truth turns rancid. It spreads through the body like an infection. It becomes depression or addiction or obsession or some other physical manifestation of the silence of what she would have said, needed to say, couldn't say."[16] The aftermath of rape lives on and in one's body, swallowed and digested into it. Silence percolates under the surface. It manifests and takes hold of the body, spreading throughout its edges and insides like contagion or poison. The cultural reality of sexual violence that we live with is a syndrome come to be seen as normal, invading certain bodies in our society. Until we let this truth out—release knowledge of a noxious, everyday reality of rape culture that is infecting some bodies and shaping an everyday fear of violation—the threat of violence will live on and inequity will continue. We need release. The valve is about to burst.

In November 2017—in the midst of the Harvey Weinstein scandal and one year after Trump was elected president—the *New York Times* published the editorial "Brave Enough to Be Angry," by recurring opinion writer Lindy West.[17] The editorial opens with a response given by actress Uma Thurman to an *Access Hollywood* reporter who inquired about Hollywood's abuse of power to which Thurman stated, "I have learned that when I've spoken in anger I usually regret the way I express myself. So I've been waiting to feel less angry. And when I'm ready, I'll say what I have to say."[18] Thurman's response went viral, taking shape in memes and short clips that circulated throughout social media networks, cheered by many, no doubt, because of the privilege Thurman holds. Nonetheless, it provided the exigency for West's editorial, which delves into longstanding and widespread misogynist norms that ask women not only to comply with and endure sexual violence but then to contain their feelings and remain silent, poisoned with the truth of what happened, infested throughout their bodies, as Gay makes clear. In other words, Thurman's account of quieted anger parallels how Gay describes the experience of remaining silent, smoldering with her own shame and hurt, swallowed deep within her because the alternative put her at greater risk. Similarly describing the expectation of silence thrust upon women, West writes, "We are seething at how long we have been ignored, seething for the ones who were long ago punished for telling the truth, seething for being told all our lives that we have no right to seethe."[19] West's essay, like Gay's memoir and Thurman's reflections, captures a public feeling of palpable injustice—bubbling, unexpressed, silenced rage that calls Ahmed's words to mind. While it emerged publicly during #MeToo, such rage has long stewed in the lives of those feminized by their gender comportment. Yet the days of quietly seething in our own bodies—clenching our fists, grinding our teeth, choking back tears, lowering our voices, *living in this silenced visceral rhetorical state of outrage*, in other words—are over. It's time that we let our boiling rage seep out and affect others. It's time that we pierce those who are apathetic to or disbelieving of the commonplaces of rape culture with our own fiercely felt attachment to pain and violence in everyday life.

A reality of rape culture in the United States has been trapped within individual bodies, percolating under the surface, long overdue for release. Like Gay and others, writing how we feel living in the aftermath of rape compels others to feel what we've felt, and the public needs such accounts, now more than ever. Writing from the place of pain is not simply a tactical rhetorical act but rather one of survival, similar to how Barbara Christian theorized the act of writing itself: "But what I write and how I write is done in order to save my own life. And I mean that literally. For me literature is a way of knowing that I am not hallucinating, that whatever I feel/know *is*. It is the affirmation that sensuality is intelligence, that sensual language is language that makes sense."[20] Protesting rape culture by carrying a dorm mattress throughout New York City, documenting the experience of bodily loss felt in a hospital room after being violated behind a dumpster, listing quite literally millions of sexual assault experiences on Twitter feeds across the globe, accounting for the horrors of rape and the desire to gain weight in order to feel safe as a result—these are acts of composing with and through the body that are for many a "refus[al] to stay in their assigned 'proper place.'"[21] Such visceral forms of writing and living make clear that "a body in touch with a world can become a body that fears the touch of a world."[22] Justice for those most subjected to rape culture is not merely about legal recognition. Justice for rape culture requires changing how we apprehend the embodied vulnerability of others around us—the pervasiveness of violence that conditions victims to remain hushed in the aftermath, trapped within a body infected by silence, rancid with culturally and historically conditioned claims seeking to deny a lived, felt reality of what happened. Justice for rape culture demands that some be bombarded with feeling the pain of merely existing in this world in the aftermath of rape, that skins crawl and stomachs sink and hearts wrench and consciences quake while being overwhelmed with the seething anger that represents what it feels like for many to live in rape culture.

NOTES

PREFACE

1. These scholars, among many others, come to mind when I think back to my earliest studies of bodies and affect: Sara Ahmed, Lauren Berlant, Judith Butler, Ann Cvetkovich, Karma Chávez, Jay Dolmage, Roxane Gay, Debra Hawhee, Jenell Johnson, Sara McKinnon, Sianne Ngai, Margaret Price, Jasbir Puar, Elaine Scarry, Eve Sedgwick, and Hortense Spillers.
2. Harrell, "Crime Against Persons."
3. James et al., *Report*, 13.
4. Spillers, "Mama's Baby"; McGuire, *At the Dark End*; Willingham, "To the Harvard Law 19"; King, "We Need to Include."
5. For more on this form of optimism, see Berlant, *Cruel Optimism*.

INTRODUCTION

1. Halicek, "Lansing/Statement," https://inourownwords.us/2018/08/08/megan-halicek.
2. While I recognize the important and necessary debates regarding the language used to call people who experience rape or sexual assault (e.g., survivor, victim), I ultimately use the term "victim" to remember the lack of choice inherent in sexual assault. Furthermore, using the term "victim" is also an attempt to avoid the term "woman" when discussing rape culture so as to not assume a particular type of body subject to sexual violence. For more on this decision, see Larson, "Survivors, Liars, and Unfit Minds."
3. From January 16, 2018, to January 24, 2018, over 204 victims offered victim impact statements in two courtrooms regarding the abuse they received by Nassar. As the case unfolded, many of these testimonies disseminated widely beyond the courtroom over this nine-day period and afterward. A simple Google search about the Nassar case and its victim impact statements will reveal the widespread coverage about the case and the victim testimonies in particular, but some key publications organized and collected these testimonies. Overwhelmingly, media and public coverage of the Nassar case validated these testimonies and cited the Nassar case as progress in the fight for justice for sexual violence. For more on these victim impact statements, see Correa and Louttit, "More than 160 Women"; May, "Here's What Happened," https://www.usatoday.com/story/news/nation-now/2018/01/30/heres-what-happened-each-day-lassar-nassars-hearing/1078324001; Rahal and Kozlowski, "204 Impact Statements," https://www.detroitnews.com/story/news/local/michigan/2018/02/08/204-impact-statements-9-days-2-counties-life-sentence-larry-nassar/1066335001;"LarryNassar's Survivors," https://www.npr.org/2018/12/07/674525176/larry-nassars-survivors-speak-and-finally-the-world-listens-and-believes.
4. Bernstein, "Sexual Politics," 143–45.
5. Buchwald, Fletcher, and Roth, "Preamble," xi.

6. Ibid.
7. Hill, "SlutWalk as Perifeminist Response," 26.
8. Pateman, "Women and Consent"; MacKinnon, *Toward a Feminist Theory*; Kimberlé Crenshaw, "Demarginalizing the Intersection"; Kimberlé Crenshaw, "Mapping the Margins"; Carrie Crenshaw, "Normality"; Picart, "Rhetorically Reconfiguring"; McKinnon, *Gendered Asylum*; Gilmore, *Tainted Witness*; Ore, *Lynching*.
9. Gilmore, *Tainted Witness*, 136.
10. While early critiques of rape that took place during the late twentieth century cited the law as a key problem in regulating female sexuality, this book traces the law's pervasive presence in public discourse today. See primarily Brownmiller, *Against Our Will*; Estrich, *Real Rape*.
11. In theorizing this "bodily intensity," I build on Jenell Johnson's theory of the "visceral public," which I describe shortly.
12. Glenn, *Unspoken*; Ratcliffe, *Rhetorical Listening*; Glenn and Ratcliffe, *Silence and Listening*.
13. Hill, "SlutWalk as Perifeminist Response," 24.
14. Bevacqua, *Rape on the Public Agenda*; Bumiller, *In an Abusive State*; Mardorossian, *Framing the Rape Victim*; Andrus, *Entextualizing Domestic Violence*; Gilmore, *Tainted Witness*; Propen and Schuster, *Rhetoric and Communication Perspectives*; Quinlan, *Technoscientific Witness*.
15. Collins, *Black Sexual Politics*, 225.
16. Second-wave feminists like Andrea Dworkin, Catharine MacKinnon, and Susan Brownmiller helped popularize the phrase's usage.
17. Bevacqua, *Rape on the Public Agenda*, 9.
18. Lonsway and Fitzgerald, "Rape Myths," 14.
19. Collins, *Black Sexual Politics*, 223.
20. Hall, "'It Can Happen to You,'" 3.
21. MacKinnon, *Toward a Feminist Theory*, 178.
22. Hall, "'It Can Happen to You,'" 3.
23. Ibid.
24. Carlson, *Crimes of Womanhood*, 75–76.
25. In addition to typifying the victim, these cases also construct a vision of the perpetrator as nonwhite and deemed outside the boundaries of normative social order.
26. Bumiller, *In an Abusive State*, 9.
27. Kimberlé Crenshaw, "Demarginalizing the Intersection," 157, emphasis in original.
28. Bumiller, *In an Abusive State*, 9.
29. Ibid., 7.
30. In fact, according to RAINN, eight out of ten victims know their rapist. See "Perpetrators of Sexual Violence," https://www.rainn.org/statistics/perpetrators-sexual-violence.
31. Collins, *Black Sexual Politics*, 217.
32. Ibid., emphasis in original.
33. For more on this history of male dominance and white supremacy, see Headlee and Biewen, "Episode 50," http://www.sceneonradio.org/episode-50-feminism-in-black-and-white-men-part-4.
34. For more on a decolonial feminist critique of gender-based violence, see Mack and Na'puti, "Our Bodies."
35. Solinger, *Pregnancy and Power*," 29.
36. Fixmer-Oraiz, *Homeland Maternity*, 7.
37. Feinstein, *When Rape Was Legal*, 3.

38. Ibid.
39. Andrus, *Entextualizing Domestic Violence*, 31.
40. Ibid., 32.
41. Ibid., 23.
42. MacKinnon, *Toward a Feminist Theory*, 172, 180.
43. "Criminal Justice System," https://www.rainn.org/statistics/criminal-justice-system.
44. Butler, *Antigone's Claim*, 21.
45. That is, US cultural and sexual norms feminize those who are penetrated by penises, which is why this archetype is always imagined as white and female, complicating who can speak about rape.
46. Gilmore, *Tainted Witness*, 2.
47. Ahmed, *Living a Feminist Life*, 65.
48. Ibid.
49. Hawhee, *Moving Bodies*, 28.
50. For more on the history of rhetoric's relationship to the body, see Chávez, "Body."
51. DeLuca, "Unruly Arguments"; Brouwer, "Precarious Visibility Politics"; Hauser, "Incongruous Bodies"; Selzer and Crowley, *Rhetorical Bodies*.
52. Hawhee, *Moving Bodies*, 7.
53. Chávez, "Body," 243.
54. Hawhee, *Moving Bodies*, 7.
55. Dolmage, *Disability Rhetoric*, 69, 5.
56. Hill, "SlutWalk as Perifeminist Response," 26.
57. Koerber, *From Hysteria to Hormones*, xiv.
58. MacKinnon, "Feminism, Marxism"; Foss and Griffin, "Feminist Perspective"; Alcoff and Gray, "Survivor Discourse"; Foss and Foss, "Personal Experience"; Foss and Griffin, "Beyond Persuasion"; Palczewski, "Survivor Testimony"; Pickering, "Women's Voices"; hooks, *Talking Back*; Gilmore, *Tainted Witness*.
59. Sutton, "Taming of Polos/Polis," 107.
60. Smith and Hyde, "Rethinking 'The Public'"; Hariman and Lucaites, "Dissent and Emotional Management"; Cloud, "Therapy, Silence, and War"; Rice, *Distant Publics*; Papacharissi, *Affective Publics*; Johnson, "'Man's Mouth Is His Castle'"; Yergeau, *Authoring Autism*.
61. Johnson, "'Man's Mouth Is His Castle,'" 3, emphasis in original.
62. Ibid., 4, emphasis in original. For more on Massumi's theory of affect, see *Parables*. In addition to Johnson, this book is indebted to Bernadette Marie Calafell and her work on theories of the flesh, which paved a foundation for rhetoricians interested in interrogating the everyday and lived experience. For more, see Calafell, "Rhetorics of Possibility."
63. Rice, *Distant Publics*, 6.
64. Scarry, *Body in Pain*, 4.
65. Ahmed, *Cultural Politics*, 27.
66. Shildrick, *Leaky Bodies*, 214–15; Johnson, "'Man's Mouth Is His Castle,'" 5.
67. Spillers, "Mama's Baby," 67.
68. Ibid.
69. Ibid., 68.
70. Ibid., 67.
71. Weheliye, *Habeas Viscus*, 11.
72. Ibid., 12.
73. For scholars engaging with a similar assessment of risk, see, Scott, *Risky Rhetoric* and Fixmer-Oraiz, *Homeland Maternity*.

74. Ahmed, *Living a Feminist Life*, 27.
75. Gilmore, *Tainted Witness*, 19.
76. Brennan, *Transmission of Affect*, 5.
77. Ibid., 3.
78. Johnson, "'Man's Mouth Is His Castle,'" 3; Hawhee, *Rhetoric in Tooth and Claw*, 6.
79. Cvetkovich, *Depression*, 4.
80. Ibid.
81. Massumi, *Parables*, 23–45.
82. Butler, *Frames of War*, 34.
83. Ibid.
84. Johnson, "'Man's Mouth Is His Castle,'" 5.
85. Spillers, "Mama's Baby," 68.
86. Johnson, "'Man's Mouth Is His Castle,'" 4.
87. Ahmed, *Cultural Politics*, 24; Scarry, *Body in Pain*, 3–26.
88. Ahmed, *Cultural Politics*, 5.
89. Jack, "Acts of Institution"; Hallenbeck, "Toward a Posthuman Perspective"; Price, "Bodymind Problem"; Walters, *Rhetorical Touch*; Teston, *Bodies in Flux*.
90. United States, *Attorney General's Commission on Pornography*, 326.
91. Butler, *Frames of War*, 2010; Puar, *Right to Maim*.

CHAPTER 1

1. In October 2019, President Trump awarded Meese the Presidential Medal of Freedom, the highest honor the US government can give. The award met much controversy not only because it was bestowed in the midst of Trump's impeachment proceedings but also given Meese's troubled history as attorney general involving three foreign affairs scandals in addition to his work with the Commission on Pornography.
2. United States, *Attorney General's Commission*, 1957.
3. United States, *Attorney General's Commission*, 326.
4. McNulty, "Federal Report," http://articles.chicagotribune.com/1986-07-10/news/8602180951_1_pornography-commission-chairman-henry-hudson-acts-of-sexual-violence.
5. United States, *Meese Commission Exposed*.
6. Fielding, "Examining an Argument"; Palczewski, "Survivor Testimony"; Hauser, "Reshaping Publics"; Vance, "Negotiating Sex."
7. For more on responses to the Meese Commission, see Burger, "Meese Report."
8. Letters analyzed in this chapter were collected from the archival papers of commission member Park Elliott Dietz at the Arthur J. Morris Law Library at the University of Virginia.
9. For more on these frameworks, see Butler, *Frames of War*; Puar, *Right to Maim*; McRuer, *Crip Times*.
10. This chapter adds to a growing body of literature in rhetorical studies that has investigated the relationship between sexuality and the nation-state. See, for example, Ono and Sloop, *Shifting Borders*; Sloop, *Disciplining Gender*; Bennett, *Banning Queer Blood*; Chávez, *Queer Migration Politics*; West, *Transforming Citizenships*; McKinnon, *Gendered Asylum*; Fixmer-Oraiz, *Homeland Maternity*.
11. Gould, *Moving Politics*; Panagia, *Political Life*; Puar, *Terrorist Assemblages*, 215.
12. Gould, *Moving Politics*, 19.
13. In assessing how risk is categorized by letter writers, I draw from the work of Scott and Fixmer-Oraiz. See Scott, *Risky Rhetoric*; Fixmer-Oraiz, *Homeland Maternity*.

14. Zarefsky, "Four Senses," 30.
15. Duggan, *Twilight of Equality*, 4, emphasis in original.
16. McRuer, *Crip Times*, 14.
17. Dingo, *Networking Arguments*, 10.
18. For a rhetorical perspective on how this era has shaped US politics, see Ian Barnard, "Rhetorical Commonsense."
19. Garland, *Culture of Control*.
20. Bumiller, *In an Abusive State*, 7.
21. Ibid., xii.
22. Butler, *Frames of War*; Butler, *Precarious Life*.
23. Butler, *Frames of War*, 1.
24. Ibid., 30.
25. Puar, *Right to Maim*, xv.
26. Ibid., 13.
27. Ibid., 11.
28. Wingard, *Branded Bodies*, 9.
29. Fixmer-Oraiz, *Homeland Maternity*, 17.
30. Kaplan, Alarcon, and Moallem, *Between Woman and Nation*; Mohanty, *Feminism Without Borders*; Grewal, *Transnational America*; Moghadam, *Globalization and Social Movements*.
31. McRuer, *Crip Times*, 8, 23–24.
32. For more on cripping, see Sandahl, "Queering the Crip"; Kafer, *Feminist, Queer, Crip*.
33. Vance, "Negotiating Sex," 361.
34. I say this not to claim or suggest that average citizens weren't writing into the commission with criticism of it, but rather to acknowledge the limits of the archive used in this study.
35. Bishop E. Harold Jensen to Alan Sears, 6 January 1986, Box 5, Folder 1, The Papers of Park Elliott Dietz for the Attorney General's Commission on Pornography, MSS 86-1, Arthur J. Morris Law Library, University of Virginia School of Law.
36. Ibid.
37. Ibid.
38. Rev. William C. Wantland to Alan Sears, 8 January 1986, Box 1, Folder 2, The Papers of Park Elliott Dietz for the Attorney General's Commission on Pornography, MSS 86-1, Arthur J. Morris Law Library, University of Virginia School of Law.
39. Butler, *Frames of War*, 3–4.
40. Jane Barnett to Park Elliott Dietz, 23 October 1985, Box 1, Folder 5, The Papers of Park Elliott Dietz for the Attorney General's Commission on Pornography, MSS 86-1, Arthur J. Morris Law Library, University of Virginia School of Law.
41. Ibid.
42. Ibid.
43. Ibid.
44. Ibid.
45. Curtis Maynard to Henry Hudson, 4 February 1986, Box 1, Folder 2, The Papers of Park Elliott Dietz for the Attorney General's Commission on Pornography, MSS 86-1, Arthur J. Morris Law Library, University of Virginia School of Law.
46. Puar, *Right to Maim*, xix.
47. Nancy Adinolfe to Edwin Meese, n.d., Box 1, Folder 2, The Papers of Park Elliott Dietz for the Attorney General's Commission on Pornography, MSS 86-1, Arthur J. Morris Law Library, University of Virginia School of Law.
48. Berlant, *Queen of America*, 16.

49. Dr. R. Donald Shafer to Alan Sears, 2 January 1986, Box 1, Folder 2, The Papers of Park Elliott Dietz for the Attorney General's Commission on Pornography, MSS 86-1, Arthur J. Morris Law Library, University of Virginia School of Law.

50. Bishop E. Harold Jensen to Alan Sears, 6 January 1986, Box 5, Folder 1, The Papers of Park Elliott Dietz for the Attorney General's Commission on Pornography, MSS 86-1, Arthur J. Morris Law Library, University of Virginia School of Law.

51. Ronald and Leslie Pasquini to Park Elliott Dietz, 16 April 2086, Box 1, Folder 5, The Papers of Park Elliott Dietz for the Attorney General's Commission on Pornography, MSS 86-1, Arthur J. Morris Law Library, University of Virginia School of Law, emphasis in original.

52. Ibid.

53. Ibid.

54. Rubin, "Blood Under the Bridge," 37.

55. Ibid.

56. Berlant, *Queen of America*; Berlant and Warner, "Sex in Public"; Warner, *Publics and Counterpublics*; Edelman, *No Future*; McRuer, *Crip Theory*.

57. Berlant, *Queen of America*, 5.

58. Berlant and Warner, "Sex in Public," 553.

59. McRuer, *Crip Times*, 14.

60. Curtis Maynard to Henry Hudson, 4 February 1986, Box 1, Folder 2, The Papers of Park Elliott Dietz for the Attorney General's Commission on Pornography, MSS 86-1, Arthur J. Morris Law Library, University of Virginia School of Law.

61. Puar, *Right to Maim*, 13.

62. Curtis Maynard to Henry Hudson, 4 February 1986, Box 1, Folder 2, The Papers of Park Elliott Dietz for the Attorney General's Commission on Pornography, MSS 86-1, Arthur J. Morris Law Library, University of Virginia School of Law.

63. Barnard, "Rhetorical Commonsense," 11.

64. While homophobia may not have been the specific source of anxiety for Maynard, fear mongering shaped this cultural moment, manifested through a range of zoning legislation and public health initiatives that targeted gay men, sex workers, immigrants, and people of color, producing a social agenda that functioned by repressing certain social groups.

65. Brown, *Undoing the Demos*, 62.

66. Eileen Roth to Park Elliott Dietz, 19 April 1986, Box 1, Folder 5, The Papers of Park Elliott Dietz for the Attorney General's Commission on Pornography, MSS 86-1, Arthur J. Morris Law Library, University of Virginia School of Law.

67. Ibid.

68. Ibid.

69. Sylvia Harbison Phillips to Henry Hudson, 17 April 1986, Box 1, Folder 4, The Papers of Park Elliott Dietz for the Attorney General's Commission on Pornography, MSS 86-1, Arthur J. Morris Law Library, University of Virginia School of Law.

70. Ibid.

71. Rev. William C. Wantland to Alan Sears, 8 January 1986, Box 1, Folder 2, The Papers of Park Elliott Dietz for the Attorney General's Commission on Pornography, MSS 86-1, Arthur J. Morris Law Library, University of Virginia School of Law.

72. Ibid.

73. Ibid.

74. Browning, *Infectious Rhythm*, 54.

75. Ibid., 77.

76. Nancy Adinolfe to Edwin Meese, n.d., Box 1, Folder 2, The Papers of Park Elliott Dietz for the Attorney General's Commission on Pornography, MSS 86-1, Arthur J. Morris Law Library, University of Virginia School of Law.

77. Sara Brown to Attorney General's Commission on Pornography, n.d., Box 1, Folder 5, The Papers of Park Elliott Dietz for the Attorney General's Commission on Pornography, MSS 86-1, Arthur J. Morris Law Library, University of Virginia School of Law.

78. Statement of Representative Frank R. Wolf before the Attorney General's Commission on Pornography, 19 June 1985, Box 1, Folder 10, The Papers of Park Elliott Dietz for the Attorney General's Commission on Pornography, MSS 86-1, Arthur J. Morris Law Library, University of Virginia School of Law.

79. Matthew F. Carney III to the Attorney General's Commission on Pornography, 25 April 1986, Box 1, Folder 5, The Papers of Park Elliott Dietz for the Attorney General's Commission on Pornography, MSS 86-1, Arthur J. Morris Law Library, University of Virginia School of Law.

80. Ibid.
81. Ibid., emphasis added.
82. Fixmer-Oraiz, *Homeland Maternity*, 4.

83. Sylvia Harbison Phillips to Henry Hudson, 17 April 1986, Box 1, Folder 4, The Papers of Park Elliott Dietz for the Attorney General's Commission on Pornography, MSS 86-1, Arthur J. Morris Law Library, University of Virginia School of Law.

84. Ibid.
85. Fixmer-Oraiz, *Homeland Maternity*, 6.
86. Ore, *Lynching*, 39.

87. Carrie Crenshaw, "'Protection' of 'Woman'"; Carrie Crenshaw, "Normality"; Gibson, "Judicial Rhetoric"; Picart, "Rhetorically Reconfiguring"; Ray and Richards, "Inventing Citizens"; Carlson, *Crimes of Womanhood*; Schuster and Propen, *Victim Advocacy*; McKinnon, *Gendered Asylum*.

88. Ryan, "Public," 15–16.
89. Sutton, "Taming of Polos/Polis," 101, 102.

90. Richard L. Dowhower to the Attorney General's Commission on Pornography, 5 October 1986, Box 5, Folder 1, The Papers of Park Elliott Dietz for the Attorney General's Commission on Pornography, MSS 86-1, Arthur J. Morris Law Library, University of Virginia School of Law.

91. Ibid.
92. Ibid.
93. Ibid., emphasis in original.
94. Ore, *Lynching*, 20.
95. Palczewski, "Survivor Testimony," 262.
96. Many thanks to Natalie Fixmer-Oraiz for helping me nuance this point.

97. While I acknowledge the archive's limitations, it is important to note that the few letters I did come across that were critical of the commission took the perspective of First Amendment rights when critiquing the commission. Kellie Everts's letter (discussed next) was the only letter I came across that took the perspective of gender equality when critiquing the commission.

98. Kellie Everts to Alan Sears, 21 March 1986, Box 1, Folder 2, The Papers of Park Elliott Dietz for the Attorney General's Commission on Pornography, MSS 86-1, Arthur J. Morris Law Library, University of Virginia School of Law.

99. Ibid., emphasis in original.
100. Ibid.
101. Duggan, *Twilight*, 70.
102. Ibid., 81, emphasis in original.

103. For a timeline of events, see Kelly and Estepa, "Brett Kavanaugh," https://www.usatoday.com/story/news/politics/onpolitics/2018/09/24/brett-kavanaugh-allegations-timeline-supreme-court/1408073002.

104. Farrow and Mayer, "Senate Democrats," https://www.newyorker.com/news/news-desk/senate-democrats-investigate-a-new-allegation-of-sexual-misconduct-from-the-supreme-court-nominee-brett-kavanaughs-college-years-deborah-ramirez.

105. Associated Press, "Memorable Quotes," https://apnews.com/article/d044d1c4577543dc89bb269d8130ea0b.

106. "Brett Kavanaugh's Opening Statement," https://www.nytimes.com/2018/09/26/us/politics/read-brett-kavanaughs-complete-opening-statement.html.

107. "Brett Kavanaugh's Opening Statement," https://www.nytimes.com/2018/09/26/us/politics/read-brett-kavanaughs-complete-opening-statement.html.

108. St. Félix, "The Ford-Kavanaugh Hearing," https://www.newyorker.com/culture/cultural-comment/the-ford-kavanaugh-hearings-will-be-remembered-for-their-grotesque-display-of-patriarchal-resentment.

109. Jennifer Slye Aniskovich et al. to Charles Grassley and Dianne Feinstein, September 14, 2018, https://www.judiciary.senate.gov/imo/media/doc/2018-09-14%2065%20Women%20who%20know%20Kavanaugh%20from%20High%20School%20-%20Kavanaugh%20Nomination.pdf.

110. Ibid.

111. Coppins, "Trump Cares About Only One Audience," https://www.theatlantic.com/politics/archive/2019/01/trump-mocks-christine-blasey-ford-rally/580069.

112. Fixmer-Oraiz, *Homeland Maternity*, 23.

113. Butler, *Frames of War*, 2–3.

114. Butler, *Precarious Life*, 33–34.

CHAPTER 2

1. Katz, "Violence Against Women," https://www.ted.com/talks/jackson_katz_violence_against_women_it_s_a_men_s_issue.

2. Ibid.

3. Ibid.

4. Ibid.

5. Ibid.

6. Ibid.

7. Mentors in Violence Prevention, "MVP Strategies," https://www.mvpstrat.com/about.

8. While I do not intend to suggest that campaigns like the ones analyzed in this chapter or those Katz supports are maliciously intended, I do seek to examine how bystander discourses produce certain logics about rape culture and who it involves, logics that serve to represent the problem and shape what responses to it are available.

9. Ore, *Lynching*, 73.

10. Barnard, "Rhetorical Commonsense," 12.

11. Ibid., 8.

12. Many thanks to Earl Brooks for helping me nuance the concept of patriarchal spectrality in relation to Ore's work.

13. Ore, *Lynching*, 50.

14. Gordon, *Ghostly Matters*, 139.

15. Young, *Responsibility for Justice*, 95–122.

16. Ibid., 105.

17. For more on the history of rape prevention, see Bevacqua, *Rape on the Public Agenda*.

18. Hall, "'It Can Happen to You,'" 3.
19. Ibid.
20. For more on the campaign and its central promotional video, see Somanader, "President Obama," https://obamawhitehouse.archives.gov/blog/2014/09/19/president-obama-launches-its-us-campaign-end-sexual-assault-campus.
21. For more on the campaign, see "Protecting Students from Sexual Assault," https://www.justice.gov/ovw/protecting-students-sexual-assault.
22. "1 is 2 Many," https://obamawhitehouse.archives.gov/1is2many.
23. Banyard, Plante, and Moynihan, "Rape Prevention," https://www.ncjrs.gov/pdffiles1/nij/grants/208701.pdf.
24. Banyard, Moynihan, and Plante, "Sexual Violence Prevention," 464.
25. McMahon, Postmus, and Koenick, "Conceptualizing the Engaging Bystander Approach," 117, 118.
26. King, "We Need to Include," https://www.thenation.com/article/need-include-black-womens-experience-movement-campus-sexual-assault.
27. Mack and McCann, "Critiquing," 329.
28. Bliss, "Black Feminism," 729.
29. Hill, "SlutWalk as a Perifeminist Response," 27.
30. Del Pilar Blanco and Peeren, *Spectralities Reader*, 2.
31. Derrida, *Specters of Marx*; Gordon, *Ghostly Matters*; Buse and Stott, *Ghosts*; Weinstock, *Spectral America*; Cho, *Haunting the Korean Diaspora*; Rabaté, *Ghosts of Modernity*; Del Pilar Blanco and Peeren, *Spectralities Reader*; Dziuban, "Spectral Turn"; Coly, *Postcolonial Hauntologies*.
32. Del Pilar Blanco and Peeren, *Spectralities Reader*, 310.
33. Coly, *Postcolonial Hauntologies*, 5.
34. Finnegan, "Recognizing Lincoln," 33.
35. Barnard, "Rhetorical Commonsense," 7.
36. Hesford and Kozol, *Haunting Violations*; Bernard-Donals, *Witnessing the Disaster*; Chambers, *Untimely Interventions*; Gunn, "Mourning Speech"; Gunn, "Mourning Humanism"; Bernard-Donals, *Forgetful Memory*; Ballif, "Writing the Event."
37. Peters, *Speaking into the Air*, 1.
38. Weinstock, *Spectral America*, 6.
39. Campt, *Listening to Images*, 6.
40. Ibid., 6.
41. Ibid., 8.
42. "It's On Us," https://www.itsonus.org. This language has since changed, but its message can be found in "Our Story," https://www.itsonus.org/our-story.
43. The White House Office of the Press Secretary, "Fact Sheet," https://obamawhitehouse.archives.gov/the-press-office/2017/01/05/fact-sheet-final-its-us-summit-and-report-white-house-task-force-protect.
44. "Take The Pledge," https://www.itsonus.org/pledge. The presence of the statements that guide the pledge have been removed from the website since the campaign's initial inception.
45. Gordon, *Ghostly Matters*, 14.
46. Somanader, "President Obama," https://obamawhitehouse.archives.gov/blog/2014/09/19/president-obama-launches-its-us-campaign-end-sexual-assault-campus.
47. Panagia, *Political Life*, 2.
48. Gordon, *Ghostly Matters*, 8.
49. Ore, *Lynching*, 48.
50. Coly, *Postcolonial Hauntologies*, 2.
51. Gordon, *Ghostly Matters*, 8.

52. The initial pledge page has since been modified on the It's On Us website. To see how the original pledge has been taken up by other colleges and universities, see, for example, "It's On Us," Stories of Cobber Life, Concordia College, accessed July 3, 2019, https://www.concordiacollege.edu/stories/details/it-s-on-us.

53. "Take The Pledge," https://www.itsonus.org/pledge.

54. Austin, *How to Do Things with Words*.

55. Ibid., 109.

56. Hariman and Lucaites, *No Caption Needed*, 2.

57. Olson, *Constitutive Visions*, 9.

58. "1 is 2 Many," https://obamawhitehouse.archives.gov/1is2many.

59. "1 is 2 Many," https://obamawhitehouse.archives.gov/1is2many.

60. Hill, "SlutWalk as a Perifeminist Response," 24.

61. Rhodes, "SlutWalk Is Not Enough."

62. Ibid., 99.

63. Jarrett, "A Renewed Call," https://obamawhitehouse.archives.gov/blog/2014/01/22/renewed-call-action-end-rape-and-sexual-assault.

64. Ibid.

65. Ibid.

66. Rhodes, "SlutWalk Is Not Enough," 102.

67. Asen, "Imagining in the Public Sphere," 347.

68. Hawhee, "Looking into Aristotle's Eyes," 141.

69. Ibid., 140.

70. Ibid.

71. Ibid.

72. Clark, *Rhetorical Landscapes*, 14.

73. Ibid.

74. Russonello, "Read Oprah Winfrey's Golden Globes Speech," https://www.nytimes.com/2018/01/07/movies/oprah-winfrey-golden-globes-speech-transcript.html.

75. Ibid.

76. Ibid.

77. McGuire, *At the Dark End*, 171.

78. Butler, *Frames of War*, 12.

79. Hill, "Ghostly Surrogates," 187.

80. Ibid.

81. Puar, *Right to Maim*, 19.

CHAPTER 3

1. Cullen, "Survivor Shares," http://will.illinois.edu/news/story/survivor-shares-experience-with-rape-kit-testing.

2. Ibid.

3. Tofte, *Testing Justice*, https://www.hrw.org/report/2009/03/31/testing-justice/rape-kit-backlog-los-angeles-city-and-county.

4. Hylton, "The Dark Side," http://nation.time.com/2013/09/07/the-dark-side-of-clearing-americas-rape-kit-backlog.

5. "What's Being Done," http://www.npr.org/2016/01/17/463358406/whats-being-done-to-address-the-countrys-backlog-of-untested-rape-kits.

6. "Neglected Law," http://www.nytimes.com/2002/05/09/opinion/a-neglected-law-enforcement-asset.html; Tofte, "A Test of Justice," http://www.washingtonpost.com/wp-dyn/content/article/2008/07/21/AR2008072102359.html.

7. Kristof, "Despite DNA," https://www.nytimes.com/2015/05/10/opinion/sunday/nicholas-kristof-despite-dna-the-rapist-got-away.html.
8. Quinlan, *Technoscientific Witness*, 7.
9. Jack, "Leviathan and the Breast Pump," 208, emphasis in original.
10. Mulla, *Violence of Care*, 227.
11. "Get Statistics," https://www.nsvrc.org/statistics.
12. Conley and O'Barr, *Just Words*, 17.
13. Kimberlé Crenshaw, "Whose Story," 405.
14. Smart, *Feminism and the Power*, 50.
15. Conley and O'Barr, *Just Words*, 21.
16. Du Mont, White, and McGregor, "Investigating the Medical"; Brewer and Ley, "Media Use"; Patterson and Campbell, "Problem"; Corrigan, "New Trial"; Mulla, *Violence of Care*; Campbell, Shaw, and Fehler-Cabral, "Shelving Justice"; Quinlan, *Technoscientific Witness*; Yung, "Rape Law Gatekeeping"; Campbell, Shaw, and Fehler-Cabral, "Evaluation of a Victim-Centered"; Campbell and Fehler-Cabral, "Why Police Couldn't."
17. Corrigan, "New Trial," 921.
18. Campbell, Shaw, and Fehler-Cabral, "Evaluation of a Victim-Centered," 381.
19. Yung, "Rape Law Gatekeeping," 209.
20. Quinlan, *Technoscientific Witness*, 13.
21. Mulla, *Violence of Care*, 42.
22. Ibid.
23. Quinlan, *Technoscientific Witness*, 13.
24. Ibid., 10.
25. While the legal outcomes do not find what happened to count as rape, I take point from Chanel Miller's testimony of the experience, which categorizes what happened as rape.
26. Rocha and Winton, "Light Sentence," https://www.latimes.com/local/lanow/la-me-ln-stanford-sexual-assault-sentence-20160607-snap-story.html.
27. While rape kits on their own do hold agency over bodies, my analysis considers human involvement, specifically the intentions and ideologies that shape the use of rape kits. In other words, while a productive argument can be made about the agency of the rape kit on its own, the analysis I offer here focuses in on the effects of human agency within this discourse and how assumptions about these kits reveal a valuing of different kinds of evidence.
28. Weheliye, *Habeas Viscus*, 4.
29. Ibid., 126.
30. Shvarts, "How I Learned," 610.
31. Weheliye, *Habeas Viscus*, 130.
32. Shvarts, "How I Learned," 606.
33. Ibid., 613.
34. Gilmore, *Tainted Witness*, 7.
35. "District Attorney Vance," https://www.manhattanda.org/district-attorney-vance-awards-38-million-grants-help-32-jurisdictions-20-states-test. All the quotes in this chapter from the "District Attorney Vance" source come from the actual press conference, embedded in this announcement at this URL. Click "Watch the Announcement" to view the press conference.
36. Ibid.
37. Tofte, *Testing Justice*, https://www.hrw.org/report/2009/03/31/testing-justice/rape-kit-backlog-los-angeles-city-and-county#.
38. Ibid.
39. Ibid.

40. "District Attorney Vance," https://www.manhattanda.org/district-attorney-vance-awards-38-million-grants-help-32-jurisdictions-20-states-test.
41. "Perpetrators of Sexual Violence," https://www.rainn.org/statistics/perpetrators-sexual-violence.
42. "District Attorney Vance," https://www.manhattanda.org/district-attorney-vance-awards-38-million-grants-help-32-jurisdictions-20-states-test.
43. Ibid.
44. Chivers, "As DNA Aids," https://www.nytimes.com/2000/02/09/nyregion/as-dna-aids-rape-inquiries-statutory-limits-block-cases.html.
45. "Criminal Justice System," https://www.rainn.org/statistics/criminal-justice-system.
46. Mulla, *Violence of Care*, 218.
47. Ibid., 41.
48. "District Attorney Vance," https://www.manhattanda.org/district-attorney-vance-awards-38-million-grants-help-32-jurisdictions-20-states-test.
49. Ibid.
50. Portnoy, "McAuliffe Signs Bill," https://www.washingtonpost.com/local/virginia-politics/mcauliffe-signs-bill-mandating-new-rules-for-rape-kits-in-va/2016/04/14/0c0f816c-01b8-11e6-9203-7b8670959b88_story.html.
51. MacKinnon, "Feminism, Marxism"; Foss and Griffin, "Feminist Perspective"; Alcoff and Gray, "Survivor Discourse"; Foss and Foss, "Personal Experience"; Foss and Griffin, "Beyond Persuasion"; Palczewski, "Survivor Testimony"; Pickering, "Women's Voices"; bell hooks, *Talking Back*; Gilmore, *Tainted Witness*.
52. Bennett, *Banning Queer Blood*, 84.
53. Prelli, *Rhetoric of Science*; Condit, *Meanings of the Gene*; Scott, *Risky Rhetoric*; Gross, *Starring the Text*; Bennett, *Banning Queer Blood*; Keränen, *Scientific Characters*; Ceccarelli, *On the Frontier*; Johnson, *American Lobotomy*; Jensen, "Improving Upon Nature."
54. "District Attorney Vance," https://www.manhattanda.org/district-attorney-vance-awards-38-million-grants-help-32-jurisdictions-20-states-test.
55. Ibid.
56. Ibid.
57. Chivers, "As DNA Aids," https://www.nytimes.com/2000/02/09/nyregion/as-dna-aids-rape-inquiries-statutory-limits-block-cases.html.
58. "District Attorney Vance," https://www.manhattanda.org/district-attorney-vance-awards-38-million-grants-help-32-jurisdictions-20-states-test.
59. Portnoy, "McAuliffe Signs Bill," https://www.washingtonpost.com/local/virginia-politics/mcauliffe-signs-bill-mandating-new-rules-for-rape-kits-in-va/2016/04/14/0c0f816c-01b8-11e6-9203-7b8670959b88_story.html.
60. Mulla, *Violence of Care*, 38.
61. Ibid., 28.
62. Ibid., 28–29.
63. Chivers, "As DNA Aids," https://www.nytimes.com/2000/02/09/nyregion/as-dna-aids-rape-inquiries-statutory-limits-block-cases.html.
64. Weheliye, *Habeas Viscus*, 132.
65. Ibid.
66. Haraway, "Situated Knowledges"; Harding, *Science Question*; Harding, *Whose Science?*; Keller, *Reflections*.
67. Jensen, *Infertility*, 28.
68. Ibid., 4.
69. Shvarts, "How I Learned," 602.

70. Quinlan, *Technoscientific Witness*, 16.
71. Ibid.
72. "District Attorney Vance," https://www.manhattanda.org/district-attorney-vance-awards-38-million-grants-help-32-jurisdictions-20-states-test.
73. Kristof, "Is Rape Serious?" https://www.nytimes.com/2009/04/30/opinion/30kristof.html.
74. Weheliye, *Habeas Viscus*, 132.
75. Wood, "'Get Home Safe,'" https://www.nytimes.com/2015/12/13/opinion/get-home-safe-my-rapist-said.html.
76. Lydersen, "Law Came Too Late," A15A, https://www.nytimes.com/2010/07/09/us/09cnckits.html.
77. Jarratt, *Rereading the Sophists*; Griffin, "Essentialist Roots"; Glenn, *Rhetoric Retold*; Glenn, *Rhetorical Feminism*.
78. Parker, "Silent No More," https://journalstar.com/news/opinion/editorial/columnists/kathleen-parker-silent-on-rape-no-more/article_4585b22b-d0b8-50bd-ad40-64e921c79c86.html; Tofte, "Test of Justice," http://www.washingtonpost.com/wp-dyn/content/article/2008/07/21/AR2008072102359.html; Gray, "Authorities Invest $80 Million," http://time.com/4029517/rape-kit-backlog-funding.
79. Lydersen, "Law Came Too Late," A15A.
80. Hanrahan, "One Woman," http://www.mtv.com/news/1962056/rape-what-it-feels-like-no-one-believes.
81. "Respect for Rape Victims," https://www.nytimes.com/2009/11/14/opinion/14sat3.html, emphasis added.
82. Condit, *Decoding Abortion Rhetoric*; Haas, "Materializing Public"; Lay, *Rhetoric of Midwifery*; Lay, Gurak, Gravon, and Myntti, *Body Talk*; Enoch, "Survival Stories"; Wells, "*Our Bodies, Ourselves*"; Jensen, *Dirty Words*; Jack, *Autism and Gender*; Jensen, "From Barren to Sterile"; Owens, *Writing Childbirth*; Stormer, *Sign of Pathology*.
83. Kohlstedt and Longino, forward to *Body Talk*, ix.
84. Bennett, "What Trump Really Meant," https://slate.com/news-and-politics/2015/08/megyn-kelly-blood-coming-out-of-her-wherever-comment-in-cnn-don-lemon-interview-it-was-classic-trump-and-not-just-because-of-his-sexism.html.
85. Koerber, *From Hysteria to Hormones*, 201.
86. For more on the relationship among hysteria, doubt, and female bodies, see Larson, "Survivors, Liars."
87. Johnson, *American Lobotomy*, 50.
88. Du Mont, White, and McGregor, "Investigating the Medical," 778.
89. Mulla, *Violence of Care*, 217.
90. Du Mont, White, and McGregor, "Investigating the Medical," 778.
91. Souto, "Rape Victim Advocates," https://www.gofundme.com/f/rdv2rg. This campaign is no longer active.
92. Dolmage, "Metis, 'Mêtis,'"; Hawhee, *Moving Bodies*; Hawhee, "Rhetoric's Sensorium."
93. Slapak-Fugate, "Who'll Conduct," https://www.chicagotribune.com/opinion/commentary/ct-rape-kit-exams-nurse-training-20160523-story.html.
94. Many thanks to Liam Randall for drawing me toward this point.
95. Johnson, "Limits of Persuasion," 341.
96. Du Mont and White, "Uses and Impacts," https://www.who.int/gender/documents/svri1_summary.pdf.
97. Mulla, *Violence of Care*, 8.
98. Lopez, "The Failure of Police Body Cameras," https://www.vox.com/policy-and-politics/2017/7/21/15983842/police-body-cameras-failures.

99. What's worse is rarely in the cases of police violence does the use of the camera actually tip toward justice—cell phone footage by bystanders, on the other hand, has become necessary for raising public awareness of the gripping reality of violence.

100. In both cases, but especially police violence, the assault can and does end in death, making the evidence found through technological processes critical and necessary.

101. Weheliye, *Habeas Viscus*, 130.

102. Ibid., 138.

CHAPTER 4

1. For the full statement, see Baker, "Here Is the Powerful Letter," https://www.buzzfeed.com/katiejmbaker/heres-the-powerful-letter-the-stanford-victim-read-to-her-ra.

2. While Miller remained anonymous throughout the trial, she has since come out publicly using her real name, Chanel Miller, most notably through the publication of her memoir in September 2019, which includes her account of the trial and her victim impact statement. I use Miller's real name throughout this chapter in an effort to recognize her identity. For her memoir, see Miller, *Know My Name*.

3. While outcomes of both cases did not determine "rape," the performances of Miller and Sulkowicz claim otherwise, which is why I distinguish their experiences as "rape."

4. See, for example, Grigoriadis, "Meet the College Women," https://www.thecut.com/2014/09/emma-sulkowicz-campus-sexual-assault-activism.html; Smith, "In a Mattress," https://nytimes.com/2014/09/22/arts/design/in-a-mattress-a-fulcrum-of-art-and-political-protest.html; Bever, "'You Took Away My Worth,'" https://www.washingtonpost.com/news/early-lead/wp/2016/06/04/you-took-away-my-worth-a-rape-victim-delivers-powerful-message-to-a-former-stanford-swimmer; Garcia, "Everyone Needs," http://www.vogue.com/article/stanford-student-sexual-assault-victim-statement; Aguilera, "House Members," https://www.nytimes.com/2016/06/17/us/politics/congress-stanford-letter.html.

5. For the full project, see Sulkowicz, *Ceci N'est Pas Un Viol*, http://www.cecinestpasunviol.com (site no longer available).

6. Smith and Hyde, "Rethinking 'The Public,'"; Hariman and Lucaites, "Dissent and Emotional Management"; Cloud, "Therapy, Silence, and War"; Rice, *Distant Publics*; Papacharissi, *Affective Publics*; Johnson, "'Man's Mouth Is His Castle.'"

7. Johnson, "'Man's Mouth Is His Castle.'"

8. Ibid., 2.

9. Ibid., 3.

10. Habermas, *Structural Transformation*.

11. Because US cultural and sexual norms feminize those who are penetrated by penises, the archetypal "victim" of rape is always female and those who experience rape are always feminized within legal codes.

12. When Miller's memoir was released in 2019, the public learned of her identity as an Asian American woman, and in her memoir, she detailed how her experience of being a woman of color further complicated her agency during the trial. For more on her case's relationship to race, see Ko, "Why It Matters," https://www.nytimes.com/2019/09/24/opinion/chanel-miller-know-my-name.html. In the wake of *Mattress Performance*, the *New York Times* reported on the performance and Sulkowicz's case, which Sulkowicz shares prompted them to grapple with their identity as gender nonbinary. For more

on the importance of acknowledging Sulkowicz's queer identity, particularly in a conversation about sexual violence, see Small, "Queer Identity," https://hyperallergic.com/458257/conversation-with-emma-sulkowicz.

13. Felski, *Beyond Feminist Aesthetics*; Fraser, "Rethinking the Public Sphere"; Griffin, "Essentialist Roots"; Asen, "Seeking the 'Counter'"; Warner, *Publics and Counterpublics*; Brouwer, "Communication as Counterpublic."

14. Fraser, "Rethinking the Public Sphere," 128.

15. See, for example, Miller, "#RapeHoax Posters" https://www.washingtonpost.com/news/morning-mix/wp/2015/05/22/rapehoax-posters-plastered-around-columbia-university-in-backlash-against-alleged-rape-victim.

16. People of the State of California v. Brock Allen Turner, No. B1577162 (2015) available at http://documents.latimes.com/stanford-brock-turner.

17. Stanford law professor Michele Dauber spearheaded the organizational efforts to recall Judge Persky, collecting nearly 95,000 signatures from county voters. On June 5, 2018, Judge Persky was recalled by voters during the 2018 California primary elections.

18. Turner's case inspired much backlash from public and legal experts, and in response, California Governor Jerry Brown signed into law two bills just months after Turner's sentencing to expand the legal definition of rape and mandatory minimum sentencing for sexual assault offenders. Many cited Miller's letter as a key effort as part of these changes, which I discuss in more detail in the conclusion. For more on the passing of these laws, see Ulloa, "California Expands Punishment," https://www.latimes.com/politics/essential/la-pol-sac-essential-politics-updates-california-expands-punishment-for-rape-1475260488-htmlstory.html.

19. While Turner did not get to the point of inserting his penis into Miller's vagina, her letter details how he groped her body with his erect penis while it remained covered by his pants.

20. S.B. 5965, 114th Cong. (2015), https://www.nysenate.gov/legislation/bills/2015/S5965.

21. For a broader discussion of affirmative consent laws, see Diehl, "Affirmative Consent"; Marciniak, "Case Against"; Delamater, "What 'Yes Means Yes' Means"; Anderson, "Campus Sexual Assault"; Humphrey, "'Let's Talk.'"

22. Marciniak, "Case Against," 61.

23. McKinnon, *Gendered Asylum*, 102.

24. Pateman, "Women and Consent"; MacKinnon, *Toward a Feminist Theory*.

25. MacKinnon, *Toward a Feminist Theory*, 180, 182.

26. Pateman, "Women and Consent," 157.

27. MacKinnon, "Rape Redefined," 439.

28. Carrie Crenshaw, "'Protection'"; Carrie Crenshaw, "Normality"; Gibson, "Judicial Rhetoric"; Ray and Richards, "Inventing Citizens"; Carlson, *Crimes of Womanhood*; Schuster and Propen, *Victim Advocacy*.

29. Marcus, "Fighting Bodies"; Hall, "'It Can Happen to You'"; Khoury, "Enough Violence."

30. Alcoff and Gray, "Survivor Discourse"; Spry, "In the Absence"; Hesford, "Reading *Rape Stories*"; Picart, "Rhetorically Reconfiguring"; Enck and McDaniel, "Playing with Fire"; Propen and Schuster, *Rhetoric and Communication*.

31. Picart, "Rhetorically Reconfiguring," 97. For more on rhetorical studies of how perceptions of "womanhood" shape public discourse, see Hesford, *Spectacular Rhetorics*; Riedner, "Lives of In-famous Women"; Hinshaw, "Regulating Girlhood"; McKinnon, *Gendered Asylum*.

32. Griffin, "Essentialist Roots," 33.

33. Fraser, "Rethinking the Public Sphere," 123.

34. Pezzullo, "Resisting 'National Breast Cancer Awareness Month,'" 357.

35. Brouwer, "ACT-ing UP"; Hauser, "Prisoners of Conscience"; Squires, "Black Press"; Pezzullo, "Resisting 'National Breast Cancer Awareness Month'"; Kaufer and Al-Malki, "War on Terror"; Dunn, "Remembering Matthew Shepard"; Elsadda, "Arab Women Bloggers"; Chávez, "Counter-Public Enclaves"; Eckert and Chadha, "Muslim Bloggers"; Jackson and Welles, "Hijacking #myNYPD."

36. To approach this intricate relationship between the body and discourse, I borrow from Johnson and Hawhee who prefer Cvetkovich's term "feeling" found in *Depression*, 4.

37. Johnson, "'Man's Mouth Is His Castle,'" 5.

38. Berlant, "Subject"; Ahmed, *Cultural Politics*; Butler, *Precarious Life*; Panagia, *Political Life*; Cvetkovich, *Depression*.

39. Cvetkovich, *Depression*, 2.

40. Baker, "Here Is the Powerful Letter."

41. Pezzullo, "Resisting 'National Breast Cancer Awareness Month,'" 347.

42. Baker, "Here Is the Powerful Letter."

43. Ibid.

44. Ibid.

45. Ibid.

46. Ibid.

47. Scarry, *Body in Pain*, 3–26.

48. Ibid., 4.

49. Baker, "Here Is the Powerful Letter."

50. Ibid.

51. Ibid.

52. Ibid.

53. Ibid.

54. Ibid.

55. Warner, "Publics and Counterpublics," 425.

56. Ibid., 417.

57. Hariman and Lucaites, *No Caption Needed*, 45.

58. Butler, *Precarious Life*, 20.

59. Ahmed, *Cultural Politics*, 27, emphasis in original.

60. Sulkowicz, *Ceci N'est Pas Un Viol*, http://www.cecinestpasunviol.com.

61. Ibid.

62. Ibid.

63. Ibid, emphasis in original.

64. Ibid.

65. There are certainly important ethics involved in viewing Sulkowicz's performance. While we can't be sure of their desires, I choose to watch the video and describe it in detail because of the important effects the video elicits for unpacking how language and feeling are in tension throughout the video, a problem that invites critique of how consent discourses problematically limit the options for knowing whether or not rape happened. With that said, I understand that some may refuse to watch the performance and may want to gloss over parts of this analysis that include description of the video. The point that I hope to illustrate is that deciphering rape requires feeling a sense of pain, a sense that is not always captured by the limited adjudicatory frameworks used to assess consent.

66. Sulkowicz, *Ceci N'est Pas Un Viol*, http://www.cecinestpasunviol.com.

67. Ibid.

68. Panagia, *Political Life*, 2–3.

69. For more, see Ulloa, "California Expands Punishment," https://www.latimes.com/politics/essential/la-pol-sac-essential-politics-updates-california-expands-punishment-for-rape-1475260488-htmlstory.html.
70. Chokshi, "As Brock Turner," https://www.nytimes.com/2016/09/01/us/as-brock-turner-is-set-to-be-freed-friday-california-bill-aims-for-harsher-penalties-for-sexual-assault.html.
71. Ahmed, *Cultural Politics*, 196.
72. Butler, *Precarious Life*, 29.

CHAPTER 5

1. "The Inception," https://justbeinc.wixsite.com/justbeinc/the-me-too-movement-cmml.
2. Ibid.
3. Zacharek, Dockterman, and Edwards, "TIME Person," https://time.com/time-person-of-the-year-2017-silence-breakers.
4. Palczewski, "Survivor Testimony"; Campbell, "Rhetoric"; MacKinnon, "Rape Redefined"; Gilmore, *Tainted Witness*.
5. Gilmore, *Tainted Witness*, 2.
6. Loken, "#BringBackOurGirls," 1101.
7. Portwood and Berridge, "Year"; Owens, *Writing Childbirth*; Carey, "Tightrope"; Stenberg, "'Tweet Me Your First Assaults.'"
8. Farrell, "Weight," 486.
9. Hawhee, *Rhetoric in Tooth*; Rice, "Rhetorical Aesthetics"; Olson, "American Magnitude."
10. Balzotti and Crosby, "Diocletian's Victory," 324.
11. Cooper and Burrell, "Modernism, Postmodernism," 93.
12. Hawhee, *Rhetoric in Tooth*, 149; Rice, "Rhetorical Aesthetics"; Olson, "American Magnitude."
13. Gould, *Moving Politics*, 27.
14. Ziegler, "Story," 417.
15. All of the tweets analyzed in this chapter were collected from published sources. This data set was collected from a LexisNexus search of over nine hundred materials, as well as MeToomentum, an information analysis of the movement's first sixth months. For more on MeToomentum, see D'Efilippo and Kocincova, "MeToomentum," http://metoomentum.com/trending.html.
16. Farrow, "From Aggressive Overtures," https://www.newyorker.com/news/news-desk/from-aggressive-overtures-to-sexual-assault-harvey-weinsteins-accusers-tell-their-stories; Kantor and Twohey, "Harvey Weinstein," https://www.nytimes.com/2017/10/05/us/harvey-weinstein-harassment-allegations.html.
17. Bennett, "'Click' Moment," https://www.nytimes.com/2017/11/05/us/sexual-harrassment-weinstein-trump.html.
18. Park, "#MeToo Reaches," https://www.cbsnews.com/news/metoo-reaches-85-countries-with-1-7-million-tweets. These numbers have since grown and are still growing to date.
19. Print and broadcast news outlets published several tweets and dedicated much time to profiling the movement. In addition, others like actress Lupita Nyong'o published their own accounts in editorials and other longform sources.
20. D'Efilippo and Kocincova, "MeToomentum," http://metoomentum.com/trending.html.

21. Ibid.
22. Ziegler, "Story," 417.
23. O'Banion, *Reorienting Rhetoric*; Browning, "Lists and Stories"; Eisenberg et al., "Communication in Emergency Medicine"; Ziegler, "Story"; Richardson, "Modern Fiction"; Fawaz, "'Open Mesh of Possibilities.'"
24. Richardson, "Modern Fiction," 328.
25. For more on feminist hashtags, see Portwood and Berridge, "Year."
26. Carey, "Tightrope," 146.
27. Winderman, "Anger's Volumes," 329.
28. Rhodes, "SlutWalk Is Not Enough," 96.
29. Ibid., 91.
30. Cintrón, "Democracy and Its Limitations," 100.
31. D'Efilippo and Kocincova, "MeToomentum," http://metoomentum.com/trending.html.
32. Gianino, "I Went Public," https://www.washingtonpost.com/news/postevery thing/wp/2017/10/18/i-went-public-with-my-sexual-assault-and-then-the-trolls-came-for-me.
33. Ibid.
34. Ibid.
35. Prokos, "16 #MeToo Tweets," https://www.theodysseyonline.com/16-metoo-tweets-everyone-needs-to-see.
36. Aristotle's treatment of *megethos* appears most prominently in discussions of epideictic rhetoric, or forms of speech that seek to "praise or blame." According to the *Rhetoric*, invoking magnitude strives "to clothe the actions with greatness and beauty." Aristotle, *On Rhetoric*, 1.9.1368a 40. Such characteristics of beauty also appear in the *Poetics*: "Again, if an object be beautiful . . . it must also be of a certain magnitude . . . a certain magnitude is necessary, and that such as may be easily embraced in one view." Aristotle, *Poetics*, 29–32.
37. Farrell, "Weight," 474.
38. Ibid.
39. Farrell, "Weight"; O'Gorman, "Longinus's Sublime Rhetoric"; O'Gorman, "Eisenhower and the American Sublime"; Balzotti and Crosby, "Diocletian's Victory Column"; Rice, "Rhetorical Aesthetics"; Olson, "American Magnitude."
40. Olson, "American Magnitude," 381.
41. Rice, "Rhetorical Aesthetics," 32.
42. Farrell, "Weight of Rhetoric," 472.
43. Olson, "American Magnitude," 387.
44. Ibid.
45. D'Efilippo and Kocincova, "MeToomentum," http://metoomentum.com/trending.html.
46. Ibid.
47. Busch, "36 'Me Too' Tweets," https://www.bustle.com/p/36-me-too-tweets-that-will-shatter-you-2920220.
48. Ibid.
49. Balzotti and Crosby, "Diocletian's Victory Column," 338.
50. Winderman, "S(anger) Goes Postal," 385.
51. Ibid.
52. Rice, "Rhetorical Aesthetics," 29.
53. Balzotti and Crosby, "Diocletian's Victory Column," 325.
54. Bielski, "We Owe," https://www.theglobeandmail.com/opinion/we-owe-sexual-abuse-survivors-more-than-metoo/article36627326.

55. Speckhard Pasque, "'We Can Do Better,'" https://madison.com/ct/news/local/govt-and-politics/we-can-do-better-madison-women-join-metoo-social-media/article_628c9419-45fd-5b08-8438-9b9d21a9c6b3.html.
56. D'Efilippo and Kocincova, "MeToomentum," http://metoomentum.com/trending.html.
57. Fawaz, "'Open Mesh of Possibilities,'" 17.
58. Ibid., 18.
59. Ibid.
60. Butler, *Frames of War*, 34.
61. Ibid.
62. Nair, "#MeToo Trends," https://yourstory.com/2017/10/metoo-trends-women-speak-sexual-abuse.
63. Busch, "36 'Me Too' Tweets," https://www.bustle.com/p/36-me-too-tweets-that-will-shatter-you-2920220.
64. Johnson, "'Man's Mouth Is His Castle,'" 5.
65. Olson, "American Magnitude," 388.
66. Browning, "Lists and Stories," 284.
67. Busch, "36 'Me Too' Tweets," https://www.bustle.com/p/36-me-too-tweets-that-will-shatter-you-2920220.
68. Johnson, "From #MeToo," https://www.nelsonstar.com/opinion/column-from-metoo-to-howiwillchange.
69. Hod, "Men Join #MeToo" https://www.thewrap.com/men-join-metoo-campaign-howiwillchange-guys-turn.
70. Irwin, "'Guys, It's Our Turn,'" https://www.independent.ie/world-news/and-finally/guys-its-our-turn-men-pledge-new-behaviour-in-response-to-metoo-36242992.html.
71. Balzotti and Crosby, "Diocletian's Victory Column," 338.
72. Rice, "Rhetorical Aesthetics," 33.
73. Olson, "American Magnitude," 388.
74. Ahmed, *Cultural Politics*, 24.
75. Rice, "Rhetorical Aesthetics," 46–47.
76. D'Efilippo and Kocincova, "MeToomentum," http://metoomentum.com/trending.html.
77. Schuller, *Biopolitics of Feeling*, 2.
78. Winderman, "Anger's Volumes," 329.
79. Chokshi and Herndon, "Jeff Flake Is Confronted," https://www.nytimes.com/2018/09/28/us/politics/jeff-flake-protesters-kavanaugh.html.
80. Ibid.
81. Ibid.
82. Ibid.
83. Ibid.
84. Presley, "Janelle Monáe Releases," https://www.npr.org/sections/allsongs/2015/08/18/385202798/janelle-mon-e-releases-visceral-protest-song-hell-you-talmbout.
85. Winderman, "Anger's Volumes," 330.
86. Hsu, "(Trans)forming #MeToo," 272.
87. "After Weinstein Sentencing," https://www.wbal.com/article/440429/110/after-weinstein-sentencing-tarana-burke-on-whats-next-for-the-metoo-movement.
88. Ibid.
89. Flores, "Between Abundance," 7.
90. Hsu, "(Trans)forming #MeToo," 283.
91. Panagia, *Political Life*, 7.

CONCLUSION

1. Brown, "How a Future Trump," https://www.miamiherald.com/news/local/article220097825.html.
2. Rogers, Haberman, and Baker, "Acosta Defends," https://www.nytimes.com/2019/07/10/us/politics/acosta-epstein.html.
3. Carroll, "Hideous Men," https://www.thecut.com/2019/06/donald-trump-assault-e-jean-carroll-other-hideous-men.html.
4. Baker and Vigdor, "'She's Not My Type,'" https://www.nytimes.com/2019/06/24/us/politics/jean-carroll-trump.html.
5. Schonbek, "Complete List," https://www.thecut.com/2020/01/harvey-weinstein-complete-list-allegations.html.
6. Douglas, *Memory of Judgment*, 4.
7. Gilmore, *Tainted Witness*, 18.
8. Mack and McCann, "Critiquing," 342.
9. Ahmed, *Living a Feminist Life*, 42.
10. For more on the trope of the angry feminist, see Tomlinson, *Feminism and Affect*.
11. Gay, *Hunger*.
12. Ibid., 4–5.
13. Ibid., 19, 16.
14. Ibid., 22.
15. Ibid., 18.
16. Ibid., 45.
17. West, "Brave Enough to Be Angry," https://www.nytimes.com/2017/11/08/opinion/anger-women-weinstein-assault.html.
18. Ibid.
19. Ibid.
20. Christian, "Race," 21, emphasis in original.
21. Butler and Athanasiou, *Dispossession*, 23.
22. Ahmed, *Living a Feminist Life*, 23.

BIBLIOGRAPHY

"After Weinstein Sentencing, Tarana Burke on What's Next for the #MeToo Movement." ABC News Radio, March 11, 2020. https://www.wbal.com/article/440429/110/after-weinstein-sentencing-tarana-burke-on-whats-next-for-the-metoo-movement.

Aguilera, Jasmine. "House Members Unite to Read Stanford Rape Victim's Letter." *New York Times*, June 16, 2016. https://www.nytimes.com/2016/06/17/us/politics/congress-stanford-letter.html.

Ahmed, Sara. *The Cultural Politics of Emotion*. New York: Routledge, 2004.

———. *Living a Feminist Life*. Durham: Duke University Press, 2017.

Alcoff, Linda, and Laura Gray. "Survivor Discourse: Transgression or Recuperation?" *Signs* 18, no. 2 (1993): 260–90.

Anderson, Michelle J. "Campus Sexual Assault Adjudication and Resistance to Reform." *Yale Law Journal* 125, no. 7 (2016): 1940–2005.

Andrus, Jennifer. *Entextualizing Domestic Violence: Language Ideology and Violence Against Women in the Anglo-American Hearsay Principle*. New York: Oxford University Press, 2015.

Aristotle. *On Rhetoric: A Theory of Civic Discourse*. Translated by George A. Kennedy. 2nd ed. Oxford: Oxford University Press, 2007.

———. *The Poetics of Aristotle*. Translated by S. H. Butcher. London: Macmillan, 1985.

Asen, Robert. "Imagining in the Public Sphere." *Philosophy and Rhetoric* 35, no. 4 (2002): 345–67.

———. "Seeking the 'Counter,' in Counterpublics." *Communication Theory* 10, no. 4 (2000): 424–46.

Associated Press. "Memorable Quotes and Exchanges from Kavanaugh-Ford Hearing." WTOP, September 28, 2018. https://apnews.com/article/d044d1c4577543dc89bb269d8130ea0b.

Austin, J. L. *How to Do Things with Words*. Edited by J. O. Urbson and Marina Sbisà. Cambridge: Harvard University Press, 1975.

Baker, Katie J. M. "Here Is the Powerful Letter the Stanford Victim Read to Her Attacker." *BuzzFeed*, June 3, 2016. Accessed April 2017. https://www.buzzfeed.com/katiejmbaker/heres-the-powerful-letter-the-stanford-victim-read-to-her-ra.

Baker, Peter, and Neil Vigdor. "'She's Not My Type': Accused Again of Sexual Assault, Trump Resorts to Old Insult." *New York Times*, June 24, 2019. https://www.nytimes.com/2019/06/24/us/politics/jean-carroll-trump.html.

Ballif, Michelle. "Writing the Event: The Impossible Possibility for Historiography." *Rhetoric Society Quarterly* 44, no. 3 (2014): 243–55.

Balzotti, Jonathan Mark, and Richard Benjamin Crosby. "Diocletian's Victory Column: Megethos and the Rhetoric of Spectacular Disruption." *Rhetoric Society Quarterly* 44, no. 4 (2014): 323–42.

Banyard, Victoria L., Mary M. Moynihan, and Elizabethe G. Plante. "Sexual Violence Prevention Through Bystander Education: An Experimental Evaluation." *Journal of Community Psychology* 35, no. 4 (2007): 463–81.

Banyard, Victoria L., Elizabethe G. Plante, and Mary M. Moynihan. *Rape Prevention Through Bystander Education: Bringing a Broader Community Perspective to Sexual Violence Prevention.* Washington, DC: National Institute of Justice, 2005. https://www.ncjrs.gov/pdffiles1/nij/grants/208701.pdf.

Barnard, Ian. "Rhetorical Commonsense and Child Molester Panic—A Queer Intervention." *Rhetoric Society Quarterly* 47, no. 1 (2017): 3–25.

Bennett, Jeffrey A. *Banning Queer Blood: Rhetorics of Citizenship, Contagion, and Resistance.* Tuscaloosa: University of Alabama Press, 2009.

Bennett, Jessica. "The 'Click' Moment: How the Weinstein Scandal Unleashed a Tsunami." *New York Times*, November 5, 2017. https://www.nytimes.com/2017/11/05/us/sexual-harrasment-weinstein-trump.html.

Bennett, Laura. "What Trump Really Meant When He Said That Megyn Kelly Had 'Blood Coming Out of Her Wherever.'" *Slate*, August 10, 2015. https://slate.com/news-and-politics/2015/08/megyn-kelly-blood-coming-out-of-her-wherever-comment-in-cnn-don-lemon-interview-it-was-classic-trump-and-not-just-because-of-his-sexism.html.

Berlant, Lauren. *Cruel Optimism.* Durham: Duke University Press, 2011.

———. *The Queen of America Goes to Washington City: Essays on Sex and Citizenship.* Durham: Duke University Press, 1997.

———. "The Subject of True Feeling: Pain, Privacy, and Politics." In *Cultural Pluralism, Identity Politics, and the Law*, edited by Austin Sarat and Thomas R. Kearns, 49–84. Ann Arbor: University of Michigan Press, 1999.

Berlant, Lauren, and Michael Warner. "Sex in Public." *Critical Inquiry* 24, no. 2 (1998): 547–66.

Bernard-Donals, Michael. *Forgetful Memory: Representation and Remembrance in the Wake of the Holocaust.* Albany: State University of New York Press, 2010.

———. *Witnessing the Disaster: Essays on Representation and the Holocaust.* Madison: University of Wisconsin Press, 2003.

Bernstein, Elizabeth. "The Sexual Politics of the 'New Abolitionism.'" *differences: A Journal of Feminist Cultural Studies* 18, no. 3 (2007): 128–51.

Bevacqua, Maria. *Rape on the Public Agenda: Feminism and the Politics of Sexual Assault.* Boston: Northeastern University Press, 2000.

Bever, Lindsey. "'You Took Away My Worth': A Sexual Assault Victim's Powerful Message to Her Stanford Attacker." *Washington Post*, June 4, 2016. https://www.washingtonpost.com/news/early-lead/wp/2016/06/04/you-took-away-my-worth-a-rape-victim-delivers-powerful-message-to-a-former-stanford-swimmer.

Bielski, Zosia. "We Owe Sexual Abuse Survivors More Than #MeToo." *Globe and Mail*, October 17, 2017. https://www.theglobeandmail.com/opinion/we-owe-sexual-abuse-survivors-more-than-metoo/article36627326.

Bliss, James. "Black Feminism Out of Place." *Signs* 41, no. 4 (2016): 727–49.

Brennan, Teresa. *The Transmission of Affect.* Ithaca: Cornell University Press, 2004.

"Brett Kavanaugh's Opening Statement: The Ford-Kavanaugh Hearin Full Transcript." *New York Times*, September 26, 2018. https://www.nytimes.com/2018/09/26/us/politics/read-brett-kavanaughs-complete-opening-statement.html.

Brewer, Paul R., and Barbara L. Ley. "Media Use and Public Perceptions of DNA Evidence." *Science Communication* 32, no. 1 (2010): 93–117.

Brouwer, Daniel C. "ACT-ing UP in Congressional Hearings." In *Counterpublics and the State*, edited by Robert Asen and Daniel C. Brouwer, 87–110. Albany: State University of New York Press, 2001.

———. "Communication as Counterpublic." In *Communication as . . . Perspectives on Theory*, edited by Gregory J. Shepard, Jeffrey St. John, and Ted Striphas, 195–208. Thousand Oaks: Sage, 2006.

———. "The Precarious Visibility Politics of Self-Stigmatization: The Case of HIV/AIDS Tattoos." *Text and Performance Quarterly* 18, no. 2 (1998): 114–36.
Brown, Julie K. "How a Future Trump Cabinet Member Gave a Serial Sex Abuser the Deal of a Lifetime." *Miami Herald*, November 28, 2018. https://www.miamiherald.com/news/local/article220097825.html.
Brown, Wendy. *Undoing the Demos: Neoliberalism's Stealth Revolution*. New York: Zone Books, 2015.
Browning, Barbara. *Infectious Rhythm: Metaphors of Contagion and the Spread of African Culture*. New York: Routledge, 1998.
Browning, Larry Davis. "Lists and Stories as Organizational Communication." *Communication Theory* 2, no. 4 (1992): 281–302.
Brownmiller, Susan. *Against Our Will*. New York: Simon and Schuster, 1975.
Buchwald, Emilie, Pamela R. Fletcher, and Martha Roth. "Preamble." In *Transforming a Rape Culture: Revised Edition*. Minneapolis: Milkweed Editions, 2005.
Bumiller, Kristin. *In an Abusive State: How Neoliberalism Appropriated the Feminist Movement Against Sexual Violence*. Durham: Duke University Press, 2008.
Burger, Robert H. "The Meese Report on Pornography and Its Respondents: A Review Article." *Library Quarterly* 57, no. 4 (1987): 436–47.
Busch, Monica. "36 'Me Too' Tweets That Will Shatter You." *Bustle*, October 17, 2017. https://www.bustle.com/p/36-me-too-tweets-that-will-shatter-you-2920220.
Buse, Peter, and Andrew Stott. *Ghosts: Deconstruction, Psychoanalysis, History*. New York: St. Martin's Press, 1999.
Butler, Judith. *Antigone's Claim: Kinship Between Life and Death*. New York: Columbia University Press, 2000.
———. *Frames of War: When Is Life Grievable?* New York: Verso, 2010.
———. *Precarious Life: The Powers of Mourning and Violence*. New York: Verso, 2004.
Butler, Judith, and Athena Athanasiou. *Dispossession: The Performative in the Political*. Malden: Polity Press, 2013.
Calafell, Bernadette Marie. "Rhetorics of Possibility: Challenging the Textual Bias of Rhetoric Through the Theory of the Flesh." In *Rhetorica in Motion: Feminist Rhetorical Methods and Methodologies*, edited by Eileen Schell and K. J. Rawson, 104–17. Pittsburgh: University of Pittsburgh Press, 2010.
Campbell, Karlyn Kohrs. "The Rhetoric of Women's Liberation: An Oxymoron." *Communication Studies* 50, no. 2 (1999): 125–37.
Campbell, Rebecca, and Giannina Fehler-Cabral. "Why Police 'Couldn't or Wouldn't' Submit Sexual Assault Kits for Forensic DNA Testing: A Focal Concerns Theory Analysis of Untested Rape Kits." *Law and Society Review* 52, no. 1 (2018): 73–105.
Campbell, Rebecca, Jessica Shaw, and Giannina Fehler-Cabral. "Evaluation of a Victim-Centered, Trauma-Informed Victim Notification Protocol for Untested Sexual Assault Kits (SAKs)." *Violence Against Women* 24, no. 4 (2018): 379–400.
———. "Shelving Justice: The Discovery of Thousands of Untested Rape Kits in Detroit." *City and Community* 14, no. 2 (2015): 151–66.
Campt, Tina M. *Listening to Images*. Durham: Duke University Press, 2017.
Carey, Tamika L. "A Tightrope of Perfection: The Rhetoric and Risk of Black Women's Intellectualism on Display in Television and Social Media." *Rhetoric Society Quarterly* 48, no. 2 (2018): 139–60.
Carlson, A. Cheree. *Crimes of Womanhood: Defining Femininity in a Court of Law*. Urbana: University of Illinois Press, 2009.
Carroll, E. Jean. "Hideous Men: Donald Trump Assaulted Me in a Bergdorf Goodman Dressing Room 23 Years Ago. But He's Not Alone on the List of Awful Men in My Life." *New York Magazine*, June 21, 2019. https://www.thecut.com/2019/06/donald-trump-assault-e-jean-carroll-other-hideous-men.html.

Ceccarelli, Leah. *On the Frontier of Science: An American Rhetoric of Exploration and Exploitation*. East Lansing: Michigan State University Press, 2013.

Chambers, Ross. *Untimely Interventions: AIDS Writing, Testimonial, and the Rhetoric of Haunting*. Ann Arbor: University of Michigan Press, 2004.

Chávez, Karma R. "The Body: An Abstract and Actual Rhetorical Concept." *Rhetoric Society Quarterly* 48, no. 3 (2018): 242–50.

———. "Counter-Public Enclaves and Understanding the Function of Rhetoric in Social Movement Coalition-Building." *Communication Quarterly* 59, no. 1 (2011): 1–18.

———. *Queer Migration Politics: Activist Rhetoric and Coalitional Possibilities*. Urbana: University of Illinois Press, 2013.

Chivers, C. J. "As DNA Aids Rape Inquiries, Statutory Limits Block Cases." *New York Times*, February 9, 2000. https://www.nytimes.com/2000/02/09/nyregion/as-dna-aids-rape-inquiries-statutory-limits-block-cases.html.

Cho, Grace M. *Haunting the Korean Diaspora: Shame, Secrecy, and the Forgotten War*. Minneapolis: University of Minnesota Press, 2008.

Chokshi, Niraj. "As Brock Turner Is Set to Be Freed Friday, California Bill Aims for Harsher Penalties for Sexual Assault." *New York Times*, August 31, 2016. https://www.nytimes.com/2016/09/01/us/as-brock-turner-is-set-to-be-freed-friday-california-bill-aims-for-harsher-penalties-for-sexual-assault.html.

Chokshi, Niraj, and Astead W. Herndon. "Jeff Flake Is Confronted on Video by Sexual Assault Survivors." *New York Times*, September 28, 2019. https://www.nytimes.com/2018/09/28/us/politics/jeff-flake-protesters-kavanaugh.html.

Christian, Barbara. "The Race for Theory." In *The Black Feminist Reader*, edited by Joy James and T. Denean Sharpley-Whiting, 11–23. Malden: Blackwell, 2000.

Cintrón, Ralph. "Democracy and Its Limitations." In *The Public Work of Rhetoric: Citizen-Scholar and Civic Engagement*, edited by John Ackerman and David Coogan, 98–117. Columbia: University of South Carolina Press, 2010.

Clark, Gregory. *Rhetorical Landscapes in America: Variations on a Theme from Kenneth Burke*. Columbia: University of South Carolina Press, 2004.

Cloud, Dana L. "Therapy, Silence, and War: Consolation and the End of Deliberation in the 'Affected' Public." *Poroi* 2, no. 1 (2003): 125–42.

Collins, Patricia Hill. *Black Sexual Politics: African Americans, Gender, and the New Racism*. New York: Routledge, 2004.

Coly, Ayo A. *Postcolonial Hauntologies: African Women's Discourses of the Female Body*. Lincoln: University of Nebraska Press, 2019.

Condit, Celeste Michelle. *Decoding Abortion Rhetoric: Communicating Social Change*. Urbana: University of Illinois Press, 1990.

———. *The Meanings of the Gene*. Madison: University of Wisconsin Press, 1999.

Conley, John M., and William O'Barr. *Just Words: Law, Language, and Power*. Chicago: University of Chicago Press, 1998.

Cooper, Robert, and Gibson Burrell. "Modernism, Postmodernism and Organizational Analysis: An Introduction." *Organizational Studies* 9, no. 1 (1988): 91–112.

Coppins, McKay. "Trump Cares About Only One Audience." *Atlantic*, January 13, 2019. https://www.theatlantic.com/politics/archive/2019/01/trump-mocks-christine-blasey-ford-rally/580069.

Correa, Carla, and Meghan Louttit. "More Than 160 Women Say Larry Nassar Sexually Abused Them. Here Are His Accusers." *New York Times*, January 24, 2018. https://www.nytimes.com/interactive/2018/01/24/sports/larry-nassar-victims.html.

Corrigan, Rose. "The New Trial by Ordeal: Rape Kits, Police Practices, and the Unintended Effects of Policy Innovation." *Law and Society Inquiry* 38, no. 4 (2013): 920–49.

Crenshaw, Carrie. "The Normality of Man and Female Otherness: (Re)Producing Patriarchal Lines of Argument in the Law and the News." *Argumentation and Advocacy* 32, no. 4 (1996): 170–84.

———. "The 'Protection' of 'Woman': A History of Legal Attitudes Toward Women's Workplace Freedom. *Quarterly Journal of Speech* 81, no. 1 (1995): 63–82.

Crenshaw, Kimberlé. "Demarginalizing the Intersection of Race and Sex: A Black Feminist Critique of Antidiscrimination Doctrine, Feminist Theory and Antiracist Politics." *University of Chicago Legal Forum* 140 (1989): 139–67.

———. "Mapping the Margins: Intersectionality, Identity Politics and Violence Against Women of Color." *Stanford Law Review* 43 (1991): 1241–99.

———. "Whose Story Is It Anyway? Feminist and Antiracist Appropriations of Anita Hill." In *Race-ing Justice, En-Gendering Power*, edited by Toni Morrison, 402–40. New York: Pantheon Books, 1992.

"The Criminal Justice System: Statistics." RAINN, March 27, 2012. Accessed July 19, 2017. https://www.rainn.org/statistics/criminal-justice-system.

Cullen, Mary. "Survivor Shares Experience with Rape Kit Testing." Illinois Public Media, May 25, 2018. http://will.illinois.edu/news/story/survivor-shares-experience-with-rape-kit-testing.

Cvetkovich, Ann. *Depression: A Public Feeling*. Durham: Duke University Press, 2012.

D'Efilippo, Valentina, and Lucia Kocincova. "MeToomentum: A Visual Analysis of the MeToo Movement." MeToomentum. Accessed December 3, 2018. http://metoomentum.com/trending.html.

Delamater, Chandler. "What 'Yes Means Yes' Means for New York Schools: The Positive Effects of New York's Efforts to Combat Campus Sexual Assault Through Affirmative Consent. *Albany Law Review* 79, no. 2 (2015–2016): 591–615.

DeLuca, Kevin. "Unruly Arguments: The Body Rhetoric of Earth First!, ACT UP, and Queer Nation." *Argumentation and Advocacy* 36, no. 1 (1991): 9–21.

Derrida, Jacques. *Specters of Marx: The State of Debt, the Work of Mourning, and the New International*. Translated by Peggy Kamuf. New York: Routledge, 1994.

Diehl, Beatrice. "Affirmative Consent in Sexual Assault: Prosecutors' Duty." *Georgetown Journal of Legal Ethics* 28, no. 3 (2015): 503–20.

Dietz, Park Elliott. The Papers of Park Elliott Dietz for the Attorney General's Commission on Pornography. MSS 86-1. 16 Boxes. Arthur J. Morris Law Library. University of Virginia School of Law. Charlottesville, Virginia. Accessed June 2017.

Dingo, Rebecca. *Networking Arguments: Rhetoric, Transnational Feminism, and Public Policy Writing*. Pittsburgh: University of Pittsburgh Press, 2012.

"District Attorney Vance Awards $38 Million in Grants to Help 32 Jurisdictions in 20 States Test Backlogged Rape Kits." Manhattan District Attorney's Office, September 10, 2015. https://www.manhattanda.org/district-attorney-vance-awards-38-million-grants-help-32-jurisdictions-20-states-test.

Dolmage, Jay. *Disability Rhetoric*. Syracuse: Syracuse University Press, 2013.

———. "Metis, 'Mêtis,' 'Mestiza,' Medusa: Rhetorical Bodies Across Rhetorical Traditions." *Rhetoric Review* 28, no. 1 (2009): 1–28.

Douglas, Lawrence. *The Memory of Judgment: Making Law and History in the Trials of the Holocaust*. New Haven: Yale University Press, 2001.

Duggan, Lisa. *The Twilight of Equality: Neoliberalism, Cultural Politics, and the Attack on Democracy*. Boston: Beacon Press, 2003.

Du Mont, Janice, and Deborah White. "The Uses and Impacts of Medico-Legal Evidence in Sexual Assault Cases: A Global Review." World Health Organization, 2007. https://www.who.int/gender/documents/svri_summary.pdf.

Du Mont, Janice, Deborah White, and Margaret J. McGregor. "Investigating the Medical Forensic Examination from the Perspectives of Sexually Assaulted Women." *Social Science and Medicine* 68, no. 4 (2009): 774–870.

Dunn, Thomas R. "Remembering Matthew Shepard: Violence, Identity, and Queer Counterpublic Memories." *Rhetoric and Public Affairs* 13, no. 4 (2010): 611–51.

Dziuban, Zuzanna. *The "Spectral Turn": Jewish Ghosts in the Polish Post-Holocaust Imaginaire*. New York: Columbia University Press, 2018.

Eckert, Stine, and Kalyani Chadha. "Muslim Bloggers in Germany: An Emerging Counterpublic." *Media, Culture and Society* 35, no. 8 (2013): 926–42.

Edelman, Lee. *No Future: Queer Theory and the Death Drive*. Durham: Duke University Press, 2004.

Eisenberg, Eric M., et al. "Communication in Emergency Medicine: Implications for Patient Safety1." *Communication Monographs* 72, no. 4 (2005): 390–413.

Elsadda, Hoda. "Arab Women Bloggers: The Emergence of Literary Counterpublics." *Middle East Journal of Culture and Communication* 3, no. 3 (2010): 312–32.

Enck, Suzanne Marie, and Blake A. McDaniel. "Playing with Fire: Cycles of Domestic Violence in Eminem and Rhianna's 'Love the Way You Lie.'" *Communication, Culture and Critique* 5, no. 4 (2012): 618–44.

Enoch, Jessica. "Survival Stories: Feminist Historiographic Approaches to Chicana Rhetorics of Sterilization Abuse." *Rhetoric Society Quarterly* 35, no. 3 (2005): 5–30.

Estrich, Susan. *Real Rape*. Cambridge: Harvard University Press, 1987.

Farrell, Thomas B. "The Weight of Rhetoric: Studies in Cultural Delirium." *Philosophy and Rhetoric* 41, no. 4 (2008): 467–87.

Farrow, Ronan. "From Aggressive Overtones to Sexual Assault: Harvey Weinstein's Accusers Tell Their Stories." *New Yorker*, October 10, 2017. https://www.newyorker.com/news/news-desk/from-aggressive-overtures-to-sexual-assault-harvey-weinsteins-accusers-tell-their-stories.

Farrow, Ronan, and Jane Mayer. "Senate Democrats Investigate a New Allegation of Sexual Misconduct, from Brett Kavanaugh's College Years." *New Yorker*, September 23, 2018. https://www.newyorker.com/news/news-desk/senate-democrats-investigate-a-new-allegation-of-sexual-misconduct-from-the-supreme-court-nominee-brett-kavanaughs-college-years-deborah-ramirez.

Fawaz, Ramzi. "'An Open Mesh of Possibilities': The Necessity of Eve Sedgwick in Dark Times." Introduction to *Reading Sedgwick*, edited by Lauren Berlant and Lee Edelman, 1–36. Durham: Duke University Press, 2019.

Feinstein, Rachel A. *When Rape Was Legal: The Untold History of Sexual Violence During Slavery*. New York: Routledge, 2019.

Felski, Rita. *Beyond Feminist Aesthetics: Feminist Literature and Social Change*. Cambridge: Harvard University Press, 1989.

Fielding, Ian. "Examining an Argument by Cause: The Weak Link Between Pornography and Violence in the Attorney General's Commission on Pornography and Final Report." In *Warranting Assent: Case Studies in Argument Evaluation*, edited by Edward Schiappa, 239–56. Albany: State University of New York Press, 1995.

Finnegan, Cara A. "Recognizing Lincoln: Image Vernaculars in Nineteenth-Century Visual Culture." *Rhetoric and Public Affairs* 8, no. 1 (2005): 31–57.

Fixmer-Oraiz, Natalie. *Homeland Maternity: US Security Culture and the New Reproductive Regime*. Urbana: University of Illinois Press, 2019.

Flores, Lisa A. "Between Abundance and Marginalization: The Imperative of Racial Rhetorical Criticism." *Review of Communication* 16, no. 1 (2016): 4–24.

Foss, Karen A., and Sonja K. Foss. "Personal Experience as Evidence in Feminist Scholarship." *Western Journal of Communication* 58, no. 1 (1994): 39–42.

Foss, Sonja K., and Cindy L. Griffin. "Beyond Persuasion: A Proposal for an Invitational Rhetoric. (Exploring Rhetoric)." *Communication Monographs* 62, no. 1 (1995): 2–19.

———. "A Feminist Perspective on Rhetorical Theory: Toward a Clarification of Boundaries." *Western Journal of Communication* 56, no. 4 (1992): 330–49.

Fraser, Nancy. "Rethinking the Public Sphere: A Contribution to the Critique of Actually Existing Democracy." In *Habermas and the Public Sphere*, edited by Craig Calhoun, 109–42. Cambridge: Massachusetts Institute of Technology Press, 1992.

Garcia, Patricia. "Everyone Needs to Read the Stanford Rape Victim's Powerful Letter to Her Attacker." *Vogue Magazine*, June 6, 2016. http://www.vogue.com/article/stanford-student-sexual-assault-victim-statement.

Garland, David. *The Culture of Control: Crime and Social Order in Contemporary Society*. Chicago: University of Chicago Press, 2001.

Gay, Roxane. *Bad Feminist: Essays*. New York: Harper Perennial, 2014.

———. *Hunger: A Memoir of (My) Body*. New York: Harper Collins, 2017.

"Get Statistics." National Sexual Violence Resource Center. Accessed July 22, 2019. https://www.nsvrc.org/statistics.

Gianino, Laura. "I Went Public with My Sexual Assault. And Then the Trolls Came for Me." *Washington Post*, October 18, 2017. https://www.washingtonpost.com/news/posteverything/wp/2017/10/18/i-went-public-with-my-sexual-assault-and-then-the-trolls-came-for-me.

Gibson, Katie L. "Judicial Rhetoric and Women's 'Place': The United States Supreme Court's Darwinian Defense of Separate Spheres." *Western Journal of Communication* 71, no. 2 (2007): 159–75.

Gilmore, Leigh. *Tainted Witness: Why We Doubt What Women Say About Their Lives*. New York: Columbia University Press, 2017.

Glenn, Cheryl. *Rhetorical Feminism and This Thing Called Hope*. Carbondale: Southern Illinois University Press, 2018.

———. *Rhetoric Retold: Regendering the Tradition from Antiquity Through the Renaissance*. Carbondale: Southern Illinois University Press, 1997.

———. *Unspoken: A Rhetoric of Silence*. Carbondale: Southern Illinois University Press, 2004.

Glenn, Cheryl, and Krista Ratcliffe. *Silence and Listening as Rhetorical Acts*. Carbondale: Southern Illinois University Press, 2011.

Gordon, Avery F. *Ghostly Matters: Haunting and the Sociological Imagination*. Minneapolis: University of Minneapolis Press, 1997.

Gould, Deborah B. *Moving Politics: Emotion and ACT UP's Fight Against AIDS*. Chicago: University of Chicago Press, 2009.

Gray, Eliza. "Authorities Invest $80 Million in Ending the Rape Kit Backlog." *Time*, September 10, 2015. http://time.com/4029517/rape-kit-backlog-funding.

Grewal, Inderpal. *Transnational America: Feminisms, Diasporas, Neoliberalisms*. Durham: Duke University Press, 2005.

Griffin, Cindy L. "The Essentialist Roots of the Public Sphere: A Feminist Critique." *Western Journal of Communication* 60, no. 1 (1996): 21–39.

Grigoriadis, Vanessa. "Meet the College Women Who Are Starting a Revolution Against Campus Sexual Assault." *New York Magazine*, September 21, 2014. https://www.thecut.com/2014/09/emma-sulkowicz-campus-sexual-assault-activism.html.

Gross, Alan. *Starring the Text*. Chicago: University of Chicago Press, 2006.

Gunn, Joshua. "Mourning Humanism, or, the Idiom of Haunting." *Quarterly Journal of Speech* 92, no. 1 (2006): 77–102.

———. "Mourning Speech: Haunting and the Spectral Voices of Nine-Eleven." *Text and Performance Quarterly* 24, no. 2 (2004): 91–114.
Haas, Christina. "Materializing Public and Private: The Spatialization of Conceptual Categories in Discourses of Abortion." In *Rhetorical Bodies*, edited by Jack Selzer and Sharon Crowley, 218–38. Madison: University of Wisconsin, Press, 1999.
Habermas, Jürgen. *The Structural Transformation of the Public Sphere: An Inquiry into a Category of Bourgeois Society*. Translated by Thomas Burger. Cambridge: Massachusetts Institute of Technology Press, 1989.
Halicek, Megan. "Lansing/Statement." In Our Words. Accessed June 11, 2019. https://inourownwords.us/2018/08/08/megan-halicek.
Hall, Rachel. "'It Can Happen to You': Rape Prevention in the Age of Risk Management." *Hypatia* 19, no. 3 (2004): 1–19.
Hallenbeck, Sarah. "Toward a Posthuman Perspective: Feminist Rhetorical Methodologies and Everyday Practices." *Advances in the History of Rhetoric* 15, no. 1 (2012): 9–27.
Hanrahan, Emma. "One Woman Tells Us What It's Like to Be Raped—And Have Your Town Turn Against You." MTV News, November 11, 2014. http://www.mtv.com/news/1962056/rape-what-it-feels-like-no-one-believes.
Haraway, Donna. "Situated Knowledges: The Science Question in Feminism and the Privilege of Partial Perspective." *Feminist Studies* 14, no. 3 (1988): 579–99.
Harding, Sandra G. *The Science Question in Feminism*. Ithaca: Cornell University Press, 1986.
———. *Whose Science? Whose Knowledge? Thinking from Women's Lives*. Ithaca: Cornell University Press, 1991.
Hariman, Robert, and John Louis Lucaites. "Dissent and Emotional Management in a Liberal-Democratic Society: The Kent State Iconic Photograph." *Rhetoric Society Quarterly* 31, no. 3 (2001): 5–31.
———. *No Caption Needed: Iconic Photographs, Public Culture, and Liberal Democracy*. Chicago: University of Chicago Press, 2007.
Harrell, Erika. "Crime Against Persons with Disabilities, 2009–2013—Statistical Tables." Bureau of Justice Statistics, U.S. Department of Justice, May 2015. https://www.bjs.gov/content/pub/pdf/capd0913st.pdf.
Hauser, Gerard A. "Incongruous Bodies: Arguments for Personal Sufficiency and Public Insufficiency." *Argumentation and Advocacy* 36, no. 1 (1999): 1–8.
———. "Prisoners of Conscience and the Counterpublic Sphere of Prison Writing: The Stones That Start the Avalanche." In *Counterpublics and the State*, edited by Robert Asen and Daniel C. Brouwer, 35–58. Albany: State University of New York Press, 2001.
———. "Reshaping Publics and Public Spheres: The Meese Commission's Report on Pornography." In *Vernacular Voices: The Rhetoric of Public and Public Spheres*. Columbia: University Of South Carolina Press, 1991: 161–88.
Hawhee, Debra. "Looking into Aristotle's Eyes: Toward a Theory of Rhetorical Vision." *Advances in the History of Rhetoric* 14, no. 2 (2011): 139–65.
———. *Moving Bodies: Kenneth Burke at the Edges of Language*. Columbia: University of South Carolina Press, 2009.
———. *Rhetoric in Tooth and Claw: Animals, Language, Sensation*. Chicago: University of Chicago Press, 2017.
———. "Rhetoric's Sensorium." *Quarterly Journal of Speech* 101, no. 1 (2015): 2–17.
Headlee, Celeste, and John Biewen. "Episode 50: Feminism in Black and White (MEN, Part 4)." Scene on Radio, August 22, 2018. https://www.sceneonradio.org/episode-50-feminism-in-black-and-white-men-part-4.

Hesford, Wendy. "Reading *Rape Stories*: Material Rhetoric and the Trauma of Representation." *College English* 62, no. 2 (1999): 192–221.

———. *Spectacular Rhetorics: Human Rights Visions, Recognitions, Feminisms.* Durham: Duke University Press, 2001.

Hesford, Wendy, and Wendy Kozol. *Haunting Violations: Feminist Criticism and the Crisis of the "Real."* Urbana: University of Illinois Press, 2000.

Hill, Annie. "SlutWalk as Perifeminist Response to Rape Logic: The Politics of Reclaiming a Name." *Communication and Critical/Cultural Studies* 13, no. 1 (2016): 23–39.

Hill, Shonagh. "Ghostly Surrogates and Unhomely Memories: Performing the Past in Marina Carr's Portia Coghlan." *Études Littéraires* 37, no. 1 (2012): 173–87.

Hinshaw, Wendy Wolters. "Regulating Girlhood: Protecting and Prosecuting Juvenile Violence." *JAC: A Journal of Rhetoric, Culture, and Politics* 33, no. 3–4 (2013): 487–506.

Hod, Itay. "Men Join #MeToo Campaign with #HowIWillChange: 'Guys It's Our Turn.'" *The Wrap*, October 18, 2017. https://www.thewrap.com/men-join-metoo-campaign-howiwillchange-guys-turn.

hooks, bell. *Talking Back: Thinking Feminist, Thinking Black.* New York: Routledge, 2014.

Hsu, V. Jo. "(Trans)forming #MeToo: Toward a Networked Response to Gender Violence." *Women's Studies in Communication* 42, no. 3 (2019): 269–86.

Humphrey, Wendy Adele. "'Let's Talk About Sex': Legislating and Educating on the Affirmative Consent Standard." *University of San Francisco Law Review* 50, no. 1 (2016): 35–74.

Hylton, Hilary. "The Dark Side of Clearing America's Rape Kit Backlog." *Time*, September 7, 2013. http://nation.time.com/2013/09/07/the-dark-side-of-clearing-americas-rape-kit-backlog.

"The Inception." The Me Too Movement. JustBeInc. Accessed July 17, 2019. https://justbeinc.wixsite.com/justbeinc/the-me-too-movement-cmml.

Irwin, Nicole. "'Guys, It's Our Turn': Men Pledge New Behaviour in Response to #MeToo." *Independent*, October 19, 2017. https://www.independent.ie/world-news/and-finally/guys-its-our-turn-men-pledge-new-behaviour-in-response-to-metoo-36242992.html.

"It's On Us." It's On Us. Accessed May 17, 2018. https://www.itsonus.org.

"It's On Us." Stories of Cobber Life. Concordia College. Accessed July 3, 2019. https://www.concordiacollege.edu/stories/details/it-s-on-us.

Jack, Jordynn. "Acts of Institution: Embodying Feminist Rhetorical Methodologies in Space and Time." *Rhetoric Review* 28, no. 3 (2009): 285–303.

———. *Autism and Gender: From Refrigerator Mothers to Computer Geeks.* Urbana: University of Illinois Press, 2014.

———. "Leviathan and the Breast Pump: Toward an Embodied Rhetoric of Wearable Technology." *Rhetoric Society Quarterly* 46, no. 3 (2016): 207–21.

Jackson, Sarah J., and Brooke Foucault Welles. "Hijacking #myNYPD: Social Media Dissent and Networked Counterpublics." *Journal of Communication* 65, no. 6 (2015): 932–52.

James, Sandy E., Jody L. Herman, Susan Rankin, Mara Keisling, Lisa Mottet, and Ma'ayan Anafi. *The Report of the 2015 U.S. Transgender Survey.* Washington, DC: National Center for Transgender Equality, 2016.

Jarratt, Susan C. *Rereading the Sophists: Classical Rhetoric Refigured.* Carbondale: Southern Illinois University Press, 1991.

Jarrett, Valerie. "A Renewed Call to Action to End Rape and Sexual Assault." National Archives and Records, January 22, 2014. Accessed May 17, 2018.

https://obamawhitehouse.archives.gov/blog/2014/01/22/renewed-call-action-end-rape-and-sexual-assault.

Jensen, Robin E. *Dirty Words: The Rhetoric of Public Sex Education, 1870–1924.* Urbana: University of Illinois Press, 2010.

———. "From Barren to Sterile: The Evolution of a Mixed Metaphor." *Rhetoric Society Quarterly* 45, no. 1 (2015): 25–46.

———. "Improving Upon Nature: The Rhetorical Ecology of Chemical Language, Reproductive Endocrinology, and the Medicalization of Infertility." *Quarterly Journal of Speech* 101, no. 2 (2015): 329–53.

———. *Infertility: Tracing the History of a Transformative Term.* University Park: Pennsylvania State University Press, 2016.

Johnson, Jenell. *American Lobotomy: A Rhetorical History.* Ann Arbor: University of Michigan Press, 2014.

———. "The Limits of Persuasion: Rhetoric and Resistance in the Last Battle of the Korean War." *Quarterly Journal of Speech* 100, no. 3 (2014): 323–47.

———. "'A Man's Mouth Is His Castle': The Midcentury Fluoridation Controversy and the Visceral Public." *Quarterly Journal of Speech* 102, no. 1 (2016): 1–20.

Johnson, Will. "From #MeToo to #HowIWillChange." *Nelson Star*, October 27, 2017. https://www.nelsonstar.com/opinion/column-from-metoo-to-howiwillchange.

Kafer, Alison. *Feminist, Queer, Crip.* Bloomington: Indiana University Press, 2013.

Kantor, Jodi, and Megan Twohey. "Harvey Weinstein Paid Off Sexual Harassment Accusers for Decades." *New York Times*, October 5, 2017. https://www.nytimes.com/2017/10/05/us/harvey-weinstein-harassment-allegations.html.

Kaplan, Caren, Norma Alacon, and Minoo Moallem. *Between Woman and Nation: Nationalisms, Transnational Feminisms, and the State.* Durham: Duke University Press, 1999.

Katz, Jackson. "Violence Against Women: It's a Men's Issue." TEDxFiDiWomen, November 2012, San Francisco, CA. Accessed July 3, 2019. https://www.ted.com/talks/jackson_katz_violence_against_women_it_s_a_men_s_issue.

Kaufer, David, and Amal Mohammed Al-Malki. "The War on Terror Through Arab-American Eyes: The Arab-American Press as a Rhetorical Counterpublic." *Rhetoric Review* 28, no. 1 (2009): 47–65.

Keller, Evelyn Fox. *Reflections on Gender and Science.* New Haven: Yale University Press, 1985.

Kelly, Erin, and Jessica Estepa. "Brett Kavanaugh: A Timeline of Allegations Against the Supreme Court Nominee." *USA Today*, September 24, 2018. https://www.usatoday.com/story/news/politics/onpolitics/2018/09/24/brett-kavanaugh-allegations-timeline-supreme-court/1408073002.

Keränen, Lisa. *Scientific Characters: Rhetoric, Politics, and Trust in Breast Cancer Research.* Tuscaloosa: University of Alabama Press, 2010.

Khoury, Nicole. "Enough Violence: The Importance of Local Action to Transnational Feminist Scholarship and Activism." *Peitho* 18, no. 1 (2015): 113–39.

King, Candace. "We Need to Include Black Women's Experience in the Movement Against Campus Sexual Assault." *Nation*, June 15, 2018. https://www.thenation.com/article/need-include-black-womens-experience-movement-campus-sexual-assault.

Ko, Lisa, "Why It Matters That 'Emily Doe' in the Brock Turner Case Is Asian-American." *New York Times*, September 24, 2019. https://www.nytimes.com/2019/09/24/opinion/chanel-miller-know-my-name.html.

Koerber, Amy. *From Hysteria to Hormones: A Rhetorical History.* University Park: Pennsylvania State University Press, 2018.

Kohlstedt, Sally Gregory, and Helen E. Longino. Forward to *Body Talk: Rhetoric, Technology, Reproduction*, edited by Mary M. Lay, Laura J. Gurak, Clare Gravon, and Cynthia Myntti, ix–xii. Madison: University of Wisconsin Press, 2000.

Kristof, Nicholas. "Despite DNA, the Rapist Got Away." *New York Times*, May 10, 2015. https://www.nytimes.com/2015/05/10/opinion/sunday/nicholas-kristof-despite-dna-the-rapist-got-away.html.

———. "Is Rape Serious?" *New York Times*, April 29, 2009. https://www.nytimes.com/2009/04/30/opinion/30kristof.html.

"Larry Nassar's Survivors Speak, And Finally the World Listens—And Believes." *Believed*, NPR, December 10, 2018. https://www.npr.org/2018/12/07/674525176/larry-nassars-survivors-speak-and-finally-the-world-listens-and-believes.

Larson, Stephanie R. "Survivors, Liars, and Unfit Minds: Rhetorical Impossibility and Rape Trauma Disclosure." *Hypatia* 44, no. 4 (2018): 681–99.

Lay, Mary M. *The Rhetoric of Midwifery: Gender, Knowledge, and Power*. New Brunswick: Rutgers University Press, 2000.

Lay, Mary M., Laura J. Gurak, Clare Gravon, and Cynthia Myntti. *Body Talk: Rhetoric, Technology, Reproduction*. Madison: University of Wisconsin Press, 2000.

Loken, Meredith. "#BringBackOurGirls and the Invisibility of Imperialism." *Feminist Media Studies* 14, no. 6 (2014): 1100–1101.

Lonsway, Kimberly A., and Louise F. Fitzgerald. "Rape Myths: In Review." *Psychology of Women Quarterly* 18, no. 2 (1994): 133–64.

Lopez, German. "The Failure of Police Body Cameras." *Vox*, July 21, 2017. https://www.vox.com/policy-and-politics/2017/7/21/15983842/police-body-cameras-failures.

Lydersen, Kari. "Law Came Too Late for Some Rape Victims." *New York Times*, July 8, 2010. https://www.nytimes.com/2010/07/09/us/09cnckits.html.

Mack, Ashley Noel, and Bryan J. McCann. "Critiquing State and Gendered Violence in the Age of #MeToo." *Quarterly Journal of Speech* 104, no. 3 (2018): 329–44.

Mack, Ashley Noel, and Tiara R. Na'puti. "Our Bodies Are Not *Terra Nullius*": Building a Decolonial Feminist Resistance to Gendered Violence." *Women's Studies in Communication* 43, no. 3 (2019): 347–70.

MacKinnon, Catharine A. "Feminism, Marxism, Method, and the State: Toward Feminist Jurisprudence." *Signs* 8, no. 4 (1983): 635–58.

———. "Rape Redefined General Essays." *Harvard Law and Policy Review* 10, no. 2 (2016): 431–78.

———. *Toward a Feminist Theory of the State*. Cambridge: Harvard University Press, 1989.

Marciniak, Allison L. "The Case Against Affirmative Consent: Why the Well-Intentioned Legislation Dangerously Misses the Mark." *University of Pittsburgh Law Review* 77, no. 2 (2015): 51–75.

Marcus, Sharon. "Fighting Bodies, Fighting Words: A Theory and Politics of Rape Prevention." In *Feminists Theorize the Political*, edited by Judith Butler and Joan W. Scott, 385–403. New York: Routledge, 2002.

Mardorossian, Carine M. *Framing the Rape Victim: Gender and Agency Reconsidered*. New Brunswick: Rutgers University Press, 2014.

Massumi, Brian. *Parables for the Virtual: Movement, Affect, Sensation*. Durham: Duke University Press, 2002.

May, Ashley. "Here's What Happened Each Day of Lassar [sic] Nassar's Hearing." *USA Today*, January 30, 2018. https://www.usatoday.com/story/news/nation-now/2018/01/30/heres-what-happened-each-day-lassar-nassars-hearing/1078324001.

McGuire, Danielle L. *At the Dark End of the Street: Black Women, Rape, and Resistance—A New History of the Civil Rights Movement from Rosa Parks to the Rise of Black Power*. New York: Vintage, 2010.

McKinnon, Sara L. *Gendered Asylum: Race and Violence in U.S. Law and Politics.* Urbana: University of Illinois Press, 2016.

McMahon, Sarah, Judy L. Postmus, and Ruth Anne Koenick. "Conceptualizing the Engaging Bystander Approach to Sexual Violence Prevention on College Campuses." *Journal of College Student Development* 52, no. 1 (2011): 115–30.

McNulty, Timothy J. "Federal Report to Meese Outlines War on Porn." *Chicago Tribune*, July 10, 1986. http://articles.chicagotribune.com/1986-07-10/news/8602180951 _1_pornography-commission-chairman-henry-hudson-acts-of-sexual-violence.

McRuer, Robert. *Crip Theory: Cultural Signs of Queerness and Disability.* New York: New York University Press, 2006.

———. *Crip Times: Disability, Globalization, and Resistance.* New York: New York University Press, 2018.

Mentors in Violence Prevention. "MVP Strategies." Accessed July 3, 2019. https://www.mvpstrat.com/about.

Miller, Chanel. *Know My Name: A Memoir.* New York: Viking, 2019.

Miller, Michael E. "#RapeHoax Posters Plastered around Columbia University in Backlash Against Alleged Rape Victim." *Washington Post*, May 22, 2015. https://www.washingtonpost.com/news/morning-mix/wp/2015/05/22/rapehoax -posters-plastered-around-columbia-university-in-backlash-against-alleged-rape -victim.

Moghadam, Valentine M. *Globalization and Social Movements: Islamism, Feminism, and the Global Justice Movement.* Lanham, MD: Rowman & Littlefield, 2009.

Mohanty, Chandra Talpade. *Feminism Without Borders: Decolonizing Theory, Practicing Solidarity.* Durham: Duke University Press, 2003.

Mulla, Sameena. *The Violence of Care: Rape Victims, Forensic Nurses, and Sexual Assault Intervention.* New York: New York University Press, 2014.

Nair, Sharika. "#MeToo Trends on Social Media as Women Speak Up About Sexual Abuse." *Your Story*, October 16, 2017. https://yourstory.com/2017/10/metoo -trends-women-speak-sexual-abuse.

"A Neglected Law Enforcement Asset." *New York Times*, May 9, 2002. http://www.nytimes .com/2002/05/09/opinion/a-neglected-law-enforcement-asset.html.

O'Banion, John D. *Reorienting Rhetoric: The Dialectic of List and Story.* University Park: Pennsylvania State University Press, 1991.

O'Gorman, Ned. "Eisenhower and the American Sublime." *Quarterly Journal of Speech* 94, no. 1 (2008): 44–72.

———. "Longinus's Sublime Rhetoric, or How Rhetoric Came into Its Own." *Rhetoric Society Quarterly* 34, no. 2 (2004): 71–89.

Olson, Christa J. "American Magnitude: Frederic Church, Hiram Bingham, and Hemispheric Vision." *Rhetoric Society Quarterly* 48, no. 4 (2017): 380–404.

———. *Constitutive Visions: Indigeneity and Commonplaces of National Identity in Republican Ecuador.* University Park: Pennsylvania State University Press, 2014.

"1 is 2 Many." National Archives and Records. Accessed May 17, 2018. https:// obamawhitehouse.archives.gov/1is2many.

Ono, Kent A., and John M. Sloop. *Shifting Borders: Rhetoric, Immigration, and California's "Proposition 187."* Philadelphia: Temple University Press, 2002.

Ore, Ersula J. *Lynching: Violence, Rhetoric, and American Identity.* Jackson: University Press of Mississippi, 2019.

"Our Story." It's On Us. Accessed May 17, 2018. https://www.itsonus.org/our-story.

Owens, Kim Hensley. *Writing Childbirth: Women's Rhetorical Agency in Labor and Online.* Carbondale: Southern Illinois University Press, 2015.

Palczewski, Catherine H. "Survivor Testimony in the Pornography Controversy: Assessing Credibility in the Minneapolis Hearings and the Attorney General's Report." In *Warranting Assent: Case Studies in Argument Evaluation*, edited by Edward Schiappa, 257–82. Albany: State University of New York Press, 1995.
Panagia, Davide. *The Political Life of Sensation*. Durham: Duke University Press, 2009.
Papacharissi, Zizi. *Affective Publics: Sentiment, Technology, and Politics*. New York: Oxford University Press, 2014.
Park, Andrea. "#MeToo Reaches 85 Countries with 1.7M Tweets." CBS News, October 24, 2017. https://www.cbsnews.com/news/metoo-reaches-85-countries-with-1-7-million-tweets.
Parker, Kathleen. "Silent No More on Rape." *Lincoln Journal Star*, March 17, 2013. https://journalstar.com/news/opinion/editorial/columnists/kathleen-parker-silent-on-rape-no-more/article_4585b22b-d0b8-50bd-ad40-64e921c79c86.html.
Pasque, Lisa Speckhard. "'We Can Do Better': Madison Women Join #MeToo Social Media Movement to Fight Sexual Assault." *Capital Times*, October 17, 2017. https://madison.com/ct/news/local/govt-and-politics/we-can-do-better-madison-women-join-metoo-social-media/article_628c9419-45fd-5b08-8438-9b9d21a9c6b3.html.
Pateman, Carole. "Women and Consent." *Political Theory* 8, no. 2 (1980): 149–68.
Patterson, Debra, and Rebecca Campbell. "The Problem of Untested Sexual Assault Kits: Why Are Some Kits Never Submitted to a Crime Laboratory?" *Journal of Interpersonal Violence* 27, no. 11 (2012): 2259–75.
People of the State of California v. Brock Allen Turner. No. B1577162 (2015) *available at* http://documents.latimes.com/stanford-brock-turner.
"Perpetrators of Sexual Violence: Statistics." RAINN. Accessed June 11, 2019. https://www.rainn.org/statistics/perpetrators-sexual-violence.
Peters, John Durham. *Speaking into the Air: A History of the Idea of Communication*. Chicago: University of Chicago Press, 1991.
Pezzullo, Phaedra C. "Resisting 'National Breast Cancer Awareness Month': The Rhetoric of Counterpublics and Their Cultural Performances." *Quarterly Journal of Speech* 89, no. 4 (2003): 345–65.
Picart, Caroline Joan S. "Rhetorically Reconfiguring Victimhood and Agency: The Violence Against Women Act's Civil Rights Clause." *Rhetoric and Public Affairs* 6, no. 1 (2003): 87–125.
Pickering, Barbara A. "Women's Voices as Evidence: Personal Testimony Is Pro-Choice Films." *Argumentation and Advocacy* 40, no. 1 (2003): 1–22.
Pilar Blanco, María del, and Esther Peeren. *The Spectralities Reader: Ghosts and Haunting in Contemporary Cultural Theory*. New York: Bloomsbury, 2013.
Portnoy, Jenna. "McAuliffe Signs Bill Mandating New Rules for Collecting, Testing Rape Kits." *Washington Post*, April 14, 2016. https://www.washingtonpost.com/local/virginia-politics/mcauliffe-signs-bill-mandating-new-rules-for-rape-kits-in-va/2016/04/14/0c0f816c-01b8-11e6-9203-7b8670959b88_story.html.
Portwood, Laura, and Susan Berridge. "The Year in Feminist Hashtags." Special issue in *Feminist Media Studies* 14, no. 6 (2014): 895–1115.
Prelli, Lawrence. *A Rhetoric of Science: Inventing Scientific Discourse*. Columbia: University of South Carolina Press, 1989.
Presley, Katie. "Janelle Monáe Releases Visceral Protest Song, 'Hell You Talmbout.'" NPR, August 18, 2015. https://www.npr.org/sections/allsongs/2015/08/18/385202798/janelle-mon-e-releases-visceral-protest-song-hell-you-talmbout.

Price, Margaret. "The Bodymind Problem and the Possibilities of Pain." *Hypatia* 30, no. 1 (2014): 268–84.

Prokos, Desaree Nicole. "16 #MeToo Tweets Everyone Needs to See." *Odyssey*, October 30, 2017. https://www.theodysseyonline.com/16-metoo-tweets-everyone-needs-to-see.

Propen, Amy D., and Mary Lay Schuster. *Rhetoric and Communication Perspectives on Domestic Violence and Sexual Assault: Policy and Protocol Through Discourse.* New York: Routledge, 2017.

"Protecting Students from Sexual Assault." Washington DC: The United States Department of Justice. Accessed May 17, 2018. https://www.justice.gov/ovw/protecting-students-sexual-assault.

Puar, Jasbir K. *The Right to Maim: Debility, Capacity, Disability.* Durham: Duke University Press, 2017.

———. *Terrorist Assemblages: Homonationalism in Queer Times.* Durham: Duke University Press, 2017.

Quinlan, Andrea. *The Technoscientific Witness of Rape: Contentious Histories of Law, Feminism, and Forensic Science.* Toronto: University of Toronto Press, 2017.

Rabaté, Jean-Michel. *The Ghosts of Modernity.* Gainesville: University Press of Florida, 2010.

Rahal, Sarah, and Kim Kozlowski. "204 Impact Statements, 9 Days, 2 Counties, A Life Sentence for Larry Nassar." *Detroit News*, February 8, 2018. https://www.detroitnews.com/story/news/local/michigan/2018/02/08/204-impact-statements-9-days-2-counties-life-sentence-larry-nassar/1066335001.

Ratcliffe, Krista. *Rhetorical Listening: Identification, Gender, Whiteness.* Carbondale: Southern Illinois University Press, 2005.

Ray, Angela G., and Cindy Koenig Richards. "Inventing Citizens, Imagining Gender Justice: The Suffrage Rhetoric of Virginia and Francis Minor." *Quarterly Journal of Speech* 93, no. 4 (2007): 375–402.

"Respect for Rape Victims." *New York Times*, November 13, 2009. https://www.nytimes.com/2009/11/14/opinion/14sat3.html.

Rhodes, Jacqueline. "SlutWalk Is Not Enough: Notes Toward a Critical Feminist Rhetoric." In *Unruly Rhetorics: Protest, Persuasion, and Publics*, edited by Jonathan Alexander, Susan C. Jarratt, and Nancy Welch, 88–104. Pittsburgh: University of Pittsburgh Press, 2018.

Rice, Jenny. *Distant Publics: Development Rhetoric and the Subject of Crisis.* Pittsburgh: University of Pittsburgh Press, 2012.

———. "The Rhetorical Aesthetics of More: On Archival Magnitude." *Philosophy and Rhetoric* 50, no. 1 (2017): 26–49.

Richardson, Brian. "Modern Fiction, the Poetics of Lists, and the Boundaries of Narrative." *Style* 50, no. 3 (2016): 327–41.

Riedner, Rachel. "Lives of In-famous Women: Gender, Political Economy, Nation-State Power, and Persuasion in a Transnational Age." *JAC: A Journal of Rhetoric, Culture, and Politics* 33, nos. 3–4 (2013): 645–69.

Rocha, Veronica, and Richard Winton. "Light Sentence for Stanford Swimmer in Sexual Assault 'Extraordinary,' Legal Experts Say." *Los Angeles Times*, June 8, 2016. https://www.latimes.com/local/lanow/la-me-ln-stanford-sexual-assault-sentence-20160607-snap-story.html.

Rogers, Katie, Maggie Haberman, and Peter Baker. "Acosta Defends His Role in Brokering Jeffry Epstein Plea Deal." *New York Times*, July 10, 2019. https://www.nytimes.com/2019/07/10/us/politics/acosta-epstein.html.

Rubin, Gayle. "Blood Under the Bridge: Reflections on 'Thinking Sex.'" *GLQ* 17, no. 1 (2011): 15–48.

Russonello, Giovanni. "Read Oprah Winfrey's Golden Globes Speech." *New York Times*, January 7, 2018. https://www.nytimes.com/2018/01/07/movies/oprah-winfrey-golden-globes-speech-transcript.html.

Ryan, Mary P. "The Public and the Private Good: Across the Great Divide in Women's History." *Journal of Women's History* 15, no. 2 (2003): 10–27.

Sandahl, Carrie. "Queering the Crip or Cripping the Queer? Intersections of Queer and Crip Identities in Solo Autobiographical Performance." *GLQ: A Journal of Lesbian and Gay Studies* 9, nos. 1–2 (2003): 25–56.

S.B. 5965, 114th Cong. (2015). https://www.nysenate.gov/legislation/bills/2015/S5965.

Scarry, Elaine. *The Body in Pain: The Making and Unmaking of the World.* New York: Oxford University Press, 1985.

Schildrick, Margrit. *Leaky Bodies and Boundaries: Feminism, Postmodernism, and (Bio) Ethics.* New York: Routledge, 1997.

Schonbek, Amelia. "The Complete List of Allegations Against Harvey Weinstein." *The Cut*, January 6, 2020, https://www.thecut.com/2020/01/harvey-weinstein-complete-list-allegations.html.

Schuller, Kyla. *The Biopolitics of Feeling: Race, Sex, and Science in the Nineteenth Century*. Durham: Duke University Press, 2017.

Schuster, Mary Lay, and Amy D. Propen. *Victim Advocacy in the Courtroom: Persuasive Practices in Domestic and Child Protection Cases*. Boston: Northeastern University Press, 2011.

Scott, J. Blake. *Risky Rhetoric: AIDS and the Cultural Practices of HIV Testing*. Carbondale: Southern Illinois University Press, 2003.

Selzer, Jack, and Sharon Crowley. *Rhetorical Bodies*. Madison: University of Wisconsin Press, 1991.

Shvarts, Aliza. "How I Learned to Stop Worrying and Love the Rape Kit." In *Feminist and Queer Information Studies Reader*, edited by Patrick Keilty and Rebecca Dean, 601–19. Sacramento: Litwin Press, 2013.

Slapak-Fugate, Terri. "Who'll Conduct the Rape Exam?" *Chicago Tribune*, May 23, 2016. https://www.chicagotribune.com/opinion/commentary/ct-rape-kit-exams-nurse-training-20160523-story.html.

Sloop, John M. *Disciplining Gender: Rhetorics of Sex Identity in Contemporary US Culture*. Amherst: University of Massachusetts Press, 2004.

Slye Aniskovich, Jennifer, et al. Letter to Charles Grassley and Dianne Feinstein, September 14, 2018. https://www.judiciary.senate.gov/imo/media/doc/2018-09-14%2065%20Women%20who%20know%20Kavanaugh%20from%20High%20School%20-%20Kavanaugh%20Nomination.pdf.

Small, Zachary. "Queer Identity in the MeToo Movement: A Conversation with Emma Sulkowicz." *Hyperallergic*, August 31, 2018. https://hyperallergic.com/458257/conversation-with-emma-sulkowicz.

Smart, Carol. *Feminism and the Power of Law*. New York: Routledge, 1989.

Smith, Craig R., and Michael J. Hyde. "Rethinking 'The Public': The Role of Emotion in Being-With-Others." *Quarterly Journal of Speech* 77, no. 4 (1991): 446–66.

Smith, Roberta. "In a Mattress, a Lever for Art and Political Protest." *New York Times*, September 21, 2014. https://nytimes.com/2014/09/22/arts/design/in-a-mattress-a-fulcrum-of-art-and-political-protest.html.

Solinger, Rickie. *Pregnancy and Power: A Short History of Reproductive Politics in America*. New York: New York University Press, 2007.

Somanader, Tanya. "President Obama Launches the 'It's On Us' Campaign to End Sexual Assault on Campus." National Archives and Records, September 19, 2014.

Accessed May 17, 2018. https://obamawhitehouse.archives.gov/blog/2014/09/19/president-obama-launches-its-us-campaign-end-sexual-assault-campus.

Souto, Melissa. "Rape Victim Advocates." GoFundMe. Accessed March 27, 2018. https://www.gofundme.com/rdv2rg.

Spillers, Hortense J. "Mama's Baby, Papa's Maybe: An American Grammar Book." *Diacritics* 17, no. 2 (1987): 64–81.

Spry, Tami. "In the Absence of Word and Body: Hegemonic Implications of 'Victim' and 'Survivor' in Women's Narratives of Sexual Violence." *Women and Language* 18, no. 2 (1995): 27–32.

Squires, Catherine. "The Black Press and the State: Attracting Unwanted (?) Attention." In *Counterpublics and the State*, edited by Robert Asen and Daniel C. Brouwer, 111–36. Albany: State University of New York Press, 2001.

Stenberg, Shari J. "'Tweet Me Your First Assaults': Writing Shame and the Rhetorical Work of #NotOkay." *Rhetoric Society Quarterly* 48, no. 2 (2018): 119–38.

St. Félix, Doreen. "The Ford-Kavanaugh Hearing Will Be Remembered as a Grotesque Display of Patriarchal Resentment." *New Yorker*, September 27, 2018. https://www.newyorker.com/culture/cultural-comment/the-ford-kavanaugh-hearings-will-be-remembered-for-their-grotesque-display-of-patriarchal-resentment.

Stormer, Nathan. *Sign of Pathology: US Medical Rhetoric on Abortion, 1800s–1960s*. University Park: Pennsylvania State University Press, 2015.

Sulkowicz, Emma. *Ceci N'est Pas Un Viol*. June 2015. Accessed April 2017. http://www.cecinestpasunviol.com (site no longer available).

Sutton, Jane. "The Taming of the Polos/Polis: Rhetoric as an Achievement Without Woman." *Southern Communication Journal* 57, no. 2 (1992): 87–119.

"Take The Pledge." It's On Us. Accessed July 3, 2019. https://www.itsonus.org/pledge.

Teston, Christa. *Bodies in Flux: Scientific Methods for Negotiating Medical Uncertainty*. Chicago: University of Chicago Press, 2017.

Tofte, Sarah. *Testing Justice: The Rape Kit Backlog in Los Angeles City and County*. New York: Human Rights Watch, 2009. https://www.hrw.org/report/2009/03/31/testing-justice/rape-kit-backlog-los-angeles-city-and-county.

———. "A Test of Justice for Rape Victims." *Washington Post*, July 22, 2008. http://www.washingtonpost.com/wp-dyn/content/article/2008/07/21/AR2008072102359.html.

Tomlinson, Barbara. *Feminism and Affect at the Scene of Argument: Beyond the Trope of the Angry Feminist*. Philadelphia: Temple University Press, 2010.

Ulloa, Jazmine. "California Expands Punishment for Rape After Brown Signs Bills Inspired by Brock Turner Case." *Los Angeles Times*, September 30, 2016. https://www.latimes.com/politics/essential/la-pol-sac-essential-politics-updates-california-expands-punishment-for-rape-1475260488-htmlstory.html.

United States. Attorney General's Commission on Pornography. *Attorney General's Commission on Pornography: Final Report*. Washington DC: United States Department of Justice, 1986.

United States. Attorney General's Commission on Pornography, and National Coalition Against Censorship (US). *Meese Commission Exposed: Proceedings of an NCAC Public Information Briefing on the Attorney General's Commission on Pornography, January 16, 1986, New York City*. New York: National Coalition Against Censorship, 1986.

Vance, Carole S. "Negotiating Sex and Gender in the Attorney General's Commission on Pornography." In *Sexualities in History: A Reader*, edited by Kim M. Phillips and Barry Reay, 359–74. New York: Routledge, 2002.

Walters, Shannon. *Rhetorical Touch: Disability, Identification, Haptics.* Columbia: University of South Carolina Press, 2014.
Warner, Michael. *Publics and Counterpublics.* New York: Zone Books, 2002.
———. "Publics and Counterpublics (Abbreviated Version)." *Quarterly Journal of Speech* 88, no. 4 (2002): 413–25.
Weheliye, Alexander G. *Habeas Viscus: Racializing Assemblages, Biopolitics, and Black Feminist Theories of the Human.* Durham: Duke University Press, 2014.
Weinstock, Jeffry Andrew. *Spectral America: Phantoms and the National Imagination.* Madison: University of Wisconsin Press, 2004.
Wells, Susan. "*Our Bodies, Ourselves*: Reading the Written Body." *Signs* 33, no. 3 (2008): 697–723.
West, Isaac. *Transforming Citizenships: Transgender Articulations of the Law.* New York: New York University Press, 2013.
West, Lindy. "Brave Enough to Be Angry." *New York Times*, November 8, 2017. https://www.nytimes.com/2017/11/08/opinion/anger-women-weinstein-assault.html.
"What's Being Done to Address the Country's Backlog of Untested Kits." NPR, January 17, 2016. http://www.npr.org/2016/01/17/463358406/whats-being-done-to-address-the-countrys-backlog-of-untested-rape-kits.
The White House Office of the Press Secretary. "Fact Sheet: Final It's On Us Summit and Report of the White House Task Force to Protect Students from Sexual Assault." January 5, 2017. Accessed July 3, 2019. https://obamawhitehouse.archives.gov/the-press-office/2017/01/05/fact-sheet-final-its-us-summit-and-report-white-house-task-force-protect.
Willingham, Kamilah. "To the Harvard Law 19: Do Better." *Medium*, March 24, 2016. https://medium.com/@kamily/to-the-harvard-law-19-do-better-1353794288f2.
Winderman, Emily. "Anger's Volumes: Rhetorics of Amplification and Aggregation in #MeToo." *Women's Studies in Communication* 42, no. 3 (2019): 327–46.
———. "S(anger) Goes Postal in *The Woman Rebel*: Angry Rhetoric as a Collectivizing Moral Emotion." *Rhetoric and Public Affairs* 17, no. 3 (2014): 381–420.
Wingard, Jennifer. *Branded Bodies, Rhetoric, and the Neoliberal State.* Lanham, MD: Lexington Books, 2013.
Wood, Alisson. "'Get Home Safe,' My Rapist Said." *New York Times*, December 12, 2015. https://www.nytimes.com/2015/12/13/opinion/get-home-safe-my-rapist-said.html.
Yergeau, M. Remi. *Authoring Autism: On Rhetoric and Neurological Queerness.* Durham: Duke University Press, 2017.
Young, Iris Marion. *Responsibility for Justice.* New York: Oxford University Press, 2011.
Yung, Corey Rayburn. "Rape Law Gatekeeping." *Boston College Law Review* 58, no. 1 (2017): 206–56.
Zacharek, Stephanie, Eliana Dockterman, and Haley Sweetland Edwards. "TIME Person of the Year 2017: The Silence Breakers." *Time*, December 18, 2018. https://time.com/time-person-of-the-year-2017-silence-breakers.
Zarefsky, David. "Four Senses of Rhetorical History." In *Doing Rhetorical History: Concepts and Cases*, edited by Kathleen J. Turner, 19–32. Tuscaloosa: University of Alabama Press, 1998.
Ziegler, Jennifer A. "The Story Behind an Organizational List: A Genealogy of Wildland Firefighters' 10 Standard Fire Orders." *Communication Monographs* 74, no. 4 (2007): 415–42.

INDEX

Italicized page references indicate illustrations. Endnotes are referenced with "n" followed by the endnote number.

ableism, 4, 56
abortion, 36, 39
academia
  college/university campus responses to sexual assault, 23, 58–59, 74–75, 79–80, 85, 112–35
  and the study of rape culture, xi–xv, 3, 16, 137
accountability, 4, 8–9, 77
ACLU. *See* American Civil Liberties Union
Acosta, Alexander, 155, 156–57
activism. *See* anti-rape activism
Adam and Eve (Biblical characters), 48–50
Adinolfe, Nancy, 37
African American women. *See* black women
Ahmed, Sara, 14, 20, 128, 134, 158, 160, 163n1
AIDS, 10, 30, 41–42, 147
Alexandre, Sandy, 50
American Civil Liberties Union (ACLU), 25
American Coalition for Traditional Values, 40–41
American Medical Association (AMA), 62
Andrus, Jennifer, 12
anti-pornography activism, 5, 25–56
  as white, ableist, and male-centric, 27
  See also pornography; US Attorney General's Commission on Pornography
Antipornography Civil Rights Ordinance (City of Minneapolis), 21, 30
anti-rape activism, 10–11
  on college campuses, 112–35
  in the digital age, 136–54
  and feeling/pain, 19
  #MeToo, 5
  and the nature of victims, 61–62
  and public performances, 23, 112–35, 142
  survivor support, 107
Aquilina, Rosemarie, 1–2

Araujo, Cheryl, 9
Archila, Ana Maria, 151–52
Aristotle, 138, 144, 189n36
Asen, Robert, 80
Asian American women
  fetishization of, 122, 176n12
"asking for it," 8–9, 51
  See also rape culture; victim blaming
Austin, J. L., 73

backlog of rape kits. *See under* rape kits
Bad Feminist (Gay), 1
Barnard College, 117
Barnett, Jane, 36
Baynard, Victoria, 63
Berlant, Lauren, xv, 163n1
Bernstein, Elizabeth, 2
Bevacqua, Maria, 8
Bialik, Mayim, 70
Bible, The, 48–50
Biden, Joe, 62–63, 75, 79–80, 92, 95–96, 97, 100, 101, 116
birth control. *See* contraception
Black, Dick, 99
#BlackGirlMagic, 142
Black Sexual Politics: African Americans, Gender, and the New Racism (Collins), 11
black women
  and change in US culture, 24
  and crimes against, viii, xiv, 11–12, 61, 71, 82–84, 152
Blanco, María del Pilar, 65
Bliss, James, 64
bodies
  as challenging rape culture, 16
  as commodity, 17–18
  nakedness as "poison," 42–43
  nonnormative, 27, 132–33
  as Othered, 32–33, 56
  and pain, 16–17

bodies *(continued)*
   and physical violence, 14–29
   as pollutants to the nation, 37
   queer, 27
   and race, class, gender, dis/ability, location, sexuality, 14–15
   and rhetorical scholarship, 20–21
   risky vs. at-risk, 18, 28–29, 30
   as sites of surveillance/regulation, 30–31, 127
   as a source of evidence, 23, 103–8
   as a source of protest, 23
   and the threat of violence, 20
   value/worthiness of, 41
"Brave Enough to Be Angry" (West), 159
Brennan, Teresa, 19
Brown, Jerry, 133, 177n18
Brown, Julie, 155
Brown, Sara, 44
Browning, Barbara, 44
Browning, Larry, 148
Brownmiller, Susan, 10
Bumiller, Kristen, 10, 31
Bureau of Justice Assistance, 62
Burke, Tarana, 136, 142, 143, 153
Butler, Judith, 13, 19–20, 21–22, 31, 35, 83, 127, 147–48, 163n1
BuzzFeed, 121, 141
bystanders (to gender-based violence), 57–67, 70–71, 77, 81
   silence of, 67–73, 77

Calafell, Bernadette Marie, 165n62
California Penal Code 261, 117
Campt, Tina, 67
campus assault, 58–59, 74–75, 79–80, 85, 112–35
   See also under academia
Carell, Steve, 75
Carey, Tamika, 142
Carlson, Cheree, 8–9
Carney, Matthew F., 46
Carroll, E. Jean, 156
Ceci N'est Pas Un Viol (or *This Is Not A Rape*) (Sulkowicz), 113, 121, 127–32, 178n65
censorship, 22
   of female sexuality/experience, 46–50
   grounded in homophobia/misogyny, 42
   opposition to, 25–26
   of pornography, 22, 34, 38
Centers for Disease Control (CDC), 62
Central Park jogger rape case (1989), 9
"Chicago Boys," 29

Chávez, Karma, 14–15, 163n1
Chicago Tribune, 108
Christian right, 39
Christian, Barbara, 160
Cintrón, Ralph, 143
cisgender privilege, 2–3, 4, 6, 9, 31, 39
Civil War (US), 11, 71
Clark, Greg, 81
"Click Moment," 139–43
   See also #MeToo
college/university campus assault. *See* campus assault
colonialism, 65
   and the foundations of rape culture, 11–12
Coly, Ayo, 66
Combined DNA Index System (CODIS), 85, 97
consent (nature of), 129–31
contraception, 39
corporeality. *See* bodies
Corrigan, Rose, 90–91
Cosby, Bill, 140
counterpublicity. *See* visceral counterpublicity
Crenshaw, Kimberlé, 10, 89
Cvetkovich, Ann, 19, 163n1

Derrida, Jacques, 65
deviance, 4, 22, 27, 30, 34, 43, 46, 53, 62, 96
Dewhurst, Colleen, 25
Dietz, Park Elliott, 34
Dingo, Rebecca, 29
disclaimer (for this book), vii
DNA evidence. *See* rape kits
Doe, Emily. *See* Miller, Chanel
Dolmage, Jay, 15, 163n1
Douglas, Lawrence, 157
Dowhower, Richard L., 48–50
Duggan, Lisa, 29, 52
Dworkin, Andrea, 10, 21, 30

End Rape on Campus, 62
   See also anti-rape activism; campus assault
energeia, 81
Epstein, Jeffrey, 97, 155, 156–57
Eve (Biblical character), 48–50
Everts, Kellie, 51
#EverydaySexism, 142

Falwell, Rev. Jerry, 39
Farrell, Thomas, 138, 144, 145, 146
Fawaz, Ramzi, 147

Federal Bureau of Investigation (FBI), 85, 97
feelings
    and visceral rhetoric, 19
Feinstein, Rachel, 12
female sexuality
    abject perceptions of, 28
    framed as a slippery slope, 50
    reduced to reproduction, 49–50
    as threatening, 48–50
    See also under women
"feminazi," 57–58
feminism
    intervention regarding sexual violence, 78–79
    and list making, 136–54
    and *megethos*, 136–54
    and rape culture, 4, 7, 16
    scholarship on victim mistrust, 137
Finnegan, Cara, 66
First Amendment, 34, 169n97
Fixmer-Oraiz, Natalie, 46–47, 55
Flake, Jeff, 151
flesh/fleshiness. *See* bodies
Flores, Lisa, 153
Ford, Christine Blasey, vii, 53–55, 155–56
    and victim blaming, 55
forensic kits (for sexual assault), vii, 5, 23, 85–111
    See also rape kits
Frames of War (Butler), 83
Freiburg School, 29
Friedan, Betty, 25

Gallagher, Maria, 151–52
Garden of Eden (Biblical setting), 48–50
Garland, David, 30
Gay, Roxane, vii, 1, 3, 24, 158–60, 163n1
    and anger, 24, 160–61
    and change in US culture, 24, 158
    and viscerality/embodiment, 24, 159
gender-based violence, 57–61, 164n34
    See also rape; sexual assault; sexual violence
gender inequality, 30, 48, 51, 120
Genesis (Book of), 48–50
genocide and sexual assault, 11–12
Georgetown Preparatory School, 53
Gianino, Laura, 144
Gillibrand, Kirsten, 116
Gilmore, Leigh, 4, 13, 137
Glamour magazine, 116
GoFundMe, 107
Golden Globes, 140

Gordon, Avery, 68
Gould, Deborah, 139

Halicek, Megan, 1–2, 4
Hall, Rachel, 8, 62
Hamm, John, 63, 68–69, *69*
Hargitay, Mariska, 92, 104
Hariman, Robert, 73, 127
hashtags. *See specific hashtags*
Hawhee, Debra, 14, 15, 19, 80–81, 138, 163n1
"Hell You Talmbout" (Monáe), 152
"he-said, she-said," 13, 51
    See also victim blaming
heteronormativity, 28, 36, 37, 56, 65–66
    as "American," 38
    and citizenship, 39
    and the ideal woman, 47
    as a measuring stick for citizenship, 42
    and pornography, 43
    and privilege, 2–3
    and rape victims as "threats," 48
    and sex as solely reproductive, 37–38
Hill Collins, Patricia, 7, 11, 15
Hill, Anita, 156–57
Hill, Annie, 7, 78
Hill, Dulé, *75*
homophobia, 41–42, 44, 168n64
Hootsuite, 141
#HowIWillChange, 148–49
Hsu, Jo, 15
Human Rights Watch, 85–86
Hunger: A Memoir of (My) Body (Gay), 158

immigrants: violence/rhetoric against, 2, 44
It's On Us (PSA), 22, 67–73, *69, 70,* 172n52

Jack, Jordynn, 88
Jensen, Bishop E. Harold, 35
Jensen, Robin, 102–3
Jim Crow, 11, 50, 59, 61
Johnson, Jenell, 16, 19, 20, 106, 109, 113, 121, 163n1
Judd, Ashley, 139
Judge, Mark, 5
Just Be Inc., 136
    See also Me Too

Katz, Jackson, 57–58
Kavanaugh, Brett, vii, 28–29, 53–55, 151, 155–57
Kelly, Megyn, 106

King, Candace, 64
Koerber, Amy, 15, 106

Lady Gaga, 62–63
Latinx activism, 151–52
Lauer, Matt, 139–40
law enforcement. *See* law
law
  and the archetype of victim, 9–10, 176n11
  and bodies, 18
  criminalization of rape, 61–65, 95–104, 116
  forensic investigation of rape, 85–111
  and gender inequality, 48
  lack of conviction for rape/sexual assault, 13, 116, 119
  lack of protection of nonwhite, nonheteronormative Others, 56, 89–90, 119
  legal definition of sexual violence, 12–13, 97–98, 112–35
  leveraging science over victims' testimony, 99–100, 102–3, 110–11
  paternalistic property laws, 12
  police body cameras, 110, 176n99
  police brutality, 110–11
  as protective of or incentivizing rape, 11–12
  and public discourse, 133–34
  state laws concerning sexual assault, 117–18, 133
  and white heteronormative male privilege, 56, 82–83
list making, 136–54
Loken, Meredith, 137
Loyola University, 85
Lucaites, John, 73, 127
Lynch, Loretta, 92, 100
lynching, 11, 60, 152
  See also Jim Crow; racism
Lynn, Barry, 25

Mack, Ashley, 157
MacKinnon, Catherine, 8, 21, 30, 118, 119
Magritte, René, 131–32
mainstream culture. *See under* United States
male privilege, 7, 56, 78, 164n33
  See also patriarchy
Marciniak, Allison, 118
masculinity
  and accountability for sexual violence, 57–58
  protection of, 57–58

Massumi, Brian, 16, 19
Matlin, Marlee, 143–44
Mattress Performance (Carry That Weight) (Sulkowicz), 112, 116, 121, 127–32, 161, 176n12
Maynard, Curtis, 36–37, 40–42
McGowan, Rose, 139
McGuire, Danielle, 83
McHale, Joel, *70*
McKinnon, Sara, 163n1
McMahon, Sarah, 63
McRuer, Robert, 29
Me Too, vii, 16, 136
  See also #MeToo
#MeToo, vii, 19, 23, 82, 136–54, 160
  impact of, 23–24
  and list generation, 138
  mainstream reaction to, 139
  origins of, 23–24, 136
  and white privilege, 142, 151, 152, 153
Meese, Edwin, 21, 26–56, 166n1
Meese Commission. *See* US Attorney General's Commission on Pornography
Meese Commission Exposed, 25
megethos, 23, 136–54, 180n36
Meili, Trisha, 9
Mentors in Violence Prevention (MVP), 58
Miami Herald, 155
Milano, Alyssa, 136–37, 139, 140
Miller, Chanel, vii, 23, 112–27, 176n2, 177n18
misogyny, 59
  biblical origins of, 48–50
  normalization of, 159–60
Monáe, Janelle, 152
Moral Majority, 38–39
Mulla, Sameena, 91, 101, 109

NAACP. *See* National Association for the Advancement of Colored People
Nassar, Larry, 1–2, 9, 23, 97, 137–38, 140, 141, 163n3
Nation, The, 64
National Association for the Advancement of Colored People, 82
National Coalition Against Censorship, 25
national identity and heteronormativity, 39–40
National Sexual Violence Resource Center, 89
neoliberalism, 28, 29
  defined 28–29
  as establishing normativity, 52

and fears of sexual predators, 1
and heteronormativity, 39
and sexual panic, 29
New Bedford rape case (1983), 9
New York Times, 86, 139
New Yorker, 54, 139
Ngai, Sianne, 163n1
1980s
   AIDS crisis, 30
   anti-pornography debates of, 26–56
   framing female sexuality as
     un-American, 46–50
   government investigation of rape (1985), 50–51
   rape culture in, 21
   victim blaming, 50–56
Not Alone (PSA), 63
#NotOkay, 142
nuclear family, 28, 36
Nungesser, Paul, 112–22, 127–32

Obama, Barack, 62–63, 70, 74, 75, 85
Olson, Christa, 73–74, 138, 144, 146
1 is 2 Many (PSA), 22, 73–78, 75
Ore, Ersula, 47, 50, 60, 71
original sin, 49
Others, 30–31, 59–60
   fear of, 32
   lack of legal protection of, 56, 119–20
   as nonwhite bodies, 30–31
   in the public sphere, 127
   and rapists as deviant, 96
   and sexual violence, 132–33

pain
   and anti-rape activism, 19
   experience of, 16–17
Palo Alto University, 155
Panagia, Davide, 133
Parks, Rosa, 82
Pasquini, Ronald and Leslie, 38–39
Pateman, Carole, 118–19
patriarchal spectrality, 22, 59–61, 66–73, 74, 81–82
patriarchy, 16, 28
   assessing rape through the male body, 116–19
   frameworks of, 159
   and rape culture, 48, 66–67
   and rape victims as "threat," 48
   and responsibility/intervention, 73–74
   and the rhetoric of containment, 28, 32
   See also rape culture
pay gap (gender based), 140

Peeren, Esther, 65
penetration
   as a legal measure of violation, 13
People of the State of California v. Brock Allen Turner, 23, 92
Perskey, Aaron, 116
Pezzullo, Phaedra, 120
phantasia, 81
Phillips, Sylvia Harbison, 43, 47
physical bodies. *See* bodies
physician misconduct, 1–2, 3
Pinochet, Augusto, 29
"porn wars," 30
   See also pornography; US Attorney General's Commission on Pornography
police. *See under* law
police brutality, 115–16, 133–34, 152
politics
   and the response to sexual violence, 2–23
   response to pornography, 25–56
   See also under law; United States
"Polluting the Censorship Debate" (Lynn), 25
pornography
   anti-pornography debates (1980s), 5, 21, 26–56
   as destructive to the male body, 42, 45–46
   as detrimental to family relationships, 37–38
   censorship of, 34, 38
   and children, 44–45
   as "contaminating" the male mind, 28, 40–46
   and the erosion of "moral values," 43
   and First Amendment rights, 33–34
   framing the effects of, 33–35
   framing female sexuality as problematic/un-American, 46–47
   as a national threat, 35–40
   and psychological/physical reactions to, 43
   and sexual violence, 33–34
   as a violation of women's rights, 30
post-feminism, 55
power
   and rape culture, 4–5, 15
Presidential Commission (1970)
   and restrictions on pornography 33–34
Price, Margaret, 163n1
"protectors" against sexual violence, 65–67
PSAs. *See* public service announcements

Puar, Jasbir, 28, 32, 37, 41, 84, 163n1
public service announcements (against sexual violence), 67–78

queer identity, 59–60
   frameworks of, 27
   as linked to corruption in mainstream culture, 37
   and the risk of rape, 9
Quinlan, Andrea, 103

racism
   and casting victims as threatening, 48
   and fears of sexuality, 43–44
   and rape culture, 59
   and sexual violence, 11–12
   and the "unseen," 65–66
   See also Jim Crow; lynching
rape
   academic study of, xi–xv, 3, 16
   aftermath of, vii, 23, 125–26, 159
   as assessed through the male body, 116–19
   criminalization of, 95–104, 112–35
   depictions of, vii, 96, 104–5, 120–32
   and discrimination (race, class, gender, dis/ability, location, and sexuality), 10, 14–15, 132–33
   forensic investigation of, 85–111
   lack of legal consequences for, 2–3, 13, 119
   as a larger social issue, 97–98, 119
   legal definition of, 12–13, 117, 118–19, 131–32
   media portrayal of, 9–10, 86
   normalization of, 7, 157
   and power, 4–5, 15
   public deliberation and the rhetoric of containment, 28, 32
   as a public health issue, 62
   public service announcements against, 67–78
   prevention of, 61–65, 80
   and stigma, 14
   survivor support, 107
   and victim blaming, 8–9, 48, 51, 86–88, 89–90
   as violation, 121
   and white privilege, 2–3
   See also rape culture; sexual assault; sexual violence
rape culture
   academic study of, xi–xv, 3, 16
   and bystanders, 57–67, 70–71, 77, 81
   and criminalization of sexual violence, 4, 97–98, 112–35
   and denial/victim blaming, 3, 4–5, 86–88
   efforts to abolish, 3, 73
   and elected officials, xiv
   and gender pay gaps, 140
   as invisible, 7
   logics concerning, 170n8
   and mainstream public discourse, 3, 157–58
   and methodologies for change, 150–54
   and #MeToo, 23–24, 138–39
   and patriarchy, 66–67
   as a term, 8, 133
   and queer identity, 59–60
   and racism, 5–6, 59–60
   as terrorism, 3
   in the United States, xiv, 7–14, 157
   See also rape
rape kits, vii, 22–23, 85–111
   administration of, 90, 104–7
   backlog of, 22–23, 85–86, 96
   as demeaning, 106–8, 124–25, 129–31
   as discounting victim testimonies, 86–88
   as evidence, 103–8, 124
   and "justice" for victims, 109
   as problematic, 94–108
   reading of, 89–94
   and rhetoric, 108–11
   science of, 99–103
   as shaped by ideologies/intentions, 173n27
Rape Trauma Syndrome, 107
Rape, Abuse & Incest National Network (RAINN), 10, 13, 62
rapist. *See* rape
Reagan, Ronald, 21, 25, 29
rhetoric
   and dismissal of sexual violence, 21, 108–11
   and feeling, 20
   in the context of violence, 20–21
   See also visceral rhetoric
"Rhetorical Aesthetics of More: On Archival Magnitude, The" (Rice), 150
Rhodes, Jacqueline, 78–79, 80, 143
Rice, Jenny, 16, 138, 144, 146, 150, 152
Richardson, Brian, 141
Rose, Charlie, 139–40
Roth, Eileen, 42–4
Rubin, Gayle, 39
Ruffalo, Mark, 149

#SayHerName, 152
Scarry, Elaine, 17, 20, 93, 124, 131, 163n1
Schuller, Kyla, 151
science
  leveraged over victim testimony, 99–100, 102–3, 110–11
Sears, Alan, 35
second-wave feminism, 8, 10, 31, 61–62, 99
  dismantling myths about rape, 53
  and moral conservatives, 31
Sedgwick, Eve, 163n1
self-care, vii
Senate Bill S5965 ("Enough is Enough"), 117–18
sex crimes. *See* rape, sexual assault, sexual violence
sex trafficking, 155
sexism
  punishment for, 74
sexual abuse. *See* sexual assault
sexual assault
  discounting victim testimonies, 86–88
  the experience of, 104–5
  forensic examination of, vii, 23, 85–111
  and incarceration, 2–3
  as invisible in rape culture, 7
  lack of conviction for, 13
  laws against, 4, 112–35
  legal definition of, 12–13
  and the male body, 116–19
  of minors, 1–2
  and misdemeanors, 1
  and power, 4–5, 15
  prevention efforts, 61–65
  in public discourse, 4
  public service announcements against, 67–78
  and race, class, gender, dis/ability, location, and sexuality, 14–15
  state laws concerning, 117–18, 133
  statistics regarding, 62, 89, 164n30
  as a weapon of racial domination, 11–12
  and white privilege, 2–3
  See also rape; rape culture; sexual violence
Sexual Assault Kit Initiative (SAKI), 86, 87, 92, 95, 97, 99, 100, 104, 110
sexual assault nurse examiners (SANE), 85
  See also rape kits
sexual promiscuity, 30, 46
sexual violence
  and bystander accountability, 57–67, 70–71, 77, 81

constructing victims and perpetrators, 65–67
cultural realities of, 115
the experience of, 104–5
ignoring/silencing victims of, 57–84, 86–88, 143
legal consequences for (or lack thereof), 13, 97–98, 112–35, 160–61
and the male body, 114, 116–19
and male responsibility for, 57
and marginalized bodies, 132–33
patriarchal definitions of, 3–4
perpetrators of, 77, 95–99
and pornography, 33–34, 36
prevention efforts, 61–65
public service announcements against, 67–78
and race, class, gender, dis/ability, location, and sexuality, 11–12, 14–15
as a "social problem," 31, 115
See also rape; rape culture; sexual assault
Sexual Violence Research Initiative, 106
sexuality
  fear of, 39, 43–44
  framing female sexuality as problematic, 46–47
sexually transmitted diseases (STDs), 37
  See also AIDS
Shafer, R. Donald, 38
Shildrick, Margrit, 17
Shvarts, Aliza, 94
silencing of victims, 16, 112–35, 143
  See also rape culture; victims
slavery, 50
  and bodies as commodity, 17–18
  and crimes against black women, 11–12
  and dehumanizing of "flesh," 17–18
  and financially incentivized rape of enslaved women, 12
  and the foundations of rape culture, 11–12
  legal protections afforded to slave owners, 12
  See also Jim Crow; racism
SlutWalk, 142
  See also anti-rape activism
Smart, Carol, 89
Smith, Debbie, 95
social media
  and activism, 136–54
  See also specific hashtags
Solinger, Rickie, 11–12
Souto, Melissa, 85, 86–87, 98, 107
Spacey, Kevin, 139–40

208   INDEX

spectrality, 65–66
Spillers, Hortense, 17, 18, 20, 152, 163n1
Sports Illustrated, 141
Stanford University, 23, 112
stigma, 14, 15, 41, 91, 105, 137, 144
Storify, 141
Sulkowicz, Emma, vii, 19, 23, 112–22, 127–32, 161, 176n12, 178n65

Taylor, Recy, vii, 61, 82–83, 84
TED Talks (on sexual violence), 57
terrorism and rape culture, 3
Thatcher, Margaret, 29
"Thinking Sex" (Rubin), 39
Thomas, Clarence, 156–57
Thurman, Uma, 159–60
Time magazine, 86
#TimesUp, 82, 140
toxic masculinity, 5, 11, 55
transgender women, 59–60
   in public discourse, 4
   and risk of violence, 2, 9
Treachery of Images, The, (Magritte), 131–32
Trump, Donald J., xiv, 106, 155, 156–57, 166n1
Turner, Brock Allen, 112–27, 177n18
tweets. *See* Twitter
Twitter, 136–54

Union, Gabrielle, 141
United States
   casting female sexuality as un-American, 46–50
   and government failure to protect women, 10, 57–84
   and heteronormative national identity, 40
   legal consequences of sexual violence in, 112–35
   mainstream sexual identity, 37–38
   mainstream views on rape, 4, 23
   moving forward in US culture, 24
   as a normative, heteronuclear state, 52–53
   and the "perversion" of sexuality, 37
   predators holding government office, 155–56
   and rape as a central component of, 1, 11, 61
   rape culture in, xiv, 7–14, 157
   and sexual violence against marginalized bodies, 82–84, 132–33
   state-sponsored rape prevention efforts, 10, 61–65, 67–78
University of Chicago, 29

US Attorney General's Commission on Pornography, 21–22, 26–56
   as affirming heteronormativity, 26–27
   compared with the prior Minneapolis hearings on pornography, 30
   and "contamination" of the male mind, 28, 40–46
   and children, 44–45
   criticism of, 25–26
   envisioning rape out of the national imaginary, 26
   focus on women's bodies instead of their experiences, 21–22, 50–56
   framing the effects of pornography, 33–35
   framing female sexuality as un-American, 46–50
   ignoring sexual violence, 26–27
   letters addressed to, 26–28, 32–33, 34–36, 37–56
   and national security, 39–40
   and protection of "worthy" lives, 31–32, 44–45
   psychological/physical reactions to porn, 43
   victim blaming/ignoring, 50–56
US Department of Education Office for Civil Rights, 117
US Electoral College, 156
US society. *See* United States
US Supreme Court
   swearing in of Brett Kavanaugh, 53–55

Vance, Carole, 34
Vance, Cyrus, 92, 99
VAWA. *See* Violence Against Women Act (VAWA)
victim blaming, 8–9, 27–28, 50–56, 57, 76–77, 143–44
   on campus, 79–80, 112–35
   discounting the experiences of victims, 50–56, 116
   historical legacy of, 27
   and the "It's On Us" PSA, 68
   leveraging science over victim testimony, 99–100, 102–3, 110–11
   mainstream archetype of, 9–10, 57–84
   as a social construct, 65–67
   and stigma, 14
victims
   acknowledgment of, 72
   and anti-rape activism, 61–62, 112–35
   as an archetype in law, 9, 10, 176n11
   as constructed in society, 65–67, 78–82
   credibility of, 90–91

examination of, 85–111
and the experience of harm, 120–32
as "haunting," 82–84
as ignored in mainstream culture, 57–84
justice for, 109, 160–61
and male "protectors," 60–61, 65–67
silencing of, 78, 112–35, 143
as a term, 163n2
violation
experience of, 20
Violence Against Women Act (VAWA), 5, 10, 22, 62–63, 67–78
Violence of Care: Rape Victims, Forensic Nurses, and Sexual Assault Intervention, The, (Mulla), 101
visceral counterpublicity, 112–35
visceral rhetoric, 14, 20, 93, 95
defined, 5–6
and the interrogation of rape culture, 21
methodology of, 19–20
as a tool for communicating women's experiences, 21
Vonnegut, Kurt, 25
Vox, 141
vulnerability, 20

Wantland, Rev. William C., 35, 43
Warner, Michael, 126–27
Washington, Kerry, 62–63
Washington Post, 86, 143
Weheliye, Alexander, 18, 93–94, 104, 111
Weinstein, Harvey, 97, 139–40, 152, 156–57
Weinstock, Jeffrey, 67
Wells-Barnett, Ida B., 152
West, Lindy, 150, 159–60
white feminism, 10, 60, 142
White House Council on Women and Girls, 62–63
White House Task Force to Protect Students from Sexual Assault, 62–63, 79
white privilege, 4, 142
and concepts of whiteness, 50

overlooking white male perpetrators, vii, 27
white supremacy, 11, 55, 79, 164n33
and the foundations of rape culture, 11–12
white women
as "bearers of moral guidance," 47
and feminine ideals, 50
and Jim Crow, 50
and patriarchy, 79
and protection of the "white maiden," 10, 50, 59, 64, 71–73
whiteness, 56, 65–66
#WhyWeWearBlack, 140
Winderman, Emily, 146
Winfrey, Oprah, 82–83
Wingard, Jennifer, 32–33
Wolf, Frank, 45
women
and the "cult of domesticity," 47
dehumanization and pornography, 46
framing female sexuality as problematic, 46–47
ignoring the female experience, 50–56
male gaze, 43, 118
as objects of the portrayal of, 106
as a sexual threat, 46–50
silencing of, 15, 123, 143
and the standards of womanhood, 120
women of color, 59–60
as fetishized, 176n12
in public discourse, 4
and risk of rape/violence, 2, 9, 152
as unseen, 65–66
women's rights, 48
Wondaland Arts Society, 152
See also Monáe, Janelle
World Health Organization, 109
World War II, 29

Young, Iris Marion, 61
Yung, Corey Rayburn, 91

Ziegler, Jennifer, 139, 141

RHETORIC AND DEMOCRATIC DELIBERATION

Other books in the series:

Karen Tracy, *Challenges of Ordinary Democracy: A Case Study in Deliberation and Dissent* / Volume 1

Samuel McCormick, *Letters to Power: Public Advocacy Without Public Intellectuals* / Volume 2

Christian Kock and Lisa S. Villadsen, eds., *Rhetorical Citizenship and Public Deliberation* / Volume 3

Jay P. Childers, *The Evolving Citizen: American Youth and the Changing Norms of Democratic Engagement* / Volume 4

Dave Tell, *Confessional Crises and Cultural Politics in Twentieth-Century America* / Volume 5

David Boromisza-Habashi, *Speaking Hatefully: Culture, Communication, and Political Action in Hungary* / Volume 6

Arabella Lyon, *Deliberative Acts: Democracy, Rhetoric, and Rights* / Volume 7

Lyn Carson, John Gastil, Janette Hartz-Karp, and Ron Lubensky, eds., *The Australian Citizens' Parliament and the Future of Deliberative Democracy* / Volume 8

Christa J. Olson, *Constitutive Visions: Indigeneity and Commonplaces of National Identity in Republican Ecuador* / Volume 9

Damien Smith Pfister, *Networked Media, Networked Rhetorics: Attention and Deliberation in the Early Blogosphere* / Volume 10

Katherine Elizabeth Mack, *From Apartheid to Democracy: Deliberating Truth and Reconciliation in South Africa* / Volume 11

Mary E. Stuckey, *Voting Deliberatively: FDR and the 1936 Presidential Campaign* / Volume 12

Robert Asen, *Democracy, Deliberation, and Education* / Volume 13

Shawn J. Parry-Giles and David S. Kaufer, *Memories of Lincoln and the Splintering of American Political Thought* / Volume 14

J. Michael Hogan, Jessica A. Kurr, Michael J. Bergmaier, and Jeremy D. Johnson, eds., *Speech and Debate as Civic Education* / Volume 15

Angela G. Ray and Paul Stob, eds., *Thinking Together: Lecturing, Learning, and Difference in the Long Nineteenth Century* / Volume 16

Sharon E. Jarvis and Soo-Hye Han, *Votes That Count and Voters Who Don't: How Journalists Sideline Electoral Participation (Without Even Knowing It)* / Volume 17

Belinda Stillion Southard, *How to Belong: Women's Agency in a Transnational World* / Volume 18

Melanie Loehwing, *Homeless Advocacy and the Rhetorical Construction of the Civic Home* / Volume 19

Kristy Maddux, *Practicing Citizenship: Women's Rhetoric at the 1893 Chicago World's Fair* / Volume 20

Craig Rood, *After Gun Violence: Deliberation and Memory in an Age of Political Gridlock* / Volume 21

Nathan Crick, *Dewey for a New Age of Fascism: Teaching Democratic Habits* / Volume 22

William Keith and Robert Danisch, *Beyond Civility: The Competing Obligations of Citizenship* / Volume 23

Lisa A. Flores, *Deportable and Disposable: Public Rhetoric and the Making of the "Illegal" Immigrant* / Volume 24

Adriana Angel, Michael L. Butterworth, and Nancy R. Gómez, eds., *Rhetorics of Democracy in the Americas* / Volume 25

Robert Asen, *School Choice and the Betrayal of Democracy: How Market-Based Education Reform Fails Our Communities* / Volume 26

www.ingramcontent.com/pod-product-compliance
Lightning Source LLC
Chambersburg PA
CBHW022052290426
44109CB00014B/1076